shattered silence

shattered silence

Melissa G. Moore

with

M. Bridget Cook

CFI
Springville, Utah

© 2009 M. Bridget Cook and Melissa G. Moore

ISBN 13: 978-1-59955-238-5

Published by CFI, an imprint of Cedar Fort, Inc., 2373 W. 700 S., Springville, UT 84663
Distributed by Cedar Fort, Inc., www.cedarfort.com

LIBRARY OF CONGRESS CATALOGING-IN-PUBLICATION DATA

Moore, Melissa G. (Melissa Grace)
  Shattered silence : the untold story of a serial killer's daughter /
Melissa G. Moore, with M. Bridget Cook.
     p. cm.
  Summary: The story of the early life of Melissa G. Moore, daughter of
convicted serial killer Keith Jesperson.
  ISBN 978-1-59955-238-5
  1. Moore, Melissa G. (Melissa Grace) 2. Jesperson, Keith Hunter, 1955- 3.
Serial murderers--Family relationships--West (U.S.) I. Cook, M. Bridget.
II. Title.
  HV6248.J475M66 2009
  364.15232092--dc22
  [B]
                              2009024370

Cover design by Nicole Williams
Cover design © 2009 by Lyle Mortimer

Printed in Canada

10 9 8 7 6 5 4 3 2 1

Printed on acid-free paper

This is my story. The events described are based upon my recollections and are true. I have changed the names of many individuals to protect their privacy.

This book is dedicated with deepest love and affection to my husband,
Samuel Moore, and our children, Aspen and Jake.
Your love has helped me to choose a better way of living.
—M. G. M.

Dedicated to BreeAnna, McKenzie, and Brent. With your love, support
and encouragement, great miracles have happened.
—M. B. C.

contents

preface

I am no stranger to terrifyingly dark nights. I know what lingering despair and isolation can do to the human soul. My story, however, is not about darkness, but about discovering my light and divinity in the midst of utter darkness—of realizing that despite the horrors of my childhood and the circumstances thrust upon me, I had *choices*.

As chaos and crises erupted all around me, I carefully watched and experimented with choices of my own. Eventually I realized that I could either choose to continue the unhealthy traditions of my family, or I could choose to break the chains. One step at a time, one choice at a time, I consciously began to create something new—something healthier . . . Despite this shift, however, hidden deep inside where no one could see—where I wouldn't *let* anyone see—a sinister black hole lurked. It refused to be filled, no matter what I did. Food didn't fill it. Material goods couldn't touch it. Relationships and religion sometimes shifted my focus, but eventually that raw, nagging darkness would intrude unbearably into everyday life. Like black holes in space that suck energy from the surrounding universe, my life was being robbed of joy and passion from within my own self.

Then quite suddenly, before I could prepare myself, before I was ready or even wanted to be, my seven-year-old daughter, Aspen, ignored the nails, locks, and buttresses of my secrecy. She asked an innocent question, expecting an honest answer.

"Mommy, where is your daddy?" my daughter asked, her eyes full of open curiosity. "Everybody has a daddy. You have to have a daddy, too, don't you?"

Aspen's questioning brought me literally to my knees. This was the child I reassured every night that there was no such thing as monsters. How was I supposed to tell her that some monsters were real? How was I supposed to tell her about her grandfather?

Your grandfather is a serial murderer. He is locked away in prison for the rest of his life because of the atrocities he has committed . . .

Being honest with Aspen would mean facing what the world considered a demon. It would also mean that I would have to face the demons within my own self. To choose change—true, honest change—meant bringing light into all of my dark places, including that seemingly unfathomable black hole within me.

I did not reveal anything to Aspen that day about her grandfather, but my mind couldn't stop racing. Should I let her grandfather be a part of her life? As a person of faith, wasn't I supposed to believe that the human soul could change? Did I give him that chance? Or were there inherent dangers lurking—the ones I had been furiously trying to protect her from?

I felt I had no clearly defined answers. I couldn't find a single book on the subject. The few people I entrusted with my inner battle seemed as bewildered as I was. This is a question that has faced millions of people—the skeleton in the family closet—and even after a millennium of human experience, most of the time, the issue is not spoken of openly. Shame and humiliation win out, and the deadly silence continues.

You are only as sick as your secrets . . .

I'd had enough of the sickness, the secret-keeping, the blame, and my racing mind. I got on the internet and wrote a letter. As I pressed send, I knew I was changing my life forever, and maybe that of many others. Magically, some of the darkness within me began to lift . . .

That one act has created a huge ripple, for I have learned that we are all connected. I am never alone. Not one of us is every really alone. And now I know I am in the perfect place at the perfect time, telling my story to those who have been searching for answers within the dark crevasses of their own souls. I know that I am bringing light into that darkness. I know that I am literally breaking the chains of horror, secrecy, and devastation, for I am a child of Light.

Do you ever wonder who you are?
Do you ever wonder as you stare into the stars?
Where you began and how you got this far . . . from home.
Have you ever walked along the shore?
Have you ever seen the water dancing back and forth?
Did you look inside to see if there was more . . . to life?

Well, there's a dream taking wing.
There's a voice that wants to sing.
Even in the deepest, darkest night.
The torch is raised to the sky.
There are hands that hold it high.
You were born to keep it burning bright.
You were made to fly.
You were meant to shine.
Child of Light.

You will never, ever stand alone.
You were never called to bare the burdens on your own.
Where there is fear, love will take control, and lead you on . . . .

Well, there's a dream taking wing.
There's a voice that wants to sing.
Even in the deepest, darkest night.
The torch is raised to the sky.
There are hands that hold it high.
You were born to keep it burning bright.
You were made to fly.
You were meant to shine.
Child of Light.

(Printed with permission. Child of Light by Mindy Gledhill, copyright 2004).

I

❦

silent cries

August 1984

I squinted into the bright blue morning sky and couldn't help the shudder that rippled through my little body. Not a single cloud wafted on the horizon, not a breeze tickled my blonde hair, yet I felt the dark storm approaching. It didn't matter that our tiny, rural town of Toppenish experienced three hundred days of sunshine a year or that our little farmhouse was settled in one of the most quiet farming communities in Washington. It didn't matter that I was only five years old. When I got one of these *knowings*, the gloom that descended was very real.

Still, I tried to shrug it off. It was a lovely day, and I had a *secret*. It was a beautiful secret that kept me tingling inside from morning until I finally fell asleep at night—I could barely contain my joy. I peered around the corner of the dusty white farmhouse, looking out carefully across the yard and out past the long alfalfa fields out toward the huge peach tree at the back of our property for any sign of life. Other than my baby sister and my little brother playing quietly with Tonka trucks around the side of the house, everything outside was still.

When I concentrated really hard, I could hear the faint and busy rustlings of my mother. She was occupied inside the house as usual, this time doing laundry. For once I wasn't sad that she wouldn't come play with me, swing me around in the grass, or sing "ring around the rosy" as I had seen other mothers do. Dad was away, trucking produce. It kept him away from home for days at a time. I was free to do what I wanted. It was a delicious feeling.

One more look to be sure, and then I quietly lifted the cellar door and slipped down inside the dank, musty room. I breathed in the air as if it were filled with the scent of luscious flowers. This was *my* house, my sanctuary. My five-year-old, hazel eyes swept the room. In my mind, I kept it as immaculately clean as my mother kept our house. There was a little table and chairs I would set for my imaginary guests or for my brother and sister when I invited them for a tea party. Not today though. My mind was on other things, and my heart was singing.

In the corner there was movement, and my mouth turned up in unadulterated pride. *My babies!* I ran to the corner and lifted the blanket on the crate. There was the stray farm cat and four of the tiniest, most fragile, beautiful creatures I had ever had the pleasure of knowing this intimately. Soft, furry, and white, with tiny mews and sweet blue eyes, they had my heart wrapped around their delicate paws.

They were old enough to recognize me now, and the kittens tumbled over each other to play and cuddle in my warm embrace. I scooped my favorite one up in my arms, and he began to lick me. I laughed out loud. How I loved him! How I loved all of them. I took the first little guy and put him in one of the front pockets of my dress, then scooped out another and put him in the other pocket. The last two I held protectively in my arms, singing lullabies to them. Suddenly I gasped and then giggled as the first one in my pocket used my dress as a ladder to crawl up almost to my shoulder.

"No, Kitty!" I scolded, putting him back down in my pocket. "You get to stay here. We're going for a trip."

I glanced over at the stray mother cat, almost for permission, and she looked at me lazily with only one eye open. She mewed just once, and then put her head down and closed her eyes. She knew she could trust me because they were my babies, after all. Walking over to the opening, I slowly peaked my head up and out of the cellar door. No one was about. Quickly, I made my way up the stairs and into the yard, heading toward the other side of our old, run-down barn. Before I could get there, my little rambunctious kitten jumped out of my pocket and onto the dusty path. I scooped him up yet again.

"Where do you think you're going?" I giggled, looking into his surprised face. He then closed his eyes, and nuzzled his soft fur against my face, purring with a tiny little roar in his throat. For that one, small moment, I thought I was in heaven. I let him nuzzle me until he got bored and wanted down. I plopped on the ground beside him and let my kittens crawl all over my legs and in the grass beside me, discovering the breeze, the moving blades of grass, and the fascinating grasshoppers. The kittens were so fun to watch, I forgot where I was.

"Here, kitty, kitty, kitty!" a voice whined in a high-pitched, sarcastic tone. My body froze. It was *him*. I didn't dare turn around. I didn't want to move a muscle. I had heard that high-pitched tone before, and I knew—all too well—what it meant.

My eyes moved wildly from side to side, frantically searching for a place to run and hide with my kitties. The barn was so dilapidated that there were only certain areas we were allowed to go in for fear it would cave in on us. He would find us there anyway. The alfalfa field? Not high enough. Neighbors were much too far away, and he'd be mad if I went there. Maybe if I ran around the barn I could lose him. Then I could run far away and hide my babies where he'd never find them. A small spurt of hope flared in my heart as I scooped them up and prepared to get onto my feet. Then I heard his footsteps much too close and knew it was too late. He was right behind me.

"Come here, Kitty," said the voice, now laughing. "I won't hurt you. I promise."

At that moment I wanted desperately to believe that promise. But I had heard it before. It was not a real promise, it was a lie. It was a lie every single time.

"No, please!" I begged. I turned to look up at my father, ignoring the tears streaming down my face and onto the dress now covered in downy cat fur. I was trying to keep all four squirming kittens clutched safely to my chest. They were scratching me now, not understanding what was going on and wanting to get down to play. "No, please, Daddy, don't hurt them! Please, please, please!"

I searched my father's eyes for some evidence of compassion, some sense that he had heard me, but all I saw was the veiled look that had come over his eyes. It matched the way his lips were twisted in a sinister half smile. I knew that look, just as I knew this particular voice of his, and I felt the blood drain out of my face. Ignoring me and my pleas, he reached for the kittens. I tried to back away, but his massive 6'6" frame towered over me and he seized them easily from my grasp.

"I wouldn't hurt you, would I?" he asked the kittens playfully, and strode over to the clothesline. Despite my fear I was . . . puzzled. This wasn't his usual behavior with cats. I shook my head, trying to keep the memories at bay. Why was he walking to the clothesline? I sidled up next to him, then watched in horror as he used clothespins to hang the kittens up on the clothesline, each kitten right next to the other. They began frantically scratching at each other in desperation to get up or down—somewhere safe. My precious little rambunctious one already had blood on his face from a wicked scratch. I was transfixed for a moment until I heard my father laughing at them.

My babies! I turned and screamed, running for the farmhouse to find my mother. It felt like I was moving through molasses to get to the front door. Horrible memories flashed into my mind, and one seemed stuck there, playing in slow motion. It was a memory of our last house in Toppenish, right next to an orchard. A stray cat had wandered into our yard, and I remembered watching Dad calling to it with that same sick, high-pitched voice. Jason and I had thought maybe we could keep this one. Jason was especially drawn to its soft, pretty coat. It seemed like Dad was being nice to it. Then my father had suddenly grabbed the stray by the throat and squeezed. The poor cat had fought him, scratching and gouging his arms in its last, desperate fight for life, but it had finally stopped moving. Dad held it up, as if inspecting it for any further signs of life, then he had thrown it on the ground like old, stinky garbage. Jason and I had been screaming uncontrollably, but my dad had ignored us and just walked away. I remembered looking into Jason's eyes in disbelief, and then I had to look away. The hurt and pain in them mirrored my own, and it was unbearable.

That was not the first time I had seen death, and I was determined I wasn't going to see it again. The screams from my memory now entwined with those erupting from my throat as I ran. I needed my mother to stop him. Surely she would save my babies.

I shot up the steps and into the farmhouse, racing to find my mother. She was quietly folding a T-shirt.

"Mommy, come quick!" I screeched. "Please, *now!*"

"What is it, Melissa?" she asked, continuing to fold the laundry.

"Daddy's going to hurt my babies—my kitties!" I frantically pulled on her arm. "You have to come quick!"

My mother pulled her arm hard, up out of my grip. She looked at me with a blank stare for a moment. It wasn't the same veiled look of threat and malice that my father had. It was simply . . . empty. Then she turned back to folding the laundry into neat little piles and neat little rows, one item of clothing at a time.

No . . . it couldn't be. Not again.

I stared at her back. I couldn't believe she wouldn't help me, especially when she had seen the gouges on Daddy's arm last time, and the poor kitty's body on the ground. Surely she had to do something. *Anything!* Because her complaints hadn't worked the time before, I could see that she wasn't willing to enter a conflict this time around. I tried pleading again.

"Please, Mom," I begged, trying not to scream so she could understand me through my panic. "Please help my babies. Please, Mom!"

My mother didn't turn around, didn't even move an inch in my direction. Feelings of desperation and frustration took over my body. What could I do? How could I save my babies? I turned and ran from the room, scraping my shin on a table in my haste to get back toward the barnyard. The pain in my leg was negligible compared to the pain in my chest. I slammed through the door, but on the top of the back steps, I stopped short.

Dad wasn't in the yard. Where was he? I couldn't see any struggling kittens dangling from the clothesline. My heart began to hope beyond hope . . .

That's when I saw them. Four tiny, helpless mounds upon the ground. They were not moving. I stared for just a moment, and then looked away, my heart crushed and crumpled like my babies' tiny bodies. I felt just as small. I was not important, and I was not powerful. My voice was silent; it wasn't heard. What I wanted, what I felt, didn't matter to anyone.

I took a breath and went over to the side of the house. Carrie and Jason were there, still playing with their trucks and action figures in the dirt as if nothing had happened. Jason kept his eyes downcast, making puttering and roaring noises with the trucks. Carrie was toddling around beside him. She looked at me for a moment, her small eyes unsure in the babyish frame of her face. My tear-stained and puffy cheeks distressed her. Carrie lost her balance and plopped on her diapered bottom. I was relieved when we broke eye contact, and I wiped my face. Quickly I kneeled down beside her in the dirt and began to play an imaginary game with her. As we got more and more into the story, it felt more real to me than what had just happened. It had to be. My characters had great adventures, they came to each other's rescue, and had happy endings whenever I wanted them to.

2

⟨⟨⟨❧⟩⟩⟩

teetering on the edge

Cold, pre-dawn light began to fill the little room I shared with Carrie. The sound of tires on the gravel lane woke me from a nightmare. Before I cried aloud again, I swallowed hard and pushed the tender feelings and memories away where they belonged—deep down inside where no one could touch them, not even me. Angrily, I ignored the small tear that had escaped my lashes. I turned over on my side, willing myself to go back to sleep, have a good dream, and escape the loneliness I felt. The bed creaked loudly. Even though Dad had already gone to work, it wouldn't do to wake Mom. If I woke up Carrie, I would really be in trouble.

For the millionth time, I missed the loft bed my grandfather had made just for me at our old house. To me it had been beautiful and unique, built right into the wall. I had loved it. But building it into the wall had also meant we couldn't take it with us when we moved, and I felt like I had left a part of me there. I wondered if people did that—left a part of themselves in places, a part that they could never get back.

I sighed, giving up on sleep. Cringing at every squeak, I snuck out of bed and over to the window, peering down the road and across the lane. My hope for another day away from home with Samantha was dashed. Her parents' car was gone, and I remembered she had said they were going on a trip. I looked at the gravel lane with longing. It had been misted with oil to keep the dust down for the hot summer. I loved to ride my pink and yellow bike to Samantha's house, carefully sliding all the way off the banana seat and unhooking my leg before the bike could tip over on me when I stopped. A gift from my dad, I cherished the freedom it gave me.

Just the afternoon before, I had ridden to Samantha's house. My friend and I were only five years old, but we loved to pretend we where fashionable teens. We played for a while inside with her mom, and I sat transfixed while she painted my toenails. I didn't have any nail polish at home, and my mother certainly didn't paint her toenails. I stared in fascination as the bright pink color went on each toe, making me feel different with every stroke. I wasn't sure if it was the smelly, slick paint, or the way her mother smiled encouragingly and joined us in our chatter. When our toes were dry, we grabbed our precious Cabbage Patch Dolls and went out to play in the field for hours.

I turned away from the window now, disappointed by Samantha's absence. The sun had begun to rise over the hills, dramatically warming the air already. It was going to be another beautiful, cloudless day. As I approached our bed, I noticed the golden light sweeping over Carrie. One arm was down, and the other was up near her hair, soft and tussled about her face. I always loved to watch her sleep. She seemed so fragile and tender, and I watched over her like a mother bear. *Sister bear*, I scolded myself. In my heart, I clutched desperately for the assurance that Daddy adored her, so it was safe to love this little girl with my whole heart.

Mom had named Carrie after *Little House on the Prairie*, and she indeed looked like the beautiful little girl running in the fields after her brother and sister, her curls bouncing. Dad said she was called Carrie because she liked to be carried. Every time he was home, she would lift her arms up to him and he would carry her around for hours on his wide shoulders.

As the room became lighter, so did my mood, and I became excited at the thought of the new day. Jason, Carrie, and I would invent fun things to do on our little acreage. There were not many kids around our little place in Toppenish, so most of the time we simply had ourselves and all of the fields around to play in. It was enough for us and our imaginations. We created all kinds of games and stories, meaning we were never bored—or at least not for long. We could always find a new adventure to pique our interest, especially Jason and me.

Jason was the captain of our days. He was often the leader in our escapades, even though he was nearly a year—to the day—younger than me. He and I looked like twins, with our oval faces and identical golden hair and hazel eyes. His eyes were turning a little more brown than hazel, but the only real difference, it seemed, was in our temperaments. I hesitated in the face of fear, but Jason would seek it out. He seemed never to be afraid.

❧❧❧

Less than an hour later, Jason got one of his wild hairs. He burst into my room, his large brown eyes full of excitement.

"Let's make a tree house, Melissa!" he cried.

"That sounds fun," I said, smiling at his enthusiasm. "But I don't think we have anything to build it with." After all, we had only one tree. Our peach tree, perched in solitary stance at the very back of our long, narrow acreage was gloriously large and delightful to climb, but there certainly were no extra branches or wood to build with.

"Maybe Mommy will let us pull stuff off of the barn," Jason said wistfully. I could see the wheels turning in his head, but I didn't think Mom would let him. I was pretty sure he didn't think so either. I became preoccupied with breakfast and helped Mom feed Carrie. When I was taking my dishes and Carrie's over to the sink, I overheard Jason begging Mom to let us pull some old boards off the barn.

"No, Jason, you may not," Mom said firmly. "It's about to fall down and it's full of old nails. You'll have to get a Tetanus shot if you even get scratched by one of them."

"I won't get scratched," he mumbled, but he seemed to back off. I didn't blame him. I didn't want to get a shot either! I had just had my kindergarten shots and the memory made my stomach do flip-flops. So did the thought of school, but I wouldn't let anyone know that.

"You'll just have to find something else to do," Mom said, and she went to grab some more canning jars. I was thankful the weather was clear, so I wouldn't have to be inside the kitchen. It was about to get stiflingly hot and humid. Jason walked mournfully to the door, looked at me, and then stomped out of the room. I got Carrie some more juice, and then we went outside to play.

Carrie loved to follow Jason around more than she did me. I liked to think it was because he was closer to her in age than I was, but whatever it was, she worshipped him.

"Yason! Yason!" she called. We both searched the yard, but couldn't find where he went. At first I suspected he was sneaking boards from the barn, but we couldn't find him there either, so the two of us went out into the alfalfa fields to play. Absorbed in our games, we got further and further away from the house and lost track of the time. Carrie suddenly sat down in the dirt and began to wail. I realized she was hungry and thirsty.

The heat made her incredibly cranky, and it was the only time I didn't like having a baby sister. I usually changed my mind once she had a nap, so I picked her up and hauled her on my hip all the way back to the house.

I was relieved to see that Mom had already made us some sandwiches. There was a plate for Jason, too, but he was nowhere to be seen. When Mom called him in, however, he came in a minute later and began gobbling down his sandwich. Carrie almost fell asleep in her chair, and Mom took her in the other room for a nap. In the meantime, Jason bolted back out the door. I finished drinking my milk and followed after him, the door banging shut behind me in my haste. I stopped and bit my lip. Listening for a moment, I was relieved not to hear any cries.

I jumped off the porch and onto the lawn, looking around. *Where was he?* Then I noticed movement way back toward the end of the field. Jason had run all the way down there. It seemed strange to move that quickly when it was so hot. Curious, I started walking slowly in that direction, only because there would be cool shade under the tree. Jason had scaled the tree now, and I could see that there was something in it. I had forgotten all about his excitement to build a tree house. There was definitely something really big up in the branches. I thought about the barn, thinking he was going to be in *big* trouble. Then I realized it couldn't be wood, and it was oddly shaped. *What in the world could it be?* I moved closer, then broke out into a curious run. I couldn't believe what I was seeing. Jason had hauled a heavy, old horse trough from the fields and all the way up and into the tree!

"Melissa!" he called to me, laughing. "Look what I did!" The large, steel trough was wedged between two big branches in the tree. It was almost as high as we ever dared climb, and I couldn't fathom how he had done it. I stopped and stared with my mouth wide open.

"Will you go get a sleeping bag for me?" he asked.

"What for?" I asked, curious.

"I want to sleep out here tonight," Jason declared, all excited. Then his face fell. "I'm sorry there's not enough room for both of us."

"That's okay," I said giggling. "We'd get squished." He looked at me and laughed, relieved I wasn't angry with him. "I'll go get your sleeping bag," I told him.

I trudged all the way back up the yard and into the house. We had just been camping with family and had brought our three-wheelers in the fiberglass trailer that Grandpa Roy had made us. On my Dad's side, it was said that the Jesperson family knew how to work and they knew how to play. The sleeping bags had all been washed and folded and put away, so I rummaged around until I got the perfect one for Jason's outdoor adventure. It came undone as I was dragging it through the house, and it got stuck in a couple of doors. Mom was so busy canning, she didn't notice what I was doing, or I'm certain she would have stopped me.

Freeing the cumbersome bag from the last doorway and out onto the porch, I dragged it down the steps and began pulling it across the yard. It felt heavy, but I wasn't about to give in, especially after the feat my little brother had accomplished getting that thing all the way up there. I would have needed a crane to do it. And I surely didn't want him calling me wimpy.

I was huffing and puffing by the time I got to the peach tree. I didn't have any more strength to get the bag up into the tree. I plopped down, grateful for the shade, and wiped my moist brow. Jason stared down at me ruefully from his little home in the tree, and then sighed and climbed down to get the sleeping bag. He dragged the bag up into the branches and into his trough. I had to admit, it looked really cool. I wanted to get in, too, even if meant we'd be squished.

I was still catching my breath when it happened. I heard a scraping sound and saw that when Jason had jumped into the sleeping bag inside the trough, it slipped forward with enough weight to move the trough off balance. I didn't have time to panic because it all happened so fast, but as I backed out of the way, I felt like I was watching apples falling . . . First Jason, then the trough—then warm, red liquid. After that, everything became a blur. When I saw him bleeding, I was so scared for Jason, and in the back of my mind I was worried that if I ran to get my mom she would ignore me. She heard Jason's howls, however, before I ever got there, and I was relieved to watch as my mother rushed to him and took care of everything, all by herself. Jason was going to be really bruised and sore for days, but he was also going to be all right.

When Dad came home, however, he wasn't happy about what had happened. He didn't spank Jason—he never punished any of us physically—but he was upset. Even though we had just been up camping and riding around on three-wheelers, sometimes going really fast, Dad had carefully ensured sure that none of us got hurt. He was the adamant protector of our physical bodies.

After he checked Jason out and knew he really was okay, he seemed to sigh, and I felt his energy shift as he got his blanket out. Carrie and Jason giggled, and I found myself giggling too because we all knew what was coming. Dad laid the blanket out carefully, whistling nonchalantly like he was the only one in the room and had no idea what would happen next. We all jumped into the middle part of the blanket and suddenly Dad bundled us up like a ball, putting us over his enormous shoulder to carry us around like a hobo with all of his belongings on his back. We were all squirming, and I couldn't help squealing in delight. I was always so amazed by how strong he was! He did it again and again, but after a while, I stood off to the side and watched as he wrapped Jason and Carrie up in the blanket and continued the hobo game. I smiled as he began to play pony with them, and finally wrestled just with Jason, but I didn't participate anymore. It wasn't that it didn't look fun; somehow it seemed safer on the outside, watching.

A few weeks later it was my first day of kindergarten. Living in Toppenish, just outside the valley, I hadn't had the opportunity to meet many people, and I certainly never compared our family with anyone else (except when Samantha had a Cabbage Patch Doll and I didn't). I was happy with our lives in Toppenish. I had no idea that Mom and Dad were having a rough time making ends meet.

One night I awakened to hear Mom and Dad fighting about my school clothes. They argued often, so I tried not to let it bother me. However, realizing they were fighting about me made me sick inside. I wanted that feeling to go away.

"I'm gone all the time to bring you and the family money, Laura!" Dad barked loudly. I covered my head with my pillow, but it didn't help much.

"You have got to learn how to cut back on what you spend on the road," said my mother, more quietly than my father, but her voice had an edge to it. "I can only do so much on the budget that we have. I did the best I could, but she needed new socks and underwear and at least a couple of nice items. It's important for her to have a few new things."

I thought about all the times I saw Mom working, doing her best to keep costs low. When she wasn't canning, she was cooking or sewing or cleaning. She even used to do the books for Grandpa, but I could tell she hadn't liked it because of the way her voice sounded whenever they talked about that time. It would get low and tight, like it was now.

Mom and Dad both loved to shop when we had the money, but they used money differently. Dad mostly spent a little bit of money all the time, like my Cabbage Patch Doll. Once in a while he would buy things like my bike and things for my mom. My mother, on the other hand, always said she would rather purchase one, really nice item than "a whole lot of junk." The argument moved from money to other things I didn't understand, but they seemed to blame each other for a lot of their unhappiness. Blame was a language I heard all of the time.

When I heard Dad talking about his life, it made me feel sad. It seemed he had a life of dreams that would never be. Born in Canada, he had always admired the rugged, outdoor life of mountaineers. He would tell anyone that listened that as he was growing up, he wanted nothing more than to join the Canadian Mounties.

"I'll never be able to do what I want," he would say sourly, then describe the severe fall he suffered during a climbing exercise in gym class. The rope had broken just as he reached the top. He told me that "part of his body also broke." He had received $30,000 in compensation when he and his father had pursued legal recourse against the school. Then my dad and his father had invested all the money into a business that didn't seem to work out very well, which he blamed on his father. He explained that his broken hip meant he lost all eligibility to become a Mountie. I had heard him tell that story lots and lots of times, and my heart always felt heavy and sad. Somewhere, deep down, I thought it was my fault he had to work so hard now. I didn't understand it, but whether it was here or at Grandpa's, money always seemed to be the biggest issue. A lot of conversations at the Jespersons revolved around money and work. My dad, his siblings, and their father worked really hard and several ran businesses or worked more than one job. Dad's work was usually heavy, physical work or projects that required him to be away from home. He had worked for an irrigation company, he framed houses, worked for a mining company, and now he trucked produce from farms and was gone for days at a time. Neither my father nor my mother knew what to do to bring in any more money or they would have already been doing it. However, it seemed to me that they still wanted to blame each other.

Dad didn't like getting into arguments with my mom. He would leave the house in a huff, often walking for hours at a time or taking a long ride on his bike. None of us minded because he seemed to be so much nicer when he came back.

In the dark, as I listened to them fighting now, I wondered if we would have to move again. My heart felt heavy at the thought. We'd lived in four places since I was a baby. First in a trailer court outside of Toppenish that I didn't remember, then we moved to Canada when I was only about two and Jason was still a baby. We lived there for two years, and Carrie was born there. Dad loved working in the mines, but his lifestyle caused some difficulties between him and my mom. Then something happened at his work that got him into trouble. His family asked us to come home, since Grandma Gladys was extremely ill, and everyone knew she was dying. We moved back to Washington and rented a home from my mother's aunt.

I missed the majestic Canadian peaks. I remembered how it felt when I pushed my way out our door so I could see the mountains—*feel* the mountains, as if I were a part of them. The wide-open spaces of Toppenish felt flat to me in comparison. People here would speak of the mountains, and for the longest time, I would squint to search for them, but all I could see were the bald, rolling hills in the distance, terraced with vineyards and surrounded by miles of apple orchards in all directions. We lived for a year in Selah before moving to this house we were in now.

I had a few vague memories of Selah, like the pool in the backyard that was never filled, the tiny table and chairs built right into the wall, and my loft bed that Grandpa Roy had made me. His gift of the loft bed helped me feel safer because mice had infested that house. At night they would come out and scuttle around in the dark. It had frightened me.

I remembered that our little place was next to a golf course where I would collect golf balls with Dad and sell them. I also remembered Dad killing our pet dog by beating his head in right in front of us, but I didn't like to remember that. I remembered Grandma Gladys (who liked to be called Glady) getting worse and worse with cancer. My mom fell quietly into despair, and my father wouldn't talk about it. I didn't want to remember that, either. I wanted to remember Grandma Glady for her soft-spoken voice and her patient and kind demeanor. Not that she was meek—in fact, far from it—she was strong, independent, and a very likeable lady. She would knit beautiful sweaters for us and she loved working on ceramics. Grandma Glady kept her hands busy, kept her home spotless, and had taken my mom under her wing. When everyone in Dad's family would tease Mom for her Christian beliefs and values, Glady would come to her aid.

I didn't want her to die, and I didn't want to move again. I liked Toppenish with its two porches and the picture window where my mom planted roses. I liked the farmyard, the peach tree, Samantha, and the dusty lane to ride my bike.

I fell into a sleep troubled with nightmares about attending school in Carrie's clothes while all the kids laughed at me. Then I was whisked away to a house, but it was on top of another house and another house . . . and I climbed and climbed until I had climbed to the top of a very tall rope and began to fall—I woke up screaming in terror.

The next day, my parents had seemed to resolve their differences, and the day was fairly normal. I was relieved, though it didn't work in my favor. Since kindergarten had started, my bedtime suddenly was strictly enforced by both of them. The problem was, Dolly Parton was playing on the television. I got very upset and started to whine because Dolly was my absolute most favorite singer in the whole, wide world! I felt like I would die if she was on TV and I couldn't see her.

"Go to bed, Melissa!" growled my father from his position in front of the TV. "It's way past your bedtime, and I'm not going to ask you again!" I ran to my room, my heart broken. I wanted to *be* Dolly Parton, with her beautiful blonde hair and her dazzling smile. She was always so happy. All that summer I had walked around the house and yard with my tape player, singing with her to *Coat of Many Colors*. I had even bought the album with my own birthday money, and I had every song memorized. Inspired by Dolly, I spent hours in the bathtub singing about Suave shampoo and conditioner and believing that someday I would be a famous singer.

When my parents ignored my tantrum, I realized it wasn't going to work. While they were distracted by the television, I decided to try a different tactic. I snuck into my parent's room and into my mom's drawers where I pulled out one of her intimate items. Putting it on, I filled it with toilet paper and socks until both cups were full. I looked in the mirror and I felt like Dolly! It was a big risk, but I snuck out to where they were watching television.

Unsure if I was in for a great laugh or loads of trouble, I strutted out in front of them and began to sing. At the look on my parents' faces, I knew all was well. Even my mom was laughing so hard she was nearly crying.

"Come here!" they said. Still laughing, they patted the space between them. *Mom and Dad all to myself?* I was on top of the world.

3

❧❧

secret recipes

Grandma Glady passed away from her cancer, and life seemed to swirl in chaos for a while. For several gloomy days after the funeral, we spent quite a bit of time helping Grandpa Roy get through his grief and learn to handle household tasks. Grandpa decided to attend a grief support group, which everyone thought would be good for him. They were not too pleased when, within a few weeks of attending, Grandpa announced he had fallen in love with a woman named Lucy, and that she was his new girlfriend. He brought her over a lot, and she seemed really nice. I liked her, but I was oblivious to the strained energy of the grown ups.

On a sunny day a few weeks after the funeral, the family was gathered at Grandpa Roy's place. He spoke to the grown ups while the kids played together. We had just started a fun game when quite suddenly it was time to go. I liked playing with my cousins and didn't want to leave, but I could see by the somber look on my parents' faces that they were not willing to negotiate. The car ride home seemed solemn as well, but Jason and Carrie and I kept ourselves busy with a backseat game and tried not to notice.

Later that night when I was supposed to be asleep, I overheard Mom and Dad speaking in low, agonized voices. I felt like I should have been shocked at the news that Grandpa Roy was marrying Lucy, but I was happy for him. I had seen Grandpa so miserable, and I didn't want him to be alone. I missed Glady and I childishly hoped Lucy would be as nice to us as Glady had been. Still, I could see that the decision made my mom and dad very uncomfortable. They whispered other things I didn't understand, like Grandpa's getting a divorce and declaring bankruptcy to pay for Glady's bills before she died. There were also rumors of something called "infidelity" while Glady was still alive. I didn't know what any of that meant, so I went to bed.

As Mom and Dad struggled with Grandpa's decision, we spent more time at our house. My father had always had difficulties getting along with his dad, and he just seemed to breathe easier at home. They had a very different relationship, in which they had to try to outdo each other. Usually Grandpa would end up the winner. He seemed to revel in teasing my dad. He would tell anyone who would listen how slow my dad was, always lagging behind everyone else. From what I saw, my father was a jogger, a biker, and an avid golfer. He seemed faster and stronger than most men his age. Grandpa had called him Sloth when he was younger and then Igor. I didn't understand either of those names, just the look on my dad's face when he was the butt of Grandpa's jokes. I didn't like to see him hurt, so I felt better about staying home. Still, I missed my cousins and wondered when we would spend time with them again.

Fortunately, I found that school was more fun than I had expected. I was so happy to be around a lot of kids and new friends. As school continued, I learned that as soon as I got on the bus, I felt fully alive, and lost myself in lessons and recess. One thing I discovered was that I absolutely loved to learn. No one had to force me to go to a place where I could learn more every day.

Grandpa got married to Lucy, and for a long while we didn't go over there very much. After some time passed, however, something shifted and family life started to get back to normal. As much as the family had tried not to accept Lucy, her naturally loving and kind ways invited people in. She genuinely cared for people, and they couldn't help but warm up to her. While no one could ever take Glady's place, even my mom came to accept and care for Lucy in a different kind of way.

Personally, I thought Lucy was magnificent, especially her cooking. She had these amazing old recipes memorized—passed down from generations of family, some of them long gone—and the food she made was delicious. Lucy also listened to me and my stories about life and school, paying close attention, so I was excited when I learned we would soon be moving next door to Grandpa and Lucy.

As time passed in Toppenish, it was becoming harder and harder for Mom and Dad to make ends meet. Lucy and Grandpa had moved into Lucy's red brick, Cape Cod–styled home, and brought his trailer onto her property. Grandpa was never one to cower from assisting family, or to let an economic opportunity go by. He offered the trailer to my parents at a price they couldn't resist and could much better afford. At this point, Dad was working away from home for days and nights at a time, trucking produce down to California and other areas of the nation. I longed for the times he would come home, grab us in his blanket and carry us around. The longer we lived next door to Grandpa, the longer Dad's times away from us seemed.

Still, Jason, Carrie, and I were in paradise. Lucy's house and our new trailer sat on miles of orchard-covered hills in the Yakima Valley, nestled in the beautiful Naches Mountains. We played for hours in the exquisitely set rows upon rows of decked-out blossoms or red bejeweled apple trees. Spring, summer, or fall, the scents were heavenly, and each season brought new delights. We wouldn't come inside until the golden light upon the mountains reminded us to go home and eat—if we weren't already full on the red, delicious apples, growing ripe in the sun.

Next door, Lucy's house often smelled of homemade cinnamon rolls. In the afternoons, I would sometimes make an impromptu visit to see the progress of the cinnamon dough, waiting for it to become scintillatingly edible. Between her housekeeping and cooking skills, Lucy was a domestic queen. Her natural ability to entertain made her an easy person to spend time with. I came to realize that part of her relaxed demeanor had to do with the glass of wine she would sip on most afternoons, but it seemed to go with her laid-back style. She also spoiled me, seeming to know what many young girls finds glamorous—designer makeup, shopping, and gossip magazines. If I had a medical need, such as a cut or headache, Lucy was always equipped to come to the rescue. Her medicine cabinet looked like the neighborhood pharmacy, and under her kitchen sink was a wet bar of pain relievers such as peach or peppermint flavored schnapps. She would take me on shopping trips to Lamonts department store, and I would stare at the beautiful displays and the price tags in wonder, especially since I was used to Kmart and discount stores. I learned that Lucy had been married to the Wiley apple mogul and had enjoyed some of the finer things of life in her day.

I was much less comfortable around Grandpa, although he spoiled me as well and always treated Carrie and me with great tenderness. Still, he was a very strict, conservative, authority figure. If we were in trouble, he would keep his voice calm, but underneath I could hear him struggling to restrain himself. I always felt that as children we should fear him, though he always called it, "respecting him." If we did not listen or obey, then the threat was the belt, especially for Jason. My grandfather had a double standard for boys and girls, and was particularly hard on his own sons and grandsons. My inner voice told me to beware and not cross him, but Grandpa never did spank or put a hand to us. I thought I knew why. I was around the corner when we first moved in, and I had heard my father say, "Don't you *ever* hit them. Don't you even touch them!"

"They're *my* grandkids, Keith!" Grandpa argued. But the look on my father's face must have been enough to quell Grandpa's response. I was thankful that my father had stood up for us. From occasional comments I overheard from Dad and his siblings, it seemed to me that they had lived with two fathers: one before he quit drinking and one after. I gathered from their hushed tones that he must have been incredibly hurtful and abusive. My dad seemed to carry the scars of that emotionally. While I had never seen that side of my grandfather to its full extent, I had seen my giant of a father belittled to bits and pieces, spoken to like a child instead of a grown man. As Grandpa became a Christian, his demeanor became more relaxed and even loving at times. To me, life was perfect. I didn't realize that the only constant I could count on in life was change.

4

❧

the burning

Life felt rich and full and comfortable in Yakima, especially in the quiet, peaceful home my mother kept for us. The only thing that was missing was Dad when he was gone on his long hauls. During that time, my parents appeared to have few arguments, or at least they did not argue in front of us. My father prided himself on the fact that he never laid a hand on my mother or any of us. I also think he prided himself on being different from his father in that respect.

One evening Dad arrived home, looking exhausted as usual. Something seemed a little different about him, but I couldn't place it. We all cheered and ran up to him to hug him. Carrie hugged his tall legs, and he picked her up.

"Let's play, Daddy!" she cried, delighted as he swung her around. He had never refused to play with us, so we weren't afraid to request a game.

"Leave your poor father alone!" scolded Mom. "He's tired. You can play with him tomorrow." But then she laughed as we ended up on the floor in giggles.

The next day, I didn't want to go to school, which was strange for me. I loved Garfield Elementary and my teachers, and I had made some great friends. Now that I was in second grade, I enjoyed my full day of learning. This morning, however, I woke up with the feeling that something was wrong, and I thought it had to do with my dad leaving again. I wanted to stay home with him every minute until it was time for him to depart. Mom wouldn't allow it, so I dragged my feet out to the bus and grudgingly got on.

At school, I actually had a good day, as I ignored the growing feeling of danger, chalking it up to missing my dad. I almost had an argument with myself—wanting to tell the feeling to shut up and go away! I hadn't felt that ominous feeling in so long; I didn't want to acknowledge it anymore. I wanted to pretend it wasn't real, or at least that it wasn't always right.

When the bell rang, I got onto the bus, making my way to the back bench. I loved sitting there because it was different from all the other seats and made me feel special, surrounded by friends. I urged the bus to go faster, hopeful that maybe Dad would still be there when I got home.

As we made our way along the winding roads from Garfield, I started feeling sick. The bus seemed hot, even with the windows down, and I felt myself sweating, which was unusual. I got more and more uncomfortable in my seat, wondering if I was going to throw up. The ominous feeling inside me had grown to a nauseating alarm. I glanced over at my buddies on the bus, wondering if I looked as horrible as I felt. I saw from their faces that something was wrong—horrendously wrong. There was a great honking alongside of us, and we looked over, our faces pressed to the glass. People were driving up, honking, waving, and pointing frantically at the rear portion of the bus. Suddenly there was a frightened shriek and I saw it—flames shooting out of the back of the vehicle. I began to scream, my howls joining those of forty or fifty other children. We all shouted at the same time as thick black, smoke and more flames enveloped us. My bus seat was on fire!

The driver stopped abruptly, and when the doors opened, the pandemonium of frightened children erupted outward as each child tried to save his own life. The heat and smoke were intense, and all I could hear was the screaming, screaming . . . .

Suddenly I was transported into a memory that I had shoved down in my attempt to forget it forever. A stray cat had gotten stuck in our burn barrel at our house in Toppenish. It couldn't get out, and its frightened moans had alerted Jason and my father. Instead of springing it loose, however, as my brother and I thought he would, Dad had poured gasoline on the pile of debris in the barrel and lit it on fire in front of us. The cat's agonized screams melded with Jason's and my own. Now I could hear our screaming again, along with the children on the bus and my father's jeering laughter. In the midst of the smoke and the mayhem, I thought I was going to die, like the stray cat. I felt that a part of me *wanted* to die . . . As everything was going black, I was suddenly whisked up and off the bus, even though the driver was still toward the front, trying to evacuate children in a safe and orderly manner through the bedlam.

Fortunately, every kid made it off the bus, and no one was seriously burned or injured. When another bus dropped me off at my stop on the other side of the orchard, I ran through the trees, blinded by tears. Normally, I loved strolling through the huge orchard and playing in and out of the trees. This time I panicked, and got lost. Everywhere I looked, the trees all looked the same. I ran on and on, never finding my way home. The friendly orchard had turned into another nightmare. *Help me.*

A short while later, I was surprised to feel that a calm had come over me. I was calm enough to recognize where I was and find my way back home. When I saw my mother, I collapsed into her arms. By the look on my tear-stained face and the smell of acrid smoke in my clothes and hair, she knew I was telling the truth about the bus. With a look of great concern, she whisked me into the house and checked my body for burns. She found only scratches from the trees, but I ignored those and quietly asked to go to my room. My mother searched my face, wondering if I had inhaled some of the smoke—usually I would enjoy her attention and play up the drama of a good story. Now all I wanted to do was escape, to feel that the bus and the barrel weren't real . . . couldn't be real.

The next morning, I was shaking uncontrollably as I slowly took each step onto my school bus. I saw one or two other pale faces and wide, frightened eyes. Now I didn't feel so alone—I had something in common with my classmates. The other memory was shoved deep inside, and I pretended, once again, that it had never happened. Searching for a seat, I refused to sit anywhere near the back, and even my eyes avoided the rumble seat. *I promise I will never ignore another warning.*

I was never made aware of what caused that small fire, but I did make it to and from school that day without another mishap. Still, it took me several weeks before I could get on a bus without trembling.

5

wrong number

It was several months before I encountered another foreboding. It came upon me strongly and suddenly, a couple of days before my father returned from a long trip. He had been away for ages this time. He was starting to spend longer periods working. He was making good money, so my parents didn't argue much with each other. While my mother didn't seem to mind his absences as much as Carrie, Jason, and I did, I could tell she missed him too. She was always eager to answer the phone to find out when he would be on his way home. A couple of times she hung up with a confused look on her face. Apparently, a lot of women had been getting wrong numbers lately.

Dad arrived home, and, as usual, we were all delighted to see him. After our play and wrestling routine, he announced he would be able to stay at home for a few days. We cheered, reveling in the idea that we would get to spend some real time with him. Since Mom always had a lengthy list of "honey-do's" for him, Dad promised to take me, Jason, and Carrie into town with him to pick up supplies so he could tackle his list. We were thrilled because it meant more time with Dad and that usually meant an ice cream, donut, or some other special treat, like Carrie's gummy worms. Often we went to the places he knew best, which were truck stops.

The next morning, Dad's energy seemed particularly high, and I noticed he whistled a lot as we shopped. He seemed eager, and I found myself feeling that same emotion in the pit of my stomach. Did he have a gift for Mom? Sometimes when he was away, he picked up something special to surprise her. He hadn't done that for a while, and I believed that must be the case. I looked forward to going home, especially because all three of us kids were getting tired.

Finally, we finished the shopping and arrived at the truck stop restaurant. I was tired, but I was even hungrier and couldn't wait to order. Suddenly a woman came up to our table. She wasn't the waitress, and as I peered at her curiously, my dad jumped up.

"Hey, kids," he said, clearing his throat. "I want to introduce you to someone. This is a friend of mine. Her name is Toni."

"Hello," she said simply, and we returned her greeting. I thought it was strange that she acted nonchalant, even shrugging like we weren't that important. But her eyes were studying us carefully. I decided to study her too. She was wiry and slim—so slim that she could wear children's-sized clothing and shoes. Her brown, thin hair was feathered back in a style she might have kept from the 1970s. I noticed that her voice was rough and coarse, like smokers get after a while, and she seemed to want to prove to my father that she was independent and tough, even. We found out that she had two young children like us, a boy and a girl who lived with her in Portland.

Dad invited her to sit and eat with us, and quite suddenly I didn't want her to. I didn't like the easy way she sat down next to my father. I didn't like the way she laughed at his jokes. And I especially didn't like the way he kept coming up with new ones to make her laugh. It was natural for my father to show off in front of women, but I found myself gritting my teeth. A couple of times, I poked his leg with my foot. *Knock it off, Dad*, I thought. *You're way overdoing it.*

Dad ignored me, and we ate together and then had dessert. Finally it was time to go, and I scooted around the bench so quickly it burned my bare legs on the vinyl.

"Nice to meet you, Toni," I murmured politely, and I noticed Dad paid for Toni's meal. That wasn't unusual. My dad was very generous, and I had seen him pay for lots of people's meals—men and women alike. He let people borrow his tools and his vehicles, and he was always helping somebody out of a pinch, even people who never returned the favor. Still, that didn't bug me nearly so bad as the way Toni tucked her arm into his on their way out, like she had known him forever.

We jumped into the car, and I was eager to get away.

"Stay here, kids," Dad said firmly, and shut the door on us. He walked away with Toni, around the corner to where she was parked. I wanted to get out and take a peek at her and what she was driving, but I knew better than to disobey. Plus, my mother would not be happy with me for judging this woman on the basis of her outward appearance and just one meeting. For a moment, I had the strangest feeling that Mom would not have really liked this woman, either, though I wasn't sure why. Only a minute or two later, Dad came back to our vehicle, and I breathed a sigh of relief. I wondered then, as we drove away, why the feeling in my stomach didn't go away.

6

❧

no brakes

A few days after Dad was gone, I was hanging out in the living room with Jason and Carrie. Mom was in the kitchen, humming happily. It was her and Dad's thirteenth anniversary, and I knew she was expecting roses. She had already gotten the vase out and had it off to the side. Flowers brought her enormous pleasure, and she planted them as often as she could at the places we had lived.

I listened to her absently as I played with Dad's racing bike. It was a huge bicycle—it had to be to fit his 6'6" frame—and we had to keep it in the living room as there wasn't room anywhere else, and it was his baby. Keeping the kickstand all the way down and over, so the back wheel was free, I played with the pedals. *Whirr . . . whirr . . .* The wheels spun quickly and quietly in one direction. I stared at the chrome, silver, and black as it went by, blurring my vision with the speed. Every once in a while, I could see a small blur of white from the brand name of the wheel, but it was too fast for my mind to seize it and read it. Faster and faster I turned the pedal, and the wheel magically continued its course with breakneck speed. *zzz . . . CLACK!* The wheel stopped short when I stood up and applied the brake.

I played with the pedals again and again. *Whirr . . . Whirr . . . Whirr . . . zzz CLACK!* Carrie came over and watched for a while, mesmerized like I was. At one point, she put her hand out to try to stop the wheel.

"No!" I screamed at her. She looked at me with such shock and hurt in her eyes, I knew she was going to cry.

"Wait, Carrie! See?" I pleaded, hoping she wouldn't run to Mom. No sounds came from the kitchen, so I turned back to Carrie. "Watch what could happen." If you touch here, it's going too fast and it could burn your skin . . . Now look at this." I stopped the wheel completely, then stuck my hand between the silver spokes. Ever so lightly, I pressed the pedal, and the wheel automatically began to turn, taking my wrist and forearm with it.

"Ouch! See?" I pointed at my arm that was all twisted up in an awkward angle to illustrate my point. "You don't want to put your hand anywhere near this thing while it's going—it's way too fast."

"Yeah," laughed Jason. "It would rip your skin right off, or even break your arm!" He made a move like he was going to come over and push harder on the pedal. I glared at him. This was supposed to be a teaching moment. He was such a . . . . such a . . . brother.

"I'm smarter than that, Jason!" Carrie pouted. I looked at her. *Yes she was.* Carrie was a little stinker sometimes because she was so amazingly smart.

I purposely let my sister take the next turn on the pedals, even though I knew Jason thought he should be next. He stuck his tongue out at me and went to turn on his video game. The last time he had played it, Dad had been here, challenging him to a match. They played for hours, and I don't think they ever knew who actually won, which was a first—Jespersons were notoriously competitive. I glanced around the immaculate living room. Mom kept this room and the rest of the house so clean that the only things even remotely out of place were my backpack and Jason's video game. Oh, and the bike.

The bike!

Quickly I turned my attention back to Carrie and breathed a sigh of relief. She was playing with the pedals like I had been, careful to keep her hands away from the wheel. I thought about how much fun she was to hang out with. Now that she was older and in kindergarten, she was fiery and independent and kept up with me and Jason with little trouble. Despite her independent streak, she was very loving and would usually listen to me, for which I was grateful. She listened to Jason more, but I was okay with that.

In a split second, I noticed my sister was concentrating so hard on making the pedals go faster and faster that she didn't notice the big bike beginning to tip. I saw what was going to happen before it did. Even though I had my hand on the bike to steady it, the second it touched down, the tire gripped the carpeted floor and sprung forward with a violent jolt. Just in time, I pulled on it, almost getting knocked off my feet as I held onto the huge frame, using all my weight to prevent it from smashing into the wall and doing any damage to the bike. I knew the bike was safe, but I was afraid the wheel brushing against the wall would make a big black mark and I pulled it away quickly, steadying myself and avoiding the teethed pedals and straps.

Carrie, however, wasn't so lucky. One pedal had scraped across her shin. It wasn't deep at all, but I could see some white where the skin had peeled off and I cringed in empathy. I was glad there wasn't blood because I could never handle it. Surprisingly, Carrie didn't cry, even as Jason rushed over to assist us.

"I'm okay," she said. With a look of irritation, she brushed her hands across the sensitive skin. Jason gave her a look of such tenderness, that I forgot I was mad at him. I went to get a band-aid for Carrie, even though she claimed she didn't need it. As I put it on, I noticed a shade of red under the white, peeled skin. No bleeding broke through, but I could tell there was going to be a big bruise there. It amazed me how quickly something could get out of my control like that. It felt disconcerting to me, and I didn't like it. I put the bike back up against the wall in its special spot. Neither Carrie nor Jason felt like messing with the machine anymore. Glancing one more time at the bandage on Carrie's shin, I went to help my mother set the table for dinner.

Later that night, after we were in bed, I heard dad come in the door. I smiled. *Happy Anniversary*, I thought, and went back to sleep

The next morning as the mid-morning sun shone on the game I was playing with Carrie, Mom came into the room.

"Girls," she said, in a firm and tight voice. I immediately knew something was wrong.

"What is it, Mom?" I asked, my eyes alert.

"Nothing," she said firmly, but then I saw her swallow hard. "I need you to pack one thing for the car that is very special to you—just one thing. We're going on a trip!" Her voice had perked up, and she tried to make it sound like it was going to be fun, then briskly left the room to give Jason the same instructions. She wouldn't answer any of my questions or theirs— just tried to make it sound like we were going on a great adventure.

Carrie and Jason grabbed their items without a second thought, ready for a new quest. I, on the other hand, couldn't decide what to take. Many of my things seemed vitally important to me, but after another moment, I knew exactly what to bring. I decided to pack my boom box, since music made everything better and was one of my biggest joys in life. I didn't sing commercials in the tub anymore or pretend I was Dolly Parton, but I did sing every chance I got. Behind me, Mom was rushing around, and I noticed she packed a few items in a bag for each of us. Then she ushered us to the door.

Quickly, I glanced back and saw Dad's bike shimmering as the door opened in the early morning light. Though it was still and silent, for a moment I swore I could see chrome, silver, and black, spinning faster and faster . . .

7

the new game

It was so sudden and unexpected. One moment I was safe in my bed in the hills of Yakima in a loving home with a mom and a dad next door to caring grandparents, then abruptly I was driving with my mother, brother, and sister into absolutely unknown territory—far from anything we had known before.

After leaving our home, we stopped to buy a few snacks, including Jo-Jos, that we ate on the way. We left Yakima for good, never to return. Mom continued to play the game that this was some great adventure. Carrie and Jason certainly wanted to believe her, but I could tell there was much more to all of this. I needed answers. For several miles, she refused to respond. I kept asking and asking until she finally broke down.

"Your father doesn't want us anymore." Great pain showed in her deep brown eyes. She paused, only briefly and then said, "We're moving to Spokane to live with my mother—your Grandma Frances—until we can get on our feet and get a place of our own." We were astonished and in total shock. It was completely silent in the car for several minutes. Then all of a sudden it seemed to hit Jason and me at about the same time, and we began to cry. When Carrie saw our distress, suddenly she knew this couldn't be good either. She joined in the sobbing, and the car seemed wrapped up in a cloud of complete misery.

Scenes flashed before my eyes—some mirrored those flashing by outside the car window though they seemed so far away and unreal, and others were invisible to anyone except me. *Didn't want us anymore . . . Spokane . . . my grandmother . . . place of our own . . .*

We have *a place of our own!* I wanted to argue. Our home in the hills, surrounded by the apple and cherry orchards and the blossoms and the golden sun in the evenings . . . A home with friends, neighbors, and Lucy and Grandpa. And it was the only place I knew where Dad would come to play with us.

Spokane . . . the word seemed so strange to me—so alien and for-eign—even though Mom said it was in the same state. What would it be like? Was it like Yakima, or Selah, or Toppenish—like something I had known? I tried to pretend this really was a glorious adventure. I pretended it was some kind of grand vacation that would be over at some point in time, and then we would be home. We were just visiting a family member, that's all. Mom said that Grandma Frances lived in a small house on the outskirts of Spokane, and that one of my mother's brothers lived with her. I remembered that my grandmother had lived in Yakima when Mom was first married, and then she had moved to Spokane. Mom was the only one of the Zerbos family who had stayed behind. The Zerbos family was very different from the Jesperson family. The Jespersons had all made their own ways far away from each other. We had been the closest to my father's par-ents, and that had been more due to economics than anything.

It took hours and hours of driving, made more difficult because we sobbed all the way there in our anguish. I couldn't help but notice as we finally neared Spokane that the road widened and there were suddenly more cars on the road than I had ever seen in my life. It seemed to me they were speeding by. Mom was a slow and conservative driver, and they were zipping past us at speeds I wasn't familiar with. The frenzied energy continued the closer we approached, and I found myself drawn in and fas-cinated in spite of myself. I had that familiar unease in my stomach, but I did my best to quiet it. Surely it was because all of this was so unknown to me. I had a sense of wanting the scenes to slow down and even pause so I could take it all in. I felt everything was moving so fast that I would always be running to catch up.

"There it is!" Mom announced as we headed down the hilltops and into the big city. My mouth dropped open and so did my sister's and brother's. We had all seen some tall buildings before, but not "skyscapers" as Carrie called them—definitely not like this, so close together. The seat belt was tight against my belly as I strained to see everything. I didn't want to miss one sight. As we got closer to downtown we were making quite a ruckus in our excitement, pointing things out to each other. My mother told us firmly that we needed to be quiet. I saw her white knuckles on the steering wheel and understood that she had to concentrate on her driving since she was in a big city now.

It was such a challenge to be calm and quiet! We were so excited to see everything, and even enjoyed the fast cars hurtling past us, honking at our mother's slow driving.

We drove past the bigger city and out into a more suburb-type area. I breathed a small sigh, grateful that we would not be living downtown. That kind of dramatic change felt like it would be way too much. As we got closer to my grandmother's house, however, I was still surprised at how close everyone lived to one another. There were no large fields or rows of apple trees between homes. Instead, the houses were literally squeezed right next to one another—and the fences! I had never seen so many fences. In our town, people generally only fenced their yard if they had animals— and that usually was an electric fence, not chain link or privacy fences. It made me feel curious as to how these people lived. My first thought was that they must all really like one another to live so close together. Then in some places, I saw iron bars on the doors and windows of shops and even homes. They seemed a little ominous to me, like tiny jails that you could go into and never come out of. Still, many of the houses were unique, in styles of architecture I'd never seen before. We started to see people of all backgrounds and ethnicities. I really was fascinated, and I began to feel a building sense of excitement to experience these new lifestyles, new ways of being.

We pulled up to Grandma's house, and I stared at it for a while. This was to be our new home. Jason, Carrie, and I were feeling rambunctious and ready to finally get out of the car. Mom stopped us.

"Play out here in the front yard," she instructed, indicating the fenced-in area out front. Jason and Carrie protested, wanting to go inside, but I sensed that Mom needed time to explain things to Grandma first, so I convinced the other two to come sit on the grass with me.

Our grandmother did not have any toys, so we just sat on the lawn. I was relieved to see kids playing in a couple different areas up and down the street. At least kids played here. We hadn't received any other instructions and were unsure of our new boundaries. I didn't know if we would be allowed to leave the fenced yard, but it was amazing to us to see so many kids. In Yakima, my closest friend lived all the way on the other side of the orchard—about a mile from my house—so I wasn't able to simply walk to her house to play. Here there were kids all over the place, and it seemed like you could step out of your door and play anytime.

Some of those kids appeared curious about the three of us, and they left the game they were playing in the street and walked over to us.

"What's your name?" asked a girl who seemed about my age. We told them who we were and that we were staying with our grandmother. As they asked us more questions, like how long we would be staying, I sized up their ages. There was another girl who seemed about my age and a younger girl about Jason's age, though I figured he probably wouldn't want to play with her since she wasn't a boy. We proceeded to ask them questions about who lived in the neighborhood and if there were any boys. I also explained that we did not know how long we were staying.

When we were finally allowed inside, I was amazed at how tiny Grandma's place was. Having just lived in a trailer, we were used to tight quarters, but this would be cramped. I felt bad for Grandma Frances, who was a very quiet woman. I wondered if our presence would bother her. She didn't say much, but offered us kind eyes and cinnamon toast. I was famished. She kept making toast, and we kept eating it. Soon I found that I had eaten too many. It was the first time I had eaten—and overeaten—for comfort.

Within twenty-four hours, my brother and sister and I had all paired up with the neighborhood kids that were our ages, and blessedly, we did not have to spend much time confined to the yard. After a short period of time, our mother also seemed to adapt into her own environment. We did not see much of her for the next few days as we busied ourselves with our new friends. Sarah Atkins and Katie Clark came to be my closest friends, and it felt good to be busy out in the neighborhood and in other people's homes instead of being in the house with Mom, my uncle and Grandma. Mom told us very little, and it was only on a need-to-know basis. We had no knowledge of the details of our parents' separation. I really didn't even have a clue about my mother's emotional state, since she was completely stone-faced around us. When we did ask questions, she refused to provide answers.

"You're too young to worry about that, Melissa," my mother said that sunny afternoon in August. "Everything is fine."

I trusted that Mom knew what she was doing. Since there was no schedule here, I made one up for a sense of security and direction. At first, I also kept track of Jason and Carrie, to make sure they were safe and I always knew where they were. Quite soon, however, it was easier for all of us to go and do our own thing, and so we did. I didn't know that this was the beginning of how life would continue on for us—each of us going in our separate directions, searching for survival and peace—each seeking what happiness we could in our individual lives. The only control we had was over our summer play, and so, why not go for it?

I didn't know what my siblings were feeling, since during the day we separated except to come together during neighborhood games. Nighttime was filled with baths, dinner, and preparing for bed. In the evenings, if we talked at all, we shared stuff about our friends and what we did for the day—never expressing our feelings, and certainly not our fears. None of us wanted to show weakness or to break the rule of silence. It wasn't that we didn't want to discuss the situation. We were simply surviving by using the only strategy we knew—pretending that it was okay and that we were happy. No one dared to break the strategy because in our new and fragile little world, we did not know any other way to deal with it.

Everything at Grandma's that week seemed so temporary, since we only had the few items of clothing Mom had packed for us, plus our one special item. Even the makeshift beds in the basement seemed to indicate to us that of course this couldn't be permanent.

A few days later, however, our father appeared in Grandma's front yard. I ran down the street, deliriously happy to see his face and his open arms, until I noticed the trailer. It was packed full of our belongings, and not one item in it belonged to Dad.

8

new discoveries,
new hope

The next morning as Dad left, I thought I was being torn in two pieces. Dad had wrestled with us, played games, and taken the three of us out to eat at a local truck stop. Mom didn't come.

"Why don't you stay here?" I pleaded to my father when we were eating. "You and Mom can work this out."

"Laura will never forgive me," he replied, his head hung low. Even though he didn't believe it would work, I could tell he was truly thinking about it. Surely being around all of us was enough to want us back, wasn't it? I tried a new tact.

"We need you, Daddy," I said. Rarely did I call him by that name anymore, usually thinking I was too grown up for it. "Mom needs you."

He was silent for a long time, and it made Jason and Carrie nervous, but I didn't care. I wanted him to hurt enough to come back to us, to see that we needed him. A few minutes later, he changed the subject, and our conversation was all but forgotten. I wanted to cry.

When Dad dropped us back at Grandma's, I wasn't the only one begging. The three of us clung to his legs in desperation.

"Please, don't leave, Daddy!" cried Carrie. Jason and I both hung on silently. I had already given my argument, but the tears streaming down my face were surely worth something. Our father untangled us, got into his vehicle, and disappeared down the road. The man that always bragged he was "the best dad in the world" had left us. I could tell it was breaking his heart too, but not enough to come back for us. Not enough.

A few short days later, my mother announced she had enrolled us in school in Spokane. Despite what I had experienced with my dad, I was surprised to hear that I would be staying longer; so long that I needed to go to school there. Disappointment welled up inside me, like a huge rock on my chest. We would have to stay in our grandmother's home while we attended school. She didn't really have room for us, and our little space in the dank darkness of the basement was less than cheerful. It was one thing to spend a summer camping out, playing outside in the sun all day. That was livable. But to suddenly realize that I would have to sleep on the uncomfortable cot in the corner of the basement—with shoeboxes for drawers—for days on end, seemed to douse any flame of happiness that I had mustered to this point. Plus, I didn't have any supplies that a normal home would have, or even my own desk to do homework. I felt unprepared. Even though my father had brought many of our belongings up from Yakima, I was still missing so much—and there was no room to put it all anyway.

Despite my misgivings, I began attending Evergreen Elementary a few weeks later. I walked into my classroom with my head held high, but inside, my stomach was turned inside out. Surely all these people could see my insecurities stamped across my forehead. My earlier love for learning forgotten, I expected that my teacher would be mean and boring, and that life would be completely sucked of all joy.

I was surprised to find out that my teacher was a tall, blond, athletic man. I was even more surprised as he began to engage with our entire class, getting to know us in an easy-going, laid-back style that was so much more inspiring than controlling. A coach and a teacher, he was passionate in working with children, and his positive energy rubbed off on us quickly. One of the first things he inspired us to do was to dream *big*. He asked us to write an essay about what we wanted to do when we grew up. He encouraged us to write as if we had no limitations—none. What would we be? At first, everyone talked about things their parents did and the kinds of jobs they were familiar with, but as the teacher engaged us, he extracted our dreams and our desires. I couldn't believe it—this exercise was so much fun. I drew a long limousine and wrote about being a movie star. Many of my classmates were similarly inspired, and some drew astronauts and presidents.

It was such a liberating feeling to dream! All of a sudden, I felt like I really *could* be anything, *have* anything, that I was only limited by my imagination. For the first time, I had a tool to deal with the uncertainty of the future. And just by making today better, I was equally excited to see what I could embrace in new days to come. I began to feel alive, and hope started to spring within me. At first I hoped for my parents to get back together, then it was to live as a family, then it was to have our own home. Some of these thoughts and emotions seemed unrealistic and childish, and yet I realized that they were the hope that was keeping me going, keeping me alive inside. I didn't realize how much of a role these dreams would play in my own future.

As much as I loved my new teacher, I found fitting in to this new school much harder than it had been in Yakima. In my old school, I was equal to everyone—*everyone* was equal to everyone! Here it seemed very different.

The first thing I noticed (especially because people noticed it about me and pointed it out) was that my clothes did not meet the expensive standards that society seemed to have set. In addition to that, I did not have involved parents who would support school activities like PTA or Girl Scouts. That also meant I did not have a group to fit into like everyone else seemed to have.

During recess, I used all kinds of tactics to avoid the other kids since they had a tendency to tease me and could be incredibly cruel. One day, the boys wanted to play dodge ball on the brick wall. My neighborhood friend, Sarah, had a different group she liked to play with at school. They played a game on the asphalt called four-square the whole time, and I was never invited. They made it very clear that I was not equal to them.

I was pleasantly surprised when one girl began to gravitate toward me. Her name was Kimberley, and she had kinky, wavy hair, braces, and two dimples when she smiled really wide. Kimberley and I would go to the top of the small hill where all the pine trees were and play house. I would make walls out of pine needles and make lines in the dirt for a kitchen, including tables and chairs, as well as the rest of the house. We had great fun.

One weekend, Kimberley invited me to her home, and I accepted. She had the same kind of dolls that my cousins did—*American Girl* dolls! In fact, she had the entire Samantha collection, with a table, tea set, and a chest for Samantha's Victorian clothes. I had so much fun playing, but the longer we played, the more clear it became that I would never own one of these dolls, much less an entire set. I suddenly felt very inferior, and it made me sad that I was even inferior to the only girl I had connected with at school.

During the school year, my father made another surprise visit to Carrie, Jason, and me. He said he simply couldn't come to Spokane without checking on his kids, which made us feel a little better. We didn't know he would be coming, so even though his visit was brief since he was only waiting for a load to pick up, we were pleased and excited to see him. Dad had more expendable income than Mom, and proved to be generous on the occasion of his visits, so I saw this as an opportunity to get at least one or two items that I needed in order to fit in. My father seemed to know how difficult it was to fit in at school. Eventually he had developed a thick skin, he said, but I had been unable to do that yet. As the school year had progressed, it had become more and more apparent that there was a huge gap between the discount clothing I wore, and the designer labels worn by the majority of the school. I had heard from my mother and father that "clothes don't make the man" but I saw how it certainly contributed. When I was walking down the hall the first day of school, every butt had a yellow Guess triangle on the pocket. Every one except mine, that is.

While Dad was there on his short visit, he agreed to take us on a little shopping excursion. We had a great time at the mall, and I worked him over really good for a pair of $60 Guess jeans. That was more money than I was given to spend on my entire wardrobe that year, but I was dying for a pair so I would feel like I could fit in. Dad knew it was expensive, but he bought them to please me. We shopped for Jason and Carrie and had a lot of fun that day at the mall. We went out to eat and did lots of other enjoyable things together. We thought about going to the movies, but Dad was low on cash.

When we stopped at the ATM machine, all of a sudden the energy around my father shifted. His body froze, and I saw him grow instantly angry. He looked at us with the coldest look I had ever seen in my life.

"W—What's the matter, Dad?" I asked, trying to still the tremor in my voice. "Did something happen?"

There was a long pause.

"Did something *happen?*" he asked, his voice menacing. "You happened! I'm nothing but a paycheck to you kids. You know when I come, I have money, so I pick up you kids, and you suck me completely dry!" His voice had risen sharply, and he didn't seem to care that everyone nearby was watching, their eyes as wide as ours.

"You're a bunch of ungrateful, selfish kids! You don't give a shit what I do to provide for you!"

I could feel this getting out of control really fast. Carrie had started to cry, and Jason's face had lost all its color. Something had to be done—fast.

"You're right, Dad," I said, quickly, looking at the ground, with my head down. "You're absolutely right. We *are* selfish. I'm selfish. I asked you to buy me those jeans, and I had no right to do that. I wanted them, and I used you as the way to get them. I'm really sorry, and I want to take them back."

The other two followed my lead.

"Yeah, Dad, we just want to take our stuff back."

Dad looked at us for a moment, the anger still raging in his eyes. We didn't do anything, didn't argue. Our heads hung low in submission, we waited. It took a moment, but I saw my dad take a breath, and then he began to melt, just a little. The cold man he had become warmed a little when we agreed with him and said he was right. We had learned that if we played by the rules, his anger would dissipate faster and no one would get hurt.

After the shopping trip was over, I was relieved that my father's trip was a brief one. I had seen him talk and act that way to our mom, but usually not to us, although money was always a big cause of stress for him. When he called to check up on us later in the week, he acted like nothing had ever happened.

As it came closer to the holidays, my mother was struggling to make ends meet. I knew I wouldn't be getting any designer clothes or toys soon, but more important was the fact that I couldn't help but feel incredibly lonely.

That entire summer and fall, I had not heard from my family in Yakima. That was probably one of the hardest things of all to face. I felt left out of my own family. I didn't understand why none of the Jespersons had called or even written a letter, but I made the excuse in my head that they did not know how to reach me. When I let myself relive past times, I missed my grandmother Lucy and her mashed potatoes and cinnamon rolls. Even more, I missed her easygoing, fun-loving manner. I missed Grandpa and the tender way he would treat me. I missed playing with my cousins and telling stories to my aunts and uncles. I had been waiting for them to make the first connection, and it did not come until my father connected us together again. The only communication I had to the close family came through my dad on the phone. He started letting us know what everyone was up to, and this filled a deep hole inside of me.

"Grandpa and Grandma want you to know they miss you and they love you," he said, and my heart swelled with pain and happiness at the same time. I missed them more than I could say, especially to my dad. If he was irritated with Grandpa, he wouldn't tell me much about them or their lives. If he was in a good mood or they were getting along well, he would give me more details that made me feel like I was still connected—almost right next door. Again the hope flared within me that I could be with my family and that we could be whole.

9

❧

the whispered prayer

Late in September, I got off the phone with Dad, and my emotions were all over the place. I went outside to breathe in the cool, fresh air and enjoy the grass for a little longer. It was getting colder, and I wondered what the weather would be like in the winter. Did it ever snow in Spokane? I tried to empty my mind and concentrate on the dry grass between my toes, but my mind was whirling. It seemed like Dad was more and more irritated with Grandpa all the time. I realized that if I listened to everything he said, I could easily hate my own grandfather. I knew Grandpa was strong-willed, and often pushed people to their limits. He was also gregarious—a genius that invented things, thought up new ideas constantly, could build just about anything, and enjoyed it when people around him knew how brilliant he was. I think that was irritating to my father, who seemed to me to also be quite brilliant—though grandpa acted as if he was slow, and even stupid sometimes. I didn't like how my grandfather treated my father, and it seemed different from how he treated his other two sons. Sometimes my grandfather teased my mother unrelentingly too.

Still, my Grandpa Roy had often shown me his tender, loving side. When I was younger, he would pick me up and take me places, drive me around on his four wheelers, and teach me things about life, nature, and what made things work. With all my heart, I missed him and wished I could see him again. I also had a feeling that Grandpa was disappointed in Dad and was getting after him for leaving us to be with Toni. I hoped that was the case, and that Dad would listen to him. Somehow I knew, however, that whatever Grandpa said made him want to do the opposite even more.

40

Observing my father and his family made me wonder about my mom and her own family's dynamics. She was very loving and caring, deep inside, but she had been through a lot and was just doing her best to survive in this brand-new situation. After being married for thirteen years and primarily being a mother and homemaker, she had been forced to work for the first time since she was a teenager. I could tell from the bags under her eyes and the extra work she took on to try to make ends meet, that this was all very hard on her.

What made it challenging for me was that Mom would never talk about it. Not one word. She wouldn't discuss any feelings or issues, unless it was to say that we couldn't afford to buy something that we might want. As I observed my mother interact with her siblings and her own mother, I realized that she had learned from her family not to talk about issues or express emotions. My mother's side of the family didn't hug, greet one another with enthusiasm, or say "I love you." It just was the way it was, and although they cared about one another deeply, their circumstances growing up reinforced this dynamic.

My mom was raised in a Byzantine Catholic home in Indiana. She was completely surrounded by family, including fifteen cousins close to her age that she spent most of her time with. They all went to church together every Sunday, and my mother grew up very sheltered. She had been taught that you got married, you had children, and you stayed together for the rest of your life. My mother didn't know of any other way to live until a tragedy happened in their family. When my mom was just seven, her mother gave birth to an infant son, and the family rejoiced. However, he contracted hepatitis from the hospital and died two weeks later.

His death had a traumatic effect on the family. Apparently my grandfather became an alcoholic and was never able to resolve his grief. After three years of struggling to make their marriage work, my grandmother had to divorce him and live on her own. This was particularly difficult during a time of horrendous social stigma for a single, divorced mother, especially one with six children. It was also very difficult for my mother to have her father suddenly leave. For more than a decade, her family never heard a thing from him, and it was hard to be estranged from much of the family life she had known for so long.

My grandmother did what she could to survive and carry on. It made her tough and resilient but emotionally unavailable to her children. Now I witnessed my mother going through the same thing. I knew this had to be difficult for her. The last thing she had been expecting was a sudden divorce, to be so abruptly left on her own and having to rely on her mother again for support and assistance. Still, she would not speak about it at all. Jason, Carrie, and I knew nothing of her inner struggles, her thoughts or emotions. I thought that would all change, but as time went on, she seemed even more withdrawn from us.

Idly, I watched people in my neighborhood in their daily activities: taking out the trash, interacting with their children, talking and laughing, going to work or coming home. I had been an observer of people since I was very young. Although I didn't have much variation to witness in the rural areas of Toppenish and Yakima, I had always enjoyed seeing the limited, but somewhat varied, ways of life around me. Now I began to pay close attention to the behavior of many other families and individuals. What made them different from each other? Why did people have different levels of abundance and show such varied signs of affection? Why did some people seem genuinely happy, others appear superficially happy, and still others appear to be cut off, disconnected, or even miserable?

I thought again about my father. He said he had chosen to be with Toni because she made him happy. Why hadn't he been happy enough with me? With his beloved Jason, and Carrie—the little girl he adored? With my mom? Fiercely, I pulled up tufts of the drying grass, and ripped them apart. Then I threw the pieces as hard as I could. With every angry thought, I pulled up more, making an ugly, bare spot in the ground. It reflected the angry questions in my mind.

If being with Toni made my father happy enough to leave us, then why did he act so miserable on the phone? Why did he spend so much resentful energy complaining about Grandpa? I didn't know the answers to any of my questions, and it made me feel more and more angry with myself and with the world.

Just then, the sounds of laughter and singing caught my attention. Bitterly, I swung my head toward the origin of the sound. A car was rounding the bend to go down our street. It was packed with five or six people, and everyone inside was laughing and noisily singing together to a song on the radio. That is, everyone except one person in the back. This young man stood out in stark contrast in his silence, looking morosely out the window. Our eyes met for a brief moment, and I couldn't help but shiver as we both looked away. I knew it was no accident that I had connected with him. I did not want to be that person. And yet that's how I felt—left out by my father.

Left out from the people I loved in Yakima. Left out emotionally from any closeness to my family here. Left out by the friends from my neighborhood once I got to school because I wasn't good enough. This time I whispered, "I do not want to be that person! How can I live my life differently so that I can be happy? Really happy?"

Once again, I didn't know the answer to my question. This time, however, as I whispered it to the wind, it felt almost as if it had turned into a sacred prayer. I felt it rise into the sky.

10

❧

holidays without home

One day after school, I trudged into my grandmother's neighborhood, feeling as bleak and colorless as my surroundings. I couldn't help but see the major transition that had taken place in the last few days. Most people had taken down all of their lights and decorations from the Christmas holidays, and we were all back to school. Instead of pure, white snow, the ground was dull and gray, mirroring the sky. I watched a lone leaf fluttering in the icy wind; the last on the bare branch of one tree. I had figured that holidays here would be a little different from I was used to, but I found each development more depressing than exciting. Normally, I was intrigued by seeing how people celebrated differently than my family and I. This year, it just seemed like everything shouted out—declaring everything I did not have.

During the month of October, the whole neighborhood had been transformed into a Halloween haven. There were decorations at most of the houses. Some of them were fun, and some were incredibly gory and creepy. I usually liked Halloween, but I had never experienced one that felt so weird and disconnected. Every advertisement on the radio and television seemed to call out: "Family Fun!" Our father was a huge Halloween fan, and it was hard not to see him during his favorite holiday. Two hundred miles was not that far away for a trucker, but since it was in the opposite direction of Dad's work, that meant we rarely got to see him.

In previous years during Halloween, our mother had preferred to stay home, while our father would dress us up and take us out for hours, and hours, and hours until we dropped. He loved trick-or-treating, and the mounds of treasures we would go home with would last for months. Carrie and Jason were especially disappointed not to see Dad, and we all went our separate ways with different friends for trick-or-treating.

When Christmas rolled around, it became especially hard on all of us. It was like the world we had always known just simply didn't exist. Christmas was Dad's second favorite holiday, and my most favorite of all. One year at grandpa's house, I had found a Santa suit and dressed up in it—pillow tummy, beard, and all—and walked around, pretending to be Old Saint Nick. Everyone laughed. I didn't understand all of the Nativity things about Christmas, but the Jespersons didn't really celebrate that part of it anyway. What I knew was that I loved being around family more than life. As a child, of course, I loved the presents, but they seemed to mean so much more when we were all enjoying them together.

It was depressing to me to know that all our cousins would be opening their gifts and then be meeting at Grandpa's house for dinner. Lucy would make her signature potatoes and rolls and yummy desserts. Then they would get the four-wheelers out and go sledding on the big mountain of snow and play games like King of the Mountain. Jason usually won, even if he wasn't the oldest. He was often the strongest.

Since my mother's family was not overtly social like the Jespersons, we didn't do much for the holiday season, except go to the St. Thomas Catholic Church with Grandmother Frances for Christmas Day. Jason, Carrie, and I became incredibly homesick.

Now, walking onto my grandmother's front walk, I paused for a moment, looking at the house. I didn't feel comfortable calling it home. It was her house, after all; it didn't feel right to call it ours. In addition, I was somehow under the delusion that if I never called it home, somehow or another we would get out of there to have a place to call our own. Every day it felt like we were visitors, or long-term campers, especially sleeping on a cot in my little nook of the basement.

The house was tiny and looked like one or two people might live there comfortably, but certainly not five or six, since it was only 300 square feet. When I walked into the house, I had to be careful not to push the door in too hard. It led right into the kitchen which was also next to the stairs. If anyone was standing there, it could knock them down. The kitchen was covered in 1960s laminate and tile, and there was a wooden banister between the kitchen and the stairwell. There was a plywood shelf above the stairwell, and the light from the kitchen gave minimal light for going up and down the stairs. Surprisingly, there was a small entrance to a tiny dining room and the front room, which was covered in burgundy-colored, marble carpeting. All the walls in the house were white, except in the dining area, which featured diagonal wood paneling. In the front room, there were floral couches, set low to the ground, and one little chair where if you pushed the arm, the leg came up.

I made my way down the small staircase and over to my corner of the basement. Dumping my backpack on my cot, I reached up and pulled down the string for the light. The naked bulb shone bleakly in the dinginess of the tiny space. Our boxes with most of our precious possessions stood stacked together in one corner, waiting for the day we could have a place of our own.

In my corner, I had stacked shoeboxes, which acted like a dresser for me. At least it was neat and tidy, keeping items off the cold, cement floor. Happy that the only homework I had was reading, I turned to go, pulling on the light cord. The entire basement went dark, since the light was fading fast outside. As quickly as I could, I made my way up the stairs and outside, stopping to breathe in the crisp clean air. I hadn't realized I was holding my breath. I searched the neighborhood for a sign of life, but everyone had gone inside to play. I had to get a playmate quickly or I'd be stuck at home, so I set out to knock on a couple of neighbors' doors, wondering who might take me in for the evening.

A week or so went by, and another school day was dawning as my mother came into my room to wake me up to get ready. The weather was still bland and cold in Spokane, but now there was fresh, new snow covering our four-square chalk outline in the street. That meant there was no point in getting ready fast. Sarah and I would be unable to play a game before the bus came.

Sarah lived right across the street in a tiny blue house that was square in shape, like ours. Most of the military '50s homes in the neighborhood were similar in size and shape. Sarah had a sister named Staci that would follow her around all the time. It was annoying to us when just the two of us wanted to hang out. Sometimes it made me grateful that Jason and Carrie didn't do the same thing. Most of the time, however, I secretly missed our camaraderie, and especially Jason's adventures.

Sarah's parents were divorced, and her father never came to visit her and Staci. I thought I had the better deal since my father made it a point to come visit at least every three months or so. Carrie made him promise he would be out for her birthday, so we only had two more months before we would see him again. Having my father visit was the only thing in my life that I believed that I actually had better than Sarah.

I did my best not to judge Sarah, but I thought she had it better than me. For one thing, she was popular in sixth grade, wore fashionable clothes, and was athletic, so she was always picked for teams. We were in different classes during the afternoon so we had other friends to play with at recess, and I could tell that also made her more comfortable. Sarah and I would ride the bus home together with our good friend Katie. We did not play with Katie after school on most days because she either had piano lessons or she would have her dad pick her up. Katie's parents were divorced as well, but her family was so different from mine. Her life was incredibly structured. Besides her lessons and visits, it was a mystery to me how her mom would be home to have fresh-baked snacks for her and her sister right after school. If her mom was staying at home, even though she was divorced, how could she afford not to work?

On my "better off scale," Katie had it better off than Sarah and me both. Her mom was attentive—and at home when her kids needed her. Their home was always clean and decorated with pictures of the girls on the wall, along with pictures of their LDS temple. Katie's family was Mormon and I had little understanding of the religion. I had been baptized in the Catholic Church back in Yakima, but I knew very little from my own church.

I could remember my First Communion. It took place just a year before my parents had separated. On weeknights, with other children my same age, I had to take lessons at the church. Remembering the Lord's Prayer by heart was our main objective. I struggled to memorize the lengthy prayer without fault. Parents of my classmates would try not to giggle as I would recite my version of the prayer: "Our Father who aren't in heaven, hollow be thy name, thy kingdom come, thy will be done . . ." I didn't understand why He was not in heaven. The Lord's Prayer did not make sense to me, but understanding it mattered little as long as I earned the opportunity to go to downtown Yakima to pick out a frilly, white dress. Being able to wear my communion dress made it worth memorizing that agonizingly long prayer.

On my Communion day, not only did the white, lacy dress look beautiful, but I also got to wear a matching tiara that I had picked out. I looked like a child bride. In my mind, I was a princess.

Now that we were in Spokane, my mother did not bring us to any Catholic church, except that one day at Christmas time. Looking up at the cross and seeing an emaciated, bloody, dying figure, Jesus or God seemed just a blur of confusion to me. In addition, I thought they would probably not care about me or my problems because Jesus had it so much worse—he was hung on a cross. In all of my hopelessness, I believed that there was no one I could turn to for comfort.

From my front window, I saw the rumbling bus come around the corner. Running to catch it as fast as I could without winter boots, I carefully hopped from one foot to the other in my old, white sneakers, my brother and sister following in my tracks so that their own sneakers wouldn't get too wet. Every day we made sure we made it to the bus on time. If we didn't, we would have to stay home alone in the boring house. There were not many material things to entertain us, and certainly no cable television.

As the bus rumbled off to pick up more kids down the street, I looked back at my grandmother's house. Another reason I had for believing that our yellow home on Nordin Street could only be temporary was because my mother did not hang one single item on the cement walls—not one calendar, not one holiday decoration. Even though I was grateful for the temporary feel, the lack of decoration gave the basement a feeling of coldness. That part I didn't like. I wanted a home like Katie's, warm and decorated with dried flowers and pictures and holiday cheer all year round. I thought of how wonderful it would feel to come home to fresh-baked cookies after school like she did. I forgot that there was a time when my mother did something similar to that in our home in Yakima. That seemed such a long time ago now, and as I settled in my seat on the bus, I settled for a brief fantasy that this bus was going to my old elementary school in Yakima, that I would get to play with my old friends there, and that I would return at night to my entire family.

Winter in Spokane dragged on, passing slowly, but finally it began to warm, and soon enough it was Carrie's birthday. We drove down to Yakima and had a party for her in mid-March, 1990, at Grandma Lucy's house. She had made Carrie a beautiful Barbie cake, and we played with our cousins like old times. For the first time, with all of my aunts, uncles, and cousins around, I noticed how big and strong my father really was.

When I was little, I thought almost all men were so tall that their heads touched the ceilings. Of course this was due to my small perspective. As I grew, I realized that this phenomenon was not true of 98.5 percent of men. My dad, however, absolutely still fit the bill. He stood 6'6" tall, and weighed 240 pounds in his leanest form, so he really *was* huge. Most men looked like children next to him.

My cousins and uncles roughhoused together as usual. Dad loved to tickle me because I was incredibly sensitive and would erupt into uncontrollable giggles. He would pin my arms back and tickle my armpits while I would scream, begging for him to stop. I could tell that he enjoyed me pleading for him to stop and liked the feeling of being in control. I would do everything I could to wiggle out of his grip, but he was far too strong. Finally I told him I was going to pee my pants. Only when I convinced him that I really was going to wet myself did he finally let me go.

Things were feeling almost like old times when chaos erupted. It seemed liked Grandpa couldn't help lecturing my father about what he was doing wrong, and the night ended badly again. Another special occasion with family ended awkwardly.

The next holiday weekend was Easter, and my grandparents made the effort to come and see us. It was the first time any family besides my father had come to spend time with us in Spokane, and I was so happy.

Our previous Easter traditions involved handmade woven fabric baskets that Grandma Glady had made us. Mine was pink and white with eyelet lace around it. Jason's was gray, blue, and red and looked like a patchwork quilt, lined inside with soft silk. Carrie's basket was yellow with pretty lace. Every year, we would open our door and see our baskets full of treats, a chocolate bunny, and one special gift. Always dressed in our Sunday best, we would attend the Catholic Church for Easter Sunday, and it was the one time each year that Dad would actually go. Mom always allowed me to put on her very special Mary Kay lip gloss, and I remembered feeling on top of the world.

This year when Easter morning dawned, Carrie received a great big pink rabbit she named Bunny Fu Fu, with whom she became inseparable. There was no room for Grandpa Roy and Lucy at our grandmother's house, so they had rented a room at a local hotel. Instead of church, we were able to swim at the hotel and bask in the company of our beloved grandparents. As I floated on my back, I studied all the adults while they watched us carefully and chatted. I couldn't figure out why they couldn't just fix the whole, messy situation between my mom and dad and make it all better. It seemed so simple to me, and I felt like they made everything complex and impossible.

All too soon, it was time to leave and say our tearful good-byes. Not only was I disappointed that we had to leave them, I hated leaving their warm embraces to go back to the real world, which had begun to seem like a mysterious and frightening place.

II

manipulation

We didn't see much of our father for a while. His employment was better now, so when he would roll into town, our mother called him "Disneyland Dad" because it would be like a big party. We would run, screaming, to greet him, jumping up and down until it was our turn for a big hug or to be picked up and spun around the yard like an airplane. That feat was no big deal for him, and he played for a couple hours and let us talk his ear off until it was time to go out together.

It was always a new adventure: roller skating, going to the movies or on the waterslides—all the things we couldn't afford to do on a daily basis. He would also buy us necessities, like underwear and socks, as well as other vital items (that although might not have been considered necessities in the normal spectrum of survival, were absolute necessities of *social* survival in the jungles of Spokane's schools).

Dad put some mysterious monetary limit on what he would spend, but to us it felt like Christmas every time he took us out. He was disappointed and frustrated to see that we were losing weight, and he would often spend as much as several hundred dollars in groceries to fill our empty cupboards and bellies before he left.

<hr>

The next time Dad rolled into town, it was early morning. He took us to breakfast, and the smell of bacon cooking was heavenly. It seemed like years since we had enjoyed bacon! We talked with Dad about the day's events and planned out what we wanted to do. I hovered on the outskirts of the discussion, feeling a little cautious, and also not wishing to take away from what Jason and Carrie wanted to create for the day. To me it was enough for us to be together. Not only was it a rare treat to be with our dad, it was also a rare treat for my siblings and I to spend the day together. Our lives had gone in multiple directions, and all away from each other.

My father seemed to sense my aloofness, and paid an extraordinary amount of attention to me. At times that took me by surprise—and sometimes it really bugged me.

As we drove from place to place, he asked how school was going, what particular subjects I was most interested in, and about my friends. We arrived at Bowl and Pitcher Park to spend part of the day. There was a suspension bridge that we loved to go on, for it was no ordinary bridge— underneath its large span, the Spokane River raged.

Dad knew I was deathly afraid of heights, so I made him promise not to tease me on the bridge. The day was cloudless and lovely, and I was enjoying the sun and the spray of the water as we made our way across the bridge. Jason had already gone far ahead and Carrie was right after him, as usual. When I was in the middle of the bridge at the unstable area, I suddenly felt the bridge dip and sway. I shrieked in terror, clinging to the railing. I turned my head to see my father bouncing up and down, chuckling. Screaming, I begged him to stop as the bridge swayed and bowed dramatically under the weight of his strong and heavy body and the huge whitecaps from the river sprayed mist on my face. He wouldn't stop, and as my hands and feet slipped on the watery boards and railings I literally thought I was going to be flung off and fall to my death in the turbulent water below. When he finally stopped, I could not wait to get to the other side. Still he bounced a couple more times for good effect. Angry, and yet still fearful for my life, I finally made it off the bridge and fell onto my knees, grateful for solid earth below me. Dad was still chuckling as he came up behind me. I couldn't help but wonder why my father seemed to like tormenting me. I wondered why it seemed to bring him such joy to do so, and it bothered me.

On the way to dinner, he softened for a moment, and told us that he had cried the day he filed the divorce papers. He said that Toni had pressured him to divorce Mom. I wondered if that was a lie. It would seem to me that he should have shed more tears when his family moved away or when his father and Lucy told him that he was acting like a fool. All it did was tick him off, but I was happy when Grandpa stood up for us. I had tried to tell my father that his rightful place was with us. Although I think he had come to realize that he had taken my mother for granted, he still believed he was meant to be with Toni. I overheard some of his conversations with his family and my mom, and he blamed his error on marrying too young. I believed the biggest mistake of his life was "that woman" as Toni was often referred to. Dad had always been so particular about the way other people in his family should treat his children, and I was surprised to witness how badly Toni treated her own. Surely he didn't like the way she talked to them, did he?

During conversations with my dad over the telephone, it was impossible not to hear how often Toni yelled at her children, calling them names and screaming at them for the smallest things. There seemed to be an inordinate amount of drama and chaos that revolved around her, and I was confused about what my father could possibly see in the woman.

I wanted to believe that he cried when he filed for the divorce. Something within me was dying to know that he really did feel some kind of remorse, some sadness for what he had done to our family. I wanted to witness more sorrow within him—enough sorrow that he might consider going back to my mother.

Soon after that, however, my father displayed less than remorse. He was rapidly becoming what some people refer to as a deadbeat dad. He fell behind on his $600 a month child support, and began visiting us less and less often with each passing month. I overheard my mother's frustrated conversations with him and felt he was not only blaming my mother, but also Toni for his lack of money. All I knew was, we felt his absence greatly. With my father gone, I felt like our family was vulnerable to the world and left without protection. That feeling of anxiety was like an "insecurity blanket"—a black cloud in which we lived, never knowing if things were going to be all right for us or if we were even safe in our own home. While I trusted my mother to provide us with food and shelter as best she could, I felt she could not provide for our safety from the terrors of the world. In my eyes, no one would mess with my father, unless they were ridiculously foolish. Because of that, I believed he could handle any problem that might come along. If only he could be there more often.

Divorce was a hard concept for me to take in. It seemed too final. Every time my father would swing into town, I would seize the opportunity to try to convince him to stay. I was relentless. It would simply not sink in for me that he had any viable reason to want to be away from us.

A few times my pleading was effective, and he would stay for another day or a few more hours, but in the end it was always short-lived. Certain that I could find his "weakness" (or should I say guilt mechanism?), I would start to beg him to come back to our family—to make it complete again. Deep inside I knew that he must know that this path with Toni was intrinsically wrong. Yet on the other hand, I also knew subconsciously that things would not be the same with my mother if he returned. She would probably always carry a grudge for his affairs and resent him for it. I couldn't blame her. I didn't like it when intense jealousy and dislike for Toni welled up inside me. I could only imagine what my mother felt, even though she wouldn't show me any feelings whatsoever.

Dad used that same argument with me—that things had changed too dramatically between him and my mom. He would say that there was no hope of going back, and that I needed to get used to it. I wanted to believe with all my heart that he was wrong, that my mother would take him back and things would go as they were before. From time to time, I could see my father weigh my arguments, considering if I was making any valid points. The fact that he would still contemplate coming home to us was a success for me. It was one step closer to the direction I wanted him to go. Could my arguments be making any headway? Would Mom consider going back to him?

One very exciting afternoon, my mother called us into our grandmother's house.

"Your father called," she said, her face looking flush with more color than I had seen for a long time. "He's on his way up to see us."

"Yes!" cried Jason and Carrie, delighting in the thought of another visit. It had been too long. My mother shushed them so she could continue.

"It looks like we may be going back to Yakima. He said he misses us all too much, and he's bringing Grandpa Roy's trailer."

We looked at her in disbelief, and after the shock wore off, we raced around, screaming, hugging each other, and jumping up and down in our excitement. Finally! We were going home!

All three of us ran to pack our things. It didn't take much time, as most of our stuff was still in boxes. After we were finished, we waited by the door, knowing we were early.

Then we waited by the door, certain he would be there any minute. We waited longer, wondering if he'd been in an accident. He should have been there by now.

Jason paced the front porch. I was writing in my journal, trying to stay focused on all the things I would do when I got home. Carrie just stood out by the front fence, her eyes searching the road and perking up at every vehicle that rounded the corner and came down our little street.

As the sun went down, there was no sign of Dad. Our mother called everyone in for dinner. As we sat around the dining room table, my mother spoke, and her voice held none of the warmth and excitement it had just hours before.

"Your father is not coming," she said quietly. "He's decided it's best if everything remains the way it is now."

Profound disappointment, sadness, and anger became etched upon the faces of my family as we all slumped around that table. I wanted to call my father up and scream at him. *Look at what you're doing to us! Look at what you're doing to me!* Instead, I took another small helping of instant potatoes and shoved all my emotions down with my food. I couldn't shove the thoughts down, however, and uncomfortable visions raced back and forth in front of my eyes.

I was unable to fathom how wonderful Toni must be if my dad was choosing her over a loyal wife and loving children. He had now moved with her twice, after leaving us. He may have been torn at times between us, but we felt totally rejected.

A month or two later, I was playing with my friend Sarah when I saw a man put a sign up in front of the tiny house just two doors down from Grandma's house on our side of the street. It said, "FOR RENT." I ran home to tell my mother about it. She looked into housing assistance and found that we could actually afford it! Within a week or two, we moved into the Nordin house, as we called it, and were delighted to have a place to call our own.

The home was similar in size to Grandmother Frances's house with the exception of the basement—there was none. The tiny house had two small, oddly-shaped bedrooms. My siblings and I shared the largest room, and the other one was for my mother.

My siblings were just as grateful as I was to leave our grandmother's house. To us it did not matter that we shared a room, or that my sister and I shared a twin bed. Carrie's head would rest at the end of the bed near the footboard and mine at the headboard. I would tickle her feet as she tried to go to sleep at night. It was a comfort to be so close to my siblings at that difficult time when everything felt so uncertain. While it seemed strange for us to be on our own, it was also gloriously wonderful, and I felt hope for a better life like I hadn't felt in months.

One afternoon, we arrived home from school to find a strange vehicle out in front of our new home. It was packed with boxes. Curious, we rushed inside to find my father sitting there. He was all smiles and had a big bear hug for each one of us. It had been only three months since we had last seen him, but it had felt like years. His presence felt as good as dew on summer grass.

"How long can you stay this time?" asked Jason. We were not prepared as a sloppy grin covered Dad's face.

"Forever," he said, and ruffled Jason's hair. I just stared at the man before me, not knowing if I could believe what he just said. *Could it really be true?* Over the next few hours, I was able to wheedle out some information from him. He apparently had reconsidered his life on a most dramatic scale and had realized he couldn't live without us. Saying good-bye to Toni, he had packed up and brought all of his belongings here. Carrie and Jason were beside themselves with joy. My heart leaped, too, but I was a little suspicious because of what he had pulled the last time he promised to be with us. Still, I played with him and talked with him and was entirely glad to have him back in our lives for good.

After we helped Dad bring all his boxes and belongings into the house, we laid on the couch and talked for a while. Our father was big enough that we could all three lay on him at the same time, and we wouldn't squish him. When he chuckled or laughed, we would bounce right off his body and come back for more. After a while we settled into a peaceful mood, no one saying much. The question that had been plaguing me all day rose to the surface.

"Dad . . . ?" I ventured.

"Yes, Missy?"

"Why, exactly, did you come back?" My voice was small and it cracked, but I wanted to know.

"Well, Melissa," he began. "I had nightmares—over and over again—

about letting you kids down. I couldn't be away from you, so I decided to come back."

He didn't put forth any further information, so again we laid in silence for a while. It didn't matter how peaceful everything was, I still had to ask the second part of the question so I would know precisely where we stood and what we were up against, if anything.

"What happened to Toni?" I asked him, wondering if she had anything to do with this.

"Toni and I are through. It's time that I did right by you." He paused and then gave me a little squeeze. "I've missed you, all of you, and I've missed your mom. She's a good woman, and I've been almost completely faithful to her for most of our married lives."

He sounded very proud of himself, and I couldn't help the ironic voice in my head that said, *I am sure that if there was a medal for being* almost *completely faithful, you would believe you deserved it, Dad.* I shook the voice away. How many months had I longed for this? To have him home with us again? I certainly wasn't going to ruin it. Still, I observed him carefully.

The first several nights, Dad slept in our room as he usually did when he came to visit. One morning, I felt the sunlight play with my eyelids before I opened them. A delicious feeling of oneness surrounded me. Carefully bracing my head on my elbow, I saw Carrie and Jason snuggled on the floor next to my father. I studied his enormous silhouette in the early morning light, and I was confused at the plethora of feelings I was experiencing for him. I loved my father, loved how he provided for us and looked after our physical and emotional needs the best he could, considering the situation he was in. Something was bothering me, however, and I was beginning to feel less and less comfortable in his presence. Was it because he had been away from us for so long? Was it because he had broken my trust? Was it because he had been living a different life, or it was simply a matter of jealousy—that I hadn't been a part of it?

I hated to admit it, but I knew that I was absolutely envious of Toni and the hold she'd had on him in the past. I was jealous of the time, energy, money, and love that he had spent on her and even her kids, when I felt like his own children and the woman that I knew still loved him were being neglected. I figured that must be most of what I was feeling, but even so, I didn't allow myself to get too close to him. My father had a different and unusual smell, for one thing, which I couldn't get a mental handle on. It seemed strange, and there was something unusual about his demeanor. It sort of reminded me of how he acted when he was around Grandpa and had pulled the wool over his eyes—like a devious inner chuckle. Somehow, the energy was very similar to that, except that there was a bit of added swagger in his manner that I hadn't picked up on before. I naturally assumed that Toni was the reason for it, so I didn't really like it. I had overriding considerations that seemed more important, anyway. I was glad Dad seemed confident and happy—I wanted my father to be happy—but more than anything, I wanted him to be with us and to know that he would stay with us.

Time flew by quickly, and we got into a routine of having Dad with us again. But by the end of the second week, I could tell something was wrong. He was agitated and anxious. I couldn't tell exactly what he was thinking, but I knew something was up. Once, before Mom got home, I overheard him arguing with someone on the phone. Could that be Toni? I couldn't tell, and he wouldn't say. By the end of three weeks, he couldn't handle it anymore. He said he had to leave.

At that moment, I could barely drag my feet out to the street to say good-bye. To see the boxes packed back up ripped my heart into tiny shreds, and I felt like I couldn't breathe. Worse still was to see the helpless, hopeless looks on Jason and Carrie's faces, mixed with the deepest sadness I had ever seen. Something switched off inside of them, and I knew what it was. Hope. There was no hope left within them. They looked like empty shells, and they mirrored what I saw in my mother's face.

I too was so sad and disappointed in my dad. I just wanted to cry, but another emotion swept over me that was even stronger. I began to burn with a feeling I had never known before. It wasn't just anger; it was intense hatred. I hated Toni like I had never hated anything or anyone before.

Shortly before Christmas in 1990, we were delighted when Grandpa Roy and Lucy called to invite us over to their place for Christmas Day dinner and festivities. To have a normal Christmas! Jason, Carrie, and I were extra helpful to Mom so we could leave early enough to spend as long as possible with our cousins. We packed ourselves, our gear, and our meager gifts into Mom's car and headed out for the Yakima area, doing our best not to be impatient with our mother's conservative, unhurried driving.

When we got there, the festivities were already in full swing, and we reunited ourselves with the cousins in short order. While it felt like it had been ages since we'd played together, within a few minutes it seemed as if no time had passed at all. The only thing that was out of the ordinary was some hushed conversation from the adults in the far corners of the room. I ignored it, reveling in the moment and praying it could last forever.

When Dad showed up suddenly to join the fun, the room went silent. We were glad he was there, but no one had told us he would be coming to see us. Since he had let us down before, we hadn't asked, and simply didn't have any expectations. It was easier that way.

Dressed in his signature blue jeans and boots, I could tell he had just combed his hair back, as his naturally wavy hair rippled lightly when he walked. Carrie got up and ran over to him. Jason and I walked over, too, but we took our time since all eyes were on us.

I could tell by my father's demeanor that things were not well on his end. As the evening progressed, I took him aside and probed him relentlessly for more information. I knew that he and Toni had become driving partners—she had been hired to do over-the-road long hauls with him. For a while, he'd seemed really happy about it. That night, however, he finally admitted that his relationship with Toni was not going well. His job wasn't going well either, and he was quick to let us know that he'd had to sell his bike and several other possessions to buy us the presents that were in his car. Apparently he had been able to come up with about $350 from the sale, so as usual, he had lavished us with gifts, including a TV and a VCR for the Nordin house. He even gave my mother some money to take home.

Jason and Carrie were ecstatic, since we were living without a television at home, but suddenly instead of feeling grateful, I felt guilty about having anything—like I somehow didn't deserve it. I wanted Dad to return my stuff so he could get his treasured possessions back.

To make matters worse, Grandpa had not told Mom that my father was coming, and he certainly hadn't told Dad that my mother would be there. It was soon apparent that Dad's folks had even tried to create some kind of romantic atmosphere for the two of them. While my Dad was happy to see us and pleased that he didn't have to travel to Spokane to do it, he was furious with his father and Lucy for the trick they had played on him. From my experience with my father, he had almost always seemed rebellious toward his father. That night, however, I felt he was ticked off on principle, and that he would rather die than do anything his father wanted him to do, even if that meant abandoning those who loved him more than life. He and Toni were about through—he had said so himself, but just because my grandfather wanted him to, I felt like Dad wouldn't even consider coming back to us.

When he left, Dad had the darkest countenance I had ever seen. When he arrived, he had been despondent. Now he was sullen, and his face was dark and clouded like the day when he was so angry with us at the ATM that we weren't sure what he was going to do. I felt unsafe, confused, and guilty—like this was somehow my fault. On the way out to the car, I couldn't believe that I had been so excited to visit. The wind felt cold and ominous. Usually at the end of such a visit I would want to rush back into the house, into the arms of Lucy and Grandpa and even my dad. Loaded down with tainted Christmas gifts in my hand, all I could feel was that I couldn't wait to get out of there.

12

⬥

the new man

January 1991 stayed cold and windy, and my siblings and I bundled up every day the best we could for school. Some of the kids looked at me weird when I would wear lots of layers of clothing with no coat, so I pretended I was like the cool, older kids who didn't want to wear a coat. I also made sure no one saw that my mittens were really socks that I layered for warmth. I carefully tucked the holey ones underneath my sweatshirts, hidden from view.

Today, for a school language arts assignment, our class was supposed to write unique and unusual descriptions about our fathers. Some of the kids groaned at the assignment, but I thought that would be a fun one because my dad had a lot of interesting character traits—and I liked using big words. I had always thought my dad was a fairly normal guy, but I had most recently discovered that not everybody's dad was like mine. In fact, nobody's dad was even close.

FUN AND UNUSUAL THINGS ABOUT MY FATHER

My father always has a pack of Juicy Fruit gum in his truck or car and he lets us chew on it as much as we want! Whenever we go anywhere with my dad, we can have any candy we want from the convenience store and delicious chocolate milk. My dad's favorite treat is donuts. He likes the rectangular ones with the brown frosting.

My dad carries a brown leather suitcase with black, silky lining. All his grubby clothes are inside and old pictures of us that have creases on them from being all worn out and loved and not being protected. One of the pictures of me is on a brown horse in my favorite Gladstone sweatshirt. Another crumbly picture is of him and my brother Jason standing next to each other, with his arm around Jason's shoulder. Since my dad is really tall, my brother looks like one of those little people from The Wizard of Oz in the picture.

My father always carries a big, fat wallet in his back pocket, so it has made worn marks on his jeans that never come out. He has a big, black comb that he keeps in his pocket, too, to comb his hair back. He likes to think he is as handsome as Elvis! He drives an enormous truck that we call his "Big Rig." He could tell you all about what size the powerful engine is, all about the spoilers and the wheels, how fast it can go and how many pounds it can pull uphill. (All I can tell you is it is big and it's a rig.) When he is not in his huge truck taking product everywhere around the United States, he likes to watch football and Star Trek in his white fruit of the looms and eat peanut butter out of the jar with a large spoon. Sometimes he opens a can of sardines and I watch in disgust as he eats the salty fish. When I was little, he gave me one to eat and laughed as I made faces. I have never eaten one since.

Dad used to wear gold and black silk boxing shorts, and he would come home all bloody and beat up from competitions. We always asked if he won, and he always said he did. I would watch him hit the heavy boxing bag and watch it sway like it was as light as a fly. Then I would try to hit it too. It wouldn't move! But it hurt my knuckles.

My dad doesn't have a lot of rules, but he does have two:

1. No Stealing! He said that if I ever want anything really bad to just ask him and he will get it for me. He says I never have to steal anything.
2. No Smoking! He says smoking is horrible for you and to never start the habit. Some of the girls he likes smoke though.

I couldn't think of how I wanted to end the paper. Thoughts of my father at the ATM, thoughts of him leaving us for Toni, and thoughts of his behavior a few weeks ago at Christmas invaded my peace of mind. I wanted this paper to be happy, like the home I wanted to get back to, like the family I desperately wanted. Maybe I needed to get out my thoughts so I wouldn't ruin this paper. Rubbing my hands together for warmth, I rummaged through my pack. It was almost as cold in our house as it was outside. Our budget was tight, so Mom said we had to keep the heat down. Keeping my jacket on, I sat down on the twin bed Carrie and I shared. I glanced quickly at the door, and satisfied that no one was around, I pulled out my journal and began to write.

> Dad told me last night that he and Toni aren't doing very well still. He made it sound like maybe she has left him for good, even though he paid a lot of bills for her and really liked her. I jumped in and told him Mom still loved him. I told him he should come back to us—that we love him and miss him and we should all be a family again. I think he's thinking about it, and I'll have to work on him some more. I don't want him to get mad at me like he does Grandpa, but can't he see that we're the best thing that ever happened to him? At least, I'd like to think we are.

I was thinking about my father when the weirdest feeling swept across my body. I didn't know what to think of it, but it made me shift uncomfortably on the bed. It was like a blackness, a deep and dark cloud, and I didn't like it. It felt kind of like how Dad had described the ghosts in Toni's house. He said it felt like something you never wanted to believe was real, but how could you explain what you felt when there was no other explanation?

I shivered, a little creeped out, and quickly turned on my radio to escape the gloom. As I began humming along to a popular song, I switched to writing in my journal about some things happening at school and a new assignment from my teacher that I was actually looking forward to. I carefully put my journal back in my backpack, behind my math book with a couple of other notebooks so it looked like any other homework.

Finally, I figured out how I wanted to end my language arts paper.

> One thing I really like about my father is that he is generous. My mother used to say that he would give the shirt off his back to someone who needed it. I think he should keep his shirt on because some people might not appreciate that. But I like how he really helps people. I like it a lot when he helps me.

A few days later, Dad informed me that Toni had found another man. He wouldn't go into too many details, just called her a whore and spat on his end of the phone. He was already feeling blue because he was unable to work as a long distance trucker. He said he had too many driving violations and had to wait it out for a short while. Instead he was collecting unemployment and he made sure to tell me that he was sending half to my mother, which meant he was broke most of the time.

I was worried about my father. For one thing, he wasn't used to *not working.* Jespersons worked all the time—that's just what they did. And if they weren't working hard, they were playing hard, but he had sold off all of his hobby possessions for our Christmas money: his eighteen-speed Twin Voyager bicycle, his fishing pole and expert reel, plus his lures and sinkers. I could tell from our calls he was frustrated and angry. I could also tell it didn't help when I reminded him once again how much we loved him and that he could get back together with us anytime.

I actually wasn't sure how much of that was true anymore. Mom had been hurt pretty deeply when he left us last time. She never said so to us, of course, but I sometimes eavesdropped on conversations to gather information on what was happening in my own family. Sometimes it was the only news Jason, Carrie, and I could get.

As a young girl, I had looked to my father as the authority to demonstrate how to navigate the world outside of our home. I had taken whatever he said as fact; he was wise and he could do no wrong . . . until he had broken my trust. When he left us, part of me locked him out of my heart so he would never be able to hurt me again. From that point on, I did not trust him. When my father lost my trust, so did every other man in the world.

At some point, my father and Toni made up. One minute they were never going to see each other again, and the next moment, they were back together "thick as thieves," as my grandfather would say. My dad had called to let me know excitedly let me know the news, and I hung up the phone, dejectedly. As Dad returned to Toni and her two children, we went back to life with our struggling, single mother. When Dad kept up with his child support payments, it helped to make the rent along with housing assistance. Still, my mother had to pay for food, heat, water, gas for the car, and a phone bill, as well as the miscellaneous other expenses that always seemed to pop up in our household. Through a lot of miracles, it seemed, she was able to provide for us. Even though daily affection was not shown to us, there was food in our bellies and we had a safe place to sleep.

I didn't know why mother didn't use food stamps like I witnessed other single mothers in our neighborhood doing. Perhaps she thought she was too classy or she was too ashamed to walk into the welfare office. There was a part of me that wanted to question it—and an even stranger part of me at the time that wished she *would* have taken welfare, so we could have all the yummy, processed foods like the neighbor kids.

After my father made his permanent decision to pursue his relationship with Toni, he would stop by Spokane to visit periodically. His "Disneyland Dad" reputation was restored; it was play, toy shopping, and games the moment he rolled into town. At the slightest glance at our sparse cupboards in the old, white-painted kitchen of the Nordin house, he would take us on a grocery-shopping spree.

Dad made it seem like nothing was off limits to throw into the shopping cart. I would carefully watch his face for any signs of disapproval on my food choices. There never was any. Not even our favorite five-gallon bucket of ice cream made him raise a brow. We chose the huge bucket of chocolate ice cream for the fact that this, at least, would outlast his visit. We would always have some after our final day with him. Jason, Carrie, and I all added to the shopping cart: boxes of pop tarts, sugary cereal, and all of the expensive, forbidden foods that our mother objected to. In a way, those sugary foods expressed to me a temporary sense of security.

13

✤

murdered

On Sunday evenings, I often found myself listening into conversations and newscasts in my grandmother's living room. Those evenings, there was never much going on in the neighborhood, since it was a day for family time in almost every house. The January snowfall made it more appealing to stay inside as well. One evening, my Grandmother Frances was lounging quietly in the living room with her legs propped up to relieve the pressure on her varicose veins. I was spinning on the wobbly, old, and off-kilter recliner beside her. My grandmother was a very introverted person, so she didn't speak much. The good thing was that not much seemed to set her off or disturb her peace, either. Therefore I was not surprised as I swung all my body weight into the recliner next to her and started to propel myself in circles that she did not tell me to sit still. Grandma was very patient. Had my mother been sitting there, she would have scolded me to go find something else to do than bother her. She would probably have told me to go outside.

It was in that wobbly recliner that I heard some breaking news. The tag line caught my attention long enough to stop the circular motion of the chair. I sat still, watching the gruesome images of a crime scene and the ongoing investigation taking place there. In late January of 1990, people in the Washington/Oregon area were disturbed by the discovery of a young Portland woman's body, found near the Columbia River Gorge. My attention piqued since the body was found in the region near my father's girlfriend's home. I worried a little that they might feel unsafe, now that a murder had taken place so close to them.

For a couple of weeks, it was simply a small story of a Jane Doe murder. As time went on, however, it turned out to be big news when a couple was arrested and implicated in the crime. Investigators reported that in late January of that year a young, twenty-three-year-old woman by the name of Taunja Bennett went to a local bar to shoot some pool, have a few drinks, and meet some new friends. She was described by those who knew her well as mentally slow and slightly retarded. That night she became quite intoxicated, according to witnesses, and left the bar. She never returned home.

I watched the television intently as the reporter discussed how a dismayed passer-by found her half-clothed and brutally beaten body just days later where it had been thrown into the ditch of a steep ravine in the switchbacks near Crown Point by the Columbia River Gorge.

An investigation took place immediately, and her physical characteristics were described in the local news. It didn't take long for Taunja to be identified by her family. A small amount of additional information had also been published, including certain aspects of the state in which the body was discovered: strangled, badly beaten, only half-clothed with a rope around her neck, and her lower lip punctured by one of her own teeth. At the time, it was reported that police had no suspects.

I continued to stay informed about the Bennett case on Sunday evenings by watching the late news before the school week would start. Within a few weeks, however, local media reported that Laverne Pavlinac, 57, and her live-in boyfriend, forty-three-year-old John Sosnovske had been arrested for the murder of Taunja Bennett. Pavlinac claimed that Sosnovske had forced her to help him rape Taunja Bennett before he killed her. They were the only suspects in the case.

I thought it was really strange that an elderly woman was involved in the rape and murder of a young woman. That didn't sit well with me because I didn't like to think that a woman, especially a "grandmotherly type" as the news described her, would do something like that. I shivered as I remembered my stranger danger classes in elementary school. We were trained that if we got lost, we should find an officer in uniform or a "grandma" (with kids, preferably). I tried to shake it off, but it reinforced the belief I was developing that I couldn't really trust anyone.

I didn't pay attention to too many of the outstanding details, but I breathed a little in relief. I was always happy to know when a killer was caught and sent to jail. I hated to think that someone who would murder young women might be on the loose somewhere.

14

❧

return of the knowing

Life finally seemed to settle into a smoother and easier routine. Every morning, I climbed out of bed, ready to tackle sixth grade. Every day I would come home to play in the neighborhood until bath time, and then it was straight to bed. It was all routine now, even sharing my bed with Carrie and my room with Jason. As a new little family, we were making it on our own.

Over the last couple of months, I had slowly but surely given up on my father getting back together with us permanently. I learned to honor his journey, and I accepted that he wouldn't be with us except for occasional visits. Between those visits and our new home, I did not think there was anything more we needed. The little brown rental home on Nordin Street was what had become permanent, and it felt like a place of safety.

One early morning when the weather couldn't decide if it was late winter or early spring, I woke up to a really queasy stomach. Not sure if I would make it through the day without the threat of spewing on a bus driver, teacher, or classmate, I decided to run the risk of missing school, and went back to bed. My mother had left for work. Jason and Carrie had caught the bus, and the house was now empty and quiet.

Missing any kind of school was a first for me. Confident that I was of age and therefore quite capable of taking care of myself, I knew I shouldn't be worried about being all alone in the house. Had I been worried at all, the flulike cramping and nausea would've drowned it out. After I went back to sleep for a while, I felt a bit better. From the bed I shared with Carrie, I grabbed the large comforter and my pillow and traipsed out to the front room to lie on the couch.

As I lay down, I was glad it felt less isolated out here. This way I knew I would hear my brother and sister coming home from school when it was time. I also knew I would be able to hear the noises of anyone else if they came by. I was wondering if I ought to turn the TV set on when suddenly my mind was filled with the image of a man trying to break into our home. I was defenseless. Over the years, I had learned that sometimes these images and pictures were not just reactions to my fear, but were valid. I attempted to relax—to tell myself that it was all in my head—but the fear made me anxious, and I had a hard time resting on the stiff couch. To make matters worse, there was a large, clear-glass, square window cut right into the door. This made it so I could see anyone who came to the door. Unfortunately, that meant they could see me as well.

I tossed and turned for a few minutes, but no matter what I did, I simply could not get comfortable with my pillow. I also could not put my fears to rest. I took my blanket and covered my head to block out some of the afternoon light and calm my racing thoughts. Finally, I began to relax. I was almost asleep when I heard a vehicle pull up in our driveway.

Who could be here? I thought. Then I knew: *I am in danger; I must lock the door fast!* Through instinct and adrenaline, I jumped up quickly and locked the front door, then ran back to my blanket on the couch and hid. I heard a door to the vehicle close, and then it was silent for a moment. *Just one person*, I thought logically. *Who could it be?* I told myself that no matter what, I could not look out. Somehow I knew I had to stay utterly still. There was the noise of feet shuffling softly on the walkway and up the three stairs. Though I couldn't see anything through the thick blanket, I could feel someone looking in from the window in the door.

At that moment, I was experiencing the same warning of extreme danger I had felt just a few times in my life. I remembered the flames on the bus and tried not to panic. *Maybe I should run to a neighbor's house?*

"Stay very still," said a soft and peaceful voice. *"Do not make one, single move."* There was no confusion about my feelings. I was not over-reacting. I felt with absolute certainty that I was in danger, and that there was a criminal right outside my door. But I also knew that I was not alone. I trusted the voice and I did not move.

Suddenly there was a knock on the wooden door. I had to steel myself not to shake and tremble. *Please don't see me*, I prayed, grateful that my comforter somewhat blended in with the couch in the dim light. I stayed frozen in my position, hardly daring to breathe for fear that whoever was at the door would see the blanket move up and down with my breath. Not moving an inch, I waited for another knock or for the sounds of the person leaving. It was eerily quiet for a long, long time. There was no sound of the vehicle door opening or shutting. I closed my eyes inside the blackness of the blanket and willed myself to see what was happening outside. I saw only a momentary flash, but it was the image of a person looking for an open window, or an unlocked back door. This time, I really did hold my breath, praying with all my might that every window and door was safely locked.

Just then, I heard the door to the vehicle open and shut. There was another long silence, and I stayed still until I heard the engine roar to life. Quickly but stealthily, avoiding the window where it was most wide and open, I carefully looked to see who had been at my door. There was a pale, beige truck and my father's silhouette in the driver's seat. Mom had not mentioned expecting him at all.

At that moment, I could have unlocked the door and stopped him from leaving, but the feeling of danger did not subside. I decided to trust my feeling, and ducked out of the way so I would not be seen. Then I laid back down on the couch to rest.

Later I realized that at the time of the incident, it did not seem odd to me that I would allow my father, who I rarely saw, to simply drive away. Between the feeling and the peaceful voice that came to intercede, there was not a question in my mind that I had been in the presence of someone who would harm me. That *knowing* somehow overshadowed the fact that it was my father, not a stranger, at the door.

Later that evening, my father came back after my mother was home from work. He slept in our room, and Carrie and Jason snuggled up next to him on the floor. They moved the beds aside to fit them all onto a couple of sleeping bags. I did not feel the need to sleep with them, nor did I want to be close to him, so I slept on my bed that was pushed up against the wall. The panic and warning had subsided, but it had not fully gone away.

How is it that my brother and sister do not feel uncomfortable? I thought. There was no reason to talk to them or my mom about it. Perhaps I was overreacting. It seemed I was the only one who did not feel at ease near him.

There was no way I could have known that just a few months previous to this, my father was in Toni's home, cleaning up blood that had splattered on the walls. Or that he had just dumped a body near our favorite family picnic spot in Oregon.

In the spring of 1990, my father and Toni moved into her mother's ranch-styled home in Portland, Oregon. The heartache continued for us when Dad picked us up to visit them that summer.

When we all walked in to her home, the cries of "Daddy! Daddy!" rang in my ears and pierced my heart. It was torture for us to watch other children having a relationship with my father in a way we used to have before the divorce.

Now I was an observer to this new family in which I did not belong. It did not feel fair that they received my father's time and attention. When I would feel these emotions, I would get angry at myself, and this brought on lingering questions of my own worth as well as a sense of shame. I felt shame for my thoughts and feelings toward this young boy and girl, and I thought that I must not have been as fun to play with as these children were, or Dad would still be with us. These feelings would intensify if my father was in a bad mood.

"You're just like your mother!" He blasted the remark at me more than once that summer, and it was usually right after he blamed her for something or had just finished complaining about what a horrible person she was. I could tell how my father felt about my mother, and being "just like your mother" meant that I was a horrible, ugly person in my father's eyes—not worthy of his presence.

My first impressions of Toni as a mother were more accurate than I had imagined. I observed her through the weeks we stayed in her home, and she often yelled and treated her two kids roughly and harshly. It seemed they couldn't do anything right, either.

Sometimes Toni would ask my father to discipline her children, including spanking them, but he would refuse. It was up to her to discipline her kids. In some ways, I liked to see her children get a bum deal, but somewhere deep inside, I knew that it was my jealousy talking. My heart hurt whenever they were yelled at, pushed around, or slapped. I knew that they deserved to be treated with patience and kindness, as all children did.

Things came to a head when Toni tried to treat me as one of her own children, or even worse. She passed on to me the rough and dirty jobs on the chore chart. It seemed unfair that I was getting the toilet cleaning duty all the time, and she didn't withhold yelling at me whenever she thought I had made a mistake. However, she never touched my body, or my siblings', and I think Dad must have laid down the law with her like he had with his father when it concerned us.

When I got home, I made sure I told my mother about the unfair treatment I received. Her expression never changed as I unloaded all the reasons why I hated Dad's girlfriend. My mother was obviously taking the higher ground, which was a great lesson—I only wish she would have commiserated with me just once. I'm sure she was sympathetic but only in an inner, silent way. From my mother's perspective Toni had taken her husband, ordered her children around, and absorbed most of the financial resources my father should have provided to her instead. I knew the situation must have been absolutely miserable for her, but if it were up to Mom, I would never know.

15

taking chances

I was genuinely thrilled that my mother had a new friend. She had spent so much time working and taking care of our needs that she had spent very little time to herself for the last two years. A genuinely warm and social woman (when she wasn't worrying about us), my mother made a loyal friend to people when they gave her a chance.

Patty lived right next door, and she quickly came to see what a gem my mother was. Her tiny white house separated our rental home from my grandmother's bright yellow house. Patty had two small boys, Nicholas and Newell. Patty's ex-husband was named Newell as well.

Petite and elegant, with fine, delicate features, Patty was visually stunning, especially with her long, black hair. My mother loved to spend her free time with Patty because of her friend's infectious laughter and humor. She saw everything in a comic light, and her life was as dramatic as it was entertaining. To my mother it made it seem like our home life was essentially peaceful and perhaps even boring by comparison! There was always some new development between Patty and one of her many sisters or with her obsessive ex-husband.

Patty was the one responsible for bringing Robert into our lives. She introduced him to my mother that summer. Patty said that Robert had hitchhiked up from Colorado. He was staying with a mutual friend of Patty and her ex. I overheard them talking the next day as I gathered a few items to spend the day at Sarah's house. Robert had just been by to visit Patty when an interesting development had happened.

"Patty, you didn't have to try to set us up!" said my mother, half sarcastically, half-resigned. "My divorce isn't even final for a couple of months."

Patty laughed. "All I said was maybe the two of you could go out, Laura. It was just a suggestion. If you wouldn't have made that face—"

"—and if he wouldn't have flipped me off—"

"—and if you wouldn't have felt *guilty!*" interjected Patty, laughing again. "Just give him a chance. I don't know him well, but he seems like a nice guy."

The next day, Robert came to pick up my mother, and I stood in stern reproach. I did not find him very attractive in looks or energy. He had fiery red hair that was receding back away from his natural hairline, and he seemed awfully short, but that was true of most men compared to my dad. I had difficulty in ascertaining his personality right away due to the fact that he was deaf, and therefore could not speak directly to me. His shirt, however, did say a lot. It was a wild, tropical print that made his red hair look mild in comparison. I did not care to write to him on the notepad that he carried around. My mother acquiesced easily, in order to be polite. Whether my concerns were valid or not, to me Robert was an intruder on the pending reunion between my parents. It would not have mattered if he were deaf or hearing, ugly or irresistibly handsome. I did not want to get to know him. They left on their date, my glowering looks following them all the way out of the door.

In the beginning, I thought Robert was simply a friend that was supporting my mother through this tough time in her life. Certainly she wouldn't be interested in more than that, would she? Certainly not with him! Slowly, his visits became more regular until he began spending the night on rare occasions. This infuriated me to no end, and created a form of rage and frustration that bottled up inside my gut and would blow unexpectedly. Robert had no right to be taking advantage of my mother and our home! I was at a loss about how to get rid of the man, so I acted in fits of temper tantrums when Robert appeared. My mother simply ignored me.

I went into my room and kicked at the bedroom wall, producing a large, thundering noise that surely even Robert could hear—and if not, at least feel. No response. Well, if my mother would ignore my tantrums, then I would have to find another way.

I sought for alternatives to get her attention and realized I would have to do something I'd never done before. In the meantime, my mother, who could not afford a doctor or a dentist, felt like we needed to see a family therapist. An idea came to me as we were in the car. We got into an argument about the need for a therapist, which I told her would not exist if there was no Robert. Calm as always, she would not engage in an argument. I felt like the reason she displayed no feelings was that she had no feelings.

"I HATE YOU!" I yelled at the top of my lungs. Her fingers clutched the steering wheel of our little blue Topaz, but there was no response. The feeling of victory, that I was winning this verbal assault came over me. Then, quite suddenly, it left as I heard a whimper and a choked cry from the only person in the front seat. Yes, I did have an effect, that was certain, but it was not the one I wanted. Not at all. Guilt flooded the space inside me where the anger had been, just moments ago. I decided to stay quiet for the remainder of the drive.

We pulled up to a professional building and my sister and brother went through the door first, anxious to get away from me, I was sure. I walked in with my head down, not wanting to see the distress I had caused on my mother's face. Finally, we all sat around a huge wooden table in a bare room. The therapist was a gentle-looking, grandfatherly sort of man that never looked at any one of us directly. At first I thought it was unprofessional, until my mother explained that he could not see; he was born blind.

"How many fingers am I holding up?" asked my brother, reaching up with seven fingers right in front of the gentleman's face. Mom and I both gasped in horror.

"Four?" the therapist asked with some humor, and Jason sat down, feeling confident that the man truly was blind. It took a few more minutes to break the ice before we could finally dive into the pressing issues that were causing strife at home.

"Melissa, what are your feelings about your parents not being together?" he asked.

"I am getting used to them not being together, but I don't like my mother's boyfriend!"

"You would not like anyone I would date," said my mother quietly. I disagreed with the point she was trying to make.

"I might not like anyone you dated," I countered, "but I *especially* don't like this one!"

"Melissa, it's not fair that you, Jason, and Carrie have accepted your father's girlfriend, Toni, but not my new boyfriend."

At that point in the conversation, I could tell that my mother was set on firmly believing that we were not going to be satisfied with any relationship she would have in the future unless it happened to be with our dad. Her belief made me more frustrated with the situation because I could not convince her otherwise. As we left, I knew Robert would continue to be a part of our existence, and I was still less than happy about it.

Over the next few weeks, I *did* try to give Robert a fair shot. He seemed quirky to me. He would write cliché jokes down on his notepad for us kids to read and then make a huge, echoing wheeze, which was his kind of laughter. That was not his fault, and I knew I had no right to be irritated with that. I could not pinpoint the exact character trait that was bothering me, and therefore I believed that the gentle therapist (and yes, my mother) might be right when he said that I was prejudiced against anyone dating my mother.

I never got an opportunity to find out if that was true or not because Robert and my mother soon became serious. Casually, Robert would bring items from his apartment over to our little home. I did not like his taste in home furnishings, and his items in our tiny house annoyed me. He brought over brightly-woven blankets, old aloe plants barely clinging to life in a clay pot, a painting of a half-nude Native American woman that looked like she was floating on a cloud, and finally, a machine that he connected to our phone line that appeared to be a typewriter.

"Robert uses that to call his relatives in Colorado," explained my mother when she noticed our curious stares. It was then that I learned Robert had been married before and that he had two sons, Norman and Robert Jr. I tried to picture what they must look like. Did they have his thick, porous skin, or the small gap between their front teeth like him? Focusing on Robert's appearance gave me a physical reason to find the man unappealing, since I could not put a finger on what it was about his energy that unnerved me. It was so shallow, and I knew it.

All I could grasp was that he really wasn't who I would want my mother to date. I had a list in my head of the person that would be right for my mother: gentle, charming, good manners, brilliant, kind, and a millionaire so we could leave this tiny house that had suddenly become even more oppressively small, the more time Robert spent there. Her boyfriend did not seem to have any more funds than my mother did.

I did not realize that it was a fantasy to wish for some handsome man to drive up in a limo and ask for my mother's hand in marriage. After all, I had seen that happen just a few weeks before at the Garland dollar movie theatre. Mom and I went to see the film, "Pretty Woman." I'm sure my mother didn't realize that her lack of funds for a babysitter contributed to my fantasy man for her, but I enjoyed watching her and Patty swoon over Richard Gere. All I could think was, *Why not?* At least I would find him appealing!

Within a few months of dating, my mother pulled me away from the JCPenney catalog one evening to tell Jason, Carrie, and me her exciting news. "Robert and I are to be married!" she announced.

Silence filled the room. All I could think was that my parents' divorce must now be final. *This is horrible!* I knew I hadn't scratched the surface of getting to know him yet, and I couldn't think that she had, either. *All those Prince Charmings that she didn't even bother to try to find. How could she settle on this man?* Neither of my siblings was pleased—this was just too much to bear in less than a year: a new home, a final divorce, and new partners for both of our parents. When would this ride slow down?

"Where are we going to live?" I asked. My mother looked at Robert, and smiled weakly.

"Here, of course!" she said. My heart sank. I was hoping for a bigger place because surely they would be merging their money together. The three of us were getting older and taller by the day, and I could not see how one more person could live in such a small space. Besides, sharing a bed with my sister was beginning to be a problem—Carrie could kick hard, even in her sleep. My mother had the smallest room, and it barely fit a single dresser and her queen bed. The only space left was a small walkway to get off the bed and slide between the dresser and the bed to get to the door. Where were Robert's things all going to fit?

I had learned that my temper tantrums did not work, kicking the walls didn't work, and of course telling my mother I hated her definitely didn't work. I was out of resources to show my disapproval for their relationship. Since that one session, we had not been back to the therapist's office, so even talking openly was out of the question—I'd actually tried that a couple of weeks previously.

Sighing, I surrendered. Maybe it was time to give Robert a chance—a fair chance. I had not been as harsh to Toni as I had been with Robert. Some of that had to do with the fact that our mother was our main caretaker. Whoever was in a relationship with her would be a full-time fixture in our lives, unlike my father's girlfriend. We saw Toni for only a few weeks in the summer or during a rare visit from them. Now that they lived in Portland, over four hundred miles away, we saw them less and less.

I made up my mind. I would give Robert a fair chance.

I knew the first step in creating a more compatible relationship with Robert would be communication. In order to get to know him, to see his good side, I needed to communicate with him so I knew what he was like, and what his preferences were. I started to notice the communication between him and my mother. I also started writing more on his pad and waiting for his response. It was only fair.

In October, 1990, Jason, Carrie, and I were at the bus stop waiting when my friend Sarah started a game of chase. She darted by the large oak tree and Jason followed her at his fastest pace. He could not stop in time to prevent him from slamming into the side of the tree trunk where Sarah was hiding. For a moment, I just watched, horrified as my brother lay in pain. Then I ran and found help from the neighbor lady who ran a child-care. Jason had suffered a serious concussion and was out of commission for several days.

When any one of us got hurt, it would literally freak Dad out. Suddenly the man we hadn't seen for months would come rolling in. This time, Dad had been planning to come and see us for Halloween, but interestingly enough, Jason's injury was bad enough for him to want to make a life change. As soon as he heard about it, our father drove straight up to Spokane and was there to help nurse his son back to health. A couple of years before when we had only been in Spokane for a short while, Dad had been involved in a serious accident while trucking and had needed to be taken to the hospital by ambulance. It had been a helpless feeling to be so far away and not be able to assist him. He had healed well, but I didn't tease him now for coming all this way for Jason. I knew exactly how he felt, and I was grateful to have him close to us again, whatever the reason.

While he was in Spokane, Dad decided he had been far away from us for too long. He decided to do something about it. Mom had already found Robert, and he was still with Toni, so the thing to do seemed to be to move to Spokane. He found a job at a local trucking company running out of the city and got the job right away. While they were looking for a place to live in the city, my father made an odd arrangement with my mother. She would allow my father and his girlfriend to live in the driveway. My father had a truck with a new camper on top of the truck bed. It was his and Toni's makeshift home until he found a better living arrangement. Not only was my father living in my driveway, so was that dreadful woman, Toni! *Why is my mother allowing this?* I wondered. I couldn't see how this incredibly uncomfortable situation could ever be approved by my mother.

Soon my father found a little apartment, and he and Toni moved in. As a driving partner, it seemed to me that my father enjoyed Toni's companionship for the most part, though from time to time he would get annoyed and express his irritation to me. We got to see him on his days off.

That year, Dad showed up to share his favorite holiday with us. He came to the Nordin House dressed as Bart Simpson for Halloween. We were preparing to go trick-or-treating when suddenly we couldn't find Carrie anywhere. We searched our little room and the yard, and then across the street and down the lane. After an hour of searching and calling her name, I had all kinds of crazy, suspicious notions going through my mind. We all tried to stay calm, but it was so unlike Carrie to disappear like this. Was it possible someone had nabbed her? It made me nervous to think about because she was such a pretty little thing, though as feisty as a rattlesnake if you bumped her cage. We went from house to house, conducting a search of our own before resorting to call 911. Dad was amazed at how many friends Carrie had in the neighborhood.

"How can one little girl know so many people?" he asked as we went to the eighth house in a row to ask if they had seen Carrie. I hesitated to reply. I didn't want him to go home feeling more helpless and responsible than he already did. It wasn't necessary for him to know that we stayed with friends as much as possible. I could tell he was already frustrated with the fact that although Robert was entering the scene in a big way, our cupboards were still pretty bare.

We were becoming more frantic, getting worried that we might have to call the police. We returned home, and suddenly we found her. Carrie was under all of her bed covers, asleep! She was only awakened by hearing all of us yelling her name as we entered the house again, and when I walked into my room, I saw Carrie sleepily pull her head out from under her thick comforter. Dad was so relieved. I could tell he'd had all kinds of scenarios going through his mind.

"Too many sickos out there," he muttered.

16

backfire

In February, 1991, news stations throughout the Northwest reported that Laverne Pavlinac's knowledge of the crime scene and the particular state of Taunja Bennett's body—including the rope—nailed the lid shut on Taunja's case. Even though Sosnovske had pleaded innocent, he had failed two lie-detector tests. When faced with the threat of the death penalty, he took a plea bargain, and both suspects were charged with murder. They were sentenced that February. Sosnovske given a life sentence, and Pavlinac a lesser sentence, though she was still to serve for ten years. Suddenly Pavlinac declared that she had made up the story to free herself of Sosnovske, whom she claimed had been abusive to her for years. While there may have been some merit to the volatility of their relationship, it was believed Pavlinac was lying to escape from having to spend the next decade behind bars. In other words, no one took her seriously.

I heard a few people talking about how they were grateful that the killers of that pretty girl were getting what was coming to them. Then they shifted their conversations to what was happening in the Gulf War and all of the hubbub that that weird Dr. Kevorkian was creating with assisted euthanasia. I had to ask my teacher what that was.

Dad's plan to live close to us backfired. Shortly after he and Toni moved to Spokane, Robert and my mother found some opportunities in Vancouver, Washington. We lived in an apartment there for a while, and

Carrie and I transferred, yet again, to another school. Jason decided to live with Dad instead of moving.

Because of the move, Carrie and I came to rely on each other and became closer as sisters while we were forced to make new friends. My sister, however, was much more vivacious and outgoing than I, so it took her less time to find new and exciting companions. I was always more cautious in making friends but found a few at school and near the complex where we lived. I missed Jason like crazy.

We had a new addition to our family as well. Mom brought home our new baby, half brother, Benjamin. He was tiny and fragile, and Carrie and I fell in love with him. Mom was very attentive to him, and she took time off work to be with him. She was very wrapped up in being his mom, and didn't even put up pictures on our apartment walls. It was interesting to see her with a new baby; a new mother all over again. I watched her and realized how she must have been with me when I was that tiny, all my needs met in her grace and affection.

Mom had worked all the way up to her delivery, and she stayed home for as long as she could with Benjamin. Money got tight, and things became tense. Soon enough, things didn't work out for our small family in Vancouver, and we decided to move back to Spokane. I was relieved. Living with Robert in such tight quarters, and in a new area with few friends had turned out to be a horrible experience. The more I learned about communicating with Robert, the less I wanted to. I found that he was petty, and would get angry with my mother over the slightest things. His signing to her would become more frenetic as he got angrier and soon I had no desire to know what it was he was saying. It seemed abusive to me, and I didn't like to see my mother being the butt of his unkind remarks, whether written or signed. His facial expressions were enough to see that he was not satisfied with her or with us the majority of the time, and there didn't seem to be anything I could do about it. However, my hopes that Mom would get wise to Robert's behavior were now overshadowed by the fact that she probably wouldn't leave the father of her new child.

Back in Spokane, we had to live in our grandmother's basement again. I was feeling despondent about the whole situation until something told me to watch for the good that happened around me. It didn't take me long to realize that being in Grandma's house seemed to temper Robert's rage considerably. He didn't seem as anxious to display his fury when he was in front of others and he put on a show that he was respectful to Mom and to us. That was one good thing. Suddenly, other good things popped into my mind. Although my cot seemed depressing and miserable, I was happy to be back near Jason again. That was another good thing. Also, I was back around friends I knew and felt the most comfortable with—at least in my neighborhood. The school I had attended previously was full, and it was the middle of the year, so I had to attend another school, Washington Elementary, for the rest of sixth grade. It was awkward sometimes for me to be in a place where everyone, except me, seemed to know each other, but I had made a few friends I felt comfortable with. That was another good thing! Best of all, each day after school I got to play with my old friends—plus I had time to daydream about the life I would create if it were all up to me. Now that was a really good thing!

As I began to get more grounded in my life in Spokane again, I saw that my mother and father had concretely moved on to new lives with their new partners. There wasn't anything more I could do to put them back together. I began to realize that I wasn't responsible for other people's choices, though I often felt responsible for their mistakes. I felt it was my fault that my father wasn't happy with us, that it must be my fault that my mother had to work so long and hard, and that it was even my fault that Robert treated her so poorly, since I was not kind to him. I also felt that it was surely my fault that we weren't able to live in more favorable circumstances with amenities that so many others seemed to take for granted.

Mom's life had become vastly different from what it had been in Yakima. She had little time for me or Carrie or Jason. She was either spending time with her new baby, her best friend Patty, or her fiancé, Robert. Or she was at work supporting us and Robert. I tried to find where I fit in her new life. I did my best not to feel resentful, but I often felt ignored from her lack of affection or interest in my school activities. I tried not to compare her to other moms—single or married—who went to their children's activities, plays, performances, games, and so forth. We didn't have money for sports, clubs, or extra-curricular activities, and mom didn't have time to serve with the PTA or Girl Scouts.

These feelings of neglect greatly increased my dislike for Robert. I began to realize how jealous I had become of her time with him, and the sheer negativity of it felt horrible to me. As the move back was sort of like a new beginning, and we were going to have to share my mother and this small space in our grandmother's house, I decided to give Robert yet another chance. Mom had seemed to settle back into a happier routine, and I thought perhaps the stress of the move to Vancouver had been hard on their relationship and was the main factor for the fighting. I conceded that I still did not know Robert very well and that it was only fair that I try to see what my mother found appealing in him.

Part of my jealousy was that while Mom was working so hard to support all of us, Robert didn't seem to work. Apparently he had some money coming in from someplace—sources that were mysterious to me—but while my mother's money went toward rent, fuel, and food, I couldn't figure out what Robert's money was used for. I reminded myself to be open, and I watched and observed Robert for signs of something praiseworthy, at least the times that I was home.

I made it a point to get involved in as many activities as I could that revolved around friends and fun. Roller-skating was high on my priorities because it was cheap and something to do on the weekends to get out of the house. It didn't hurt that it was a hugely popular thing for kids my age. It was easy to tell which kids where popular and skilled at skating by looking at their roller skates. If they were rentals, then they were new to the sport. If they had their own skates, they were likely part of the in-crowd at school and had some skills. Sarah Atkins, who was still my close friend and neighbor, would dress up in form-fitting, stonewashed Jordache jeans. On top she wore an oversized T-shirt tied to the side. She had the cool mall bangs look and topped it off with Ray Ban sunglasses. I would wear my generic-brand clothes from Kmart and did my best to match the look. We made quite a pair.

One time, during an outing with my father, he took Carrie, Jason, and me to Patterson's Roller Rink on the north side of Spokane. Patterson's smelled like theatre popcorn and played all the latest music. On the sides of the rink it showcased orange, cube-shaped lockers. The deep red carpet on the floor matched the same carpet on the benches. The kids who were skilled skaters would always go to the center of the roller rink to show off and perform tricks. The center of the rink was the scariest place for me, since it did not have any walls to cling to. I liked to be within easy skating distance of the wall in case I felt myself starting to fall. Also, if I did stumble along the wall, only a few people might notice, which was much better than to fall in the center where everyone would see me.

Carrie and I strapped on our brown leather skates with red wheels, while Jason and Dad tried out the new thing—roller blades. Dad looked like an athletic giant. It always amazed me how lithe he was for such a big man. His tremendous height was added to by the roller blades and it made his head almost touch the ceiling. As he took the floor, he began skating circles around the inner part of the rink, like the skilled kids I was used to seeing in there. I was suddenly aware that he was tall enough to knock into the disco ball in the center of the rink! I watched carefully, worried that he might actually do that, and perhaps even knock it down. He was aware of his body in alignment with the ball, however, and never even came close to hitting it. I breathed a sigh of relief.

My father had other ideas of fun, though. Quickly building momentum, he began to skate as fast as he could. I watched in horrified fascination as people moved out of his way, fast—terrified that he would plow into them. Although he was skillful and handled his body well, it was apparent he was there for himself, and didn't care if he frightened anyone or not. He never slowed down, just skated around people. I watched as several children and adults left the wooden rink to sit on the sidelines. They waited until Dad took a break and left the floor before they would even re-enter the rink. Soon a rock 'n roll song came on that my dad thought would be fun to skate to. I noticed that as soon as Dad flew back on the rink floor, people peeled off in waves, scrambling for safety once again. I had been proud of how my father could handle his body like an athlete, but it embarrassed me to see him so oblivious to the chaos in his wake. Part of me wondered if he really didn't know, or if he was chuckling silently inside? Other skilled skaters didn't frighten people off of the floor. They skillfully—and respectfully—skated around others with less skill.

A slower song came on. I jumped as Dad was suddenly right beside me.

"Do you want to skate with me?" he asked. I shook my head, turning red as all eyes were on me. At that moment, I didn't want people knowing he was my dad. In addition to that, I was one of those people who had been getting out of the way when he was skating! I was afraid of what could happen if he fell down and took me with him.

"Suit yourself, Prissy Missy." He picked up Carrie with ease, and they skated together, having a grand old time. Carrie stuck her tongue out at me, as if to say, "Na, na, na, na, na, na!"

I watched my father and my sister out on the floor. I was feeling wistful and so confused. Dad only called me Prissy Missy when he felt I was too concerned about what other people thought. On the one hand, I really *did* want to be a part of the fun. On the other, yes, I probably *did* care too much about what other people thought. But at least I cared! I thought about all the people that had to scatter before him, and I didn't know where to draw the line. I didn't know when to jump in and enjoy life and when to respect other people enough to allow them the same privilege.

17

hazard

I couldn't wait to grow up! My grade school years behind me, I was ready for the summer and ready to be and act like the BWOC—the big woman on campus. I felt that the older I got, the more control I would have over my own life. So many times I had felt as powerless as the flag on a rope of tug-o'-war; going this way and that, depending on who was strongest on the ends of the rope.

Dad broke the news that we would be staying with him for the whole summer, and we could hardly believe our luck. Anything was better than living in Grandma's small house with Robert and my mother. And being with Dad likely meant long trips, and playing hard—the Jesperson kind of summer fun that we hadn't experienced for some time, but that we still remembered well.

Along with the excitement, I was also experiencing some nervousness. Since that time I had been home sick and my father came to our house, I had never felt comfortable being alone with him. I reminded myself that I would always have Jason or Carrie around and that we were going to be spending much of the summer with Toni and her children, but Toni was another reason for my nervousness. I was resigned to the fact that I would have to come to terms with her as well, since she had become a permanent figure in our lives.

That night in my journal, I vented my anxieties and even my frustrations about my parents and their relationship choices. It was frustrating that neither of them seemed to have the judgment I would have had if I were able to pick out their new partners for them. As unrealistic as I knew that was, certain traits of their partners really bothered me. Just as I would have preferred to see my mom with a more compassionate, loving, and supportive partner, I would have loved to see my father with someone kind and tender as well. Toni seemed the opposite of that to me—hard and cruel. There was nothing soft or lovely about her, although she seemed to be obsessed with having my father by her side. He returned that obsession. I realized that Toni *needed* my dad, and that maybe he found that need appealing.

After I hid my journal under my cot that night, I tried to recall what it was like for Mom and Dad when they were together during their thirteen years of marriage. I could remember them loving each other, even though they spent little time together. In my memories, they seemed to live completely separate lives—their three children being the only common ground. While they could agree most of the time on how to parent us, everything else seemed like it had been amiss. I realized my parents had been married for several years before I was born, and I couldn't help but wonder what the early years of their marriage were like before children came along to tie them together.

Before the divorce, my parents had made some friends across town in Selah. Sterling had been my father's friend since childhood. His wife, Amanda was from Germany, and she and my mom had been close. A year before I was born, Sterling and Amanda had a son they named Gavin. They and my parents would get together once in a while whenever my father had returned from one of his long hauls. While they visited, Jason and Gavin would play with Gavin's train set, but the boys would not allow Carrie or me to touch it. I wanted so badly to play with the bristle trees and look more closely at the detail of the trains. After they would finish playing with the train, the boys would allow us to play in their next game. When we went outside, the boys played gunmen, and Carrie and I were the targets for them. It got old fast, so Carrie and I learned to bring toys of our own. But then we got annoyed when the boys would sneak up on us as we were playing Barbies

As a young girl, I thought Gavin was cute and charming. I knew I didn't understand him—or any boy—and that, of course, made him more appealing. From a young age, my father would call me "boy crazy" and every time he did, I would feel embarrassed. I was naturally curious about the differences between boys and girls. Barbie and Ken and small snippets of adult conversations offered little insight, and often only added to my confusion.

My parents were acquainted with another couple as well, Ted and Sylvia. On occasions when we visited them, Carrie and I would play with their daughter, Alicia, while Jason played with her older brother, Forrest. Alicia was quite bossy, but she did have all the information I was looking for in the boy department. With all of her great personal wisdom (and the information she had gathered from other children in her apartment complex), she explained the differences between boys and girls. Alicia had also kissed a boy while playing house, but I didn't think the boy was cute, so I didn't want to learn anything he might have to teach me. Sometime later, Alicia and her parents moved to Vancouver, Washington, and I didn't see them again.

My first kiss came on a different visit to Sterling and Amanda's house. While I couldn't remember how I got my little five-year-old self in the closet, I remembered kissing Gavin. Remembering it now brought a blush to my cheeks. That little peck probably would have been no big deal if it hadn't been for the humiliation we felt when our parents caught us! The ride home was even more horrible. My father had grilled me to find out why I would kiss a boy. I denied the kiss and told him we were looking for a missing toy in the closet.

I had not seen Gavin or his parents for many years. My father casually mentioned that they had just moved to Oregon. Then he sprung the surprise—he had decided we should visit them! We all piled our suitcases and meager belongings into his station wagon, prepared for an adventure.

Traveling with Dad was always fun and spontaneous. We were never sure what it would entail. Dad pulled up in an older station wagon. It was fairly roomy for a trip, but it didn't have air conditioning. He liked Buicks and Oldsmobiles; their barrel seats seemed to fit him better and were more comfortable for driving because of his large frame.

As we left the city limits, our father let us turn on the radio and take turns flipping stations. We sang lots of popular songs and old songs, our voices raised together. He usually let us listen to and sing whatever we wanted.

We headed southwest along the freeway toward Pasco. Suddenly, "Hazard," a Richard Marx song, came on. It had come out in '91, but had only recently become popular. Jason went to change it, but we stopped him, and then we all began singing. When we got to the chorus, we all took a deep breath and sang the chorus really loud; Dad's booming voice, Carrie's high one, and Jason's and mine blending in, somewhere in the middle.

Like all the most popular songs, it felt like "Hazard" came on the radio fifty times an hour. As we headed toward Oregon, we made terrific time on the highway, and finally pulled in to eat at a truck stop. Most of the waitresses seemed to know Dad, and he had his usual fun, flirting and making comments that now made me blush. Had he always acted this way? I realized he had—I just hadn't always known what his comments meant. I was relieved when our stomachs were full and it was time to get back on the road.

The scenery outside our windows became more lush, green, and filled with trees of all kinds. Instead of staying on I-84, Dad took us on the Columbia River Gorge Scenic Highway. The foliage was so much thicker than in Spokane, and between the gorge, the bridges, and the vistas, it was absolutely breathtaking. I was in charge of the radio now, which was helping to take my mind off the heat of the afternoon. Jason was staring out the back window, the breeze blowing his blond hair askew. Carrie had fallen asleep, and Dad was whistling to the song on the radio. Then he stopped.

"I know how to kill someone and get away with it," my father said casually, as he skillfully rounded another switchback. I looked at him quizzically.

"That was random," I said. Then I noticed his detective novel in the pocket of the door. Like the magazine piles in his truck, the car floor was littered with detective magazines now. *Another one of Dad's phases,* I thought. First there was the boxing phase . . . then there was the golfing phase . . . then there was the biking phase . . . then there was the *Crocodile Dundee* phase, complete with the hat, jacket, and accent (and boy was I glad that one was over). Now it was apparently the detective phase.

"You have to be very careful not to leave fingerprints," he said measuredly, "and you have to change your shoes so that the police can't identify your foot prints. Since I have large shoes, I would be an easier candidate to trace once in custody." I felt listless, and it was still too hot. I thought his conversation topic odd and not at all interesting. Neither Jason or I bothered to respond, and he dropped it.

I noticed that we were getting off the freeway and entering a tunnel that led to a large parking lot.

"Where are we going, Dad?" Jason asked.

"We're at Multnomah Falls, kiddos," he said, pulling into a parking space. "Wake Carrie, she's going to want to see it. It's the second tallest waterfall in the U.S. It will be a nice place to cool off and get a snack."

He was right, it was nice—more than nice. I looked up into the mountains and thought it was the most beautiful site I had ever seen. As we made our way along the path to the bottom of the falls, there were many large and even ancient trees, and the smell of cedar was strong in the air. A soft spray misted our cheeks at the base of the short waterfall. Looking up, we saw a decorative cement bridge that broke the lengthy upper fall into two sections. There was a trail that led up to the bridge and beyond. At the bottom of the waterfall, where we headed, there was a small pool of fresh water and the stream that took the water to the Columbia River. I took off my flip-flops and entered the shallow, icy water to cool off from the summer heat.

"Anyone want to go for a run to the top of the waterfall?" my dad asked. He was always up for a physical challenge and so was Jason. I started up the trail, dragging behind them, but I was not able to keep up their fast pace and quickly gave up. I could tell my father was disappointed by my lack of fitness. For a moment I felt let down as well, but that disappointment left when I walked back to the stream. I sat on a large rock and put my feet back in the water. Then I wrenched them out quickly. There were some weird looking creatures in the water that looked like lobsters, crawling over the slippery river rocks, their long antennas wiggling. I didn't want to touch one because they had pinchers.

When my family returned, Dad explained that the creatures were called crawdads, and that they were edible. I was not even slightly interested in eating them, but they were fascinating to watch. My brother wanted to take one home. Running back to the car, Jason and Dad brought over a white bucket. They decided he could take just one, so Jason searched for the biggest crawdads he could find and placed them in the bucket to compare them back on land. After he made his choice, we walked back to the car with his trophy. It had been so nice to cool off, and now that we were back to the hot car, I felt like I had to crawl into an oven. The heated leather stung my legs, giving me goose bumps. Luckily, we only had a couple more hours to drive before we reached the Portland area. As we drew closer and closer, I hoped I had prepared myself enough to see Toni.

Then Dad announced something completely unexpected. He said our first stop on our journey was to go see Ted and Sylvia and their two kids, Alicia and Forrest. I breathed a huge but silent sigh of relief. Yes! Friendly company! I wondered at Dad's sudden announcement, though. It was mysterious. Did he not want to see Toni, either? I didn't think that was the case, but it was so spontaneous, I wasn't sure what was going on his head. And I wondered if Ted and Sylvia had any clue we were coming . . .

18

❧

seaside splendor

Across the Columbia River from Portland, on the Washington side, was Vancouver. I had fallen in love with the rolling hills and trees of the beautiful city when we lived there before. Ted and Sylvia were now living in a two-story duplex, and we pulled up—all four of us and our luggage. It was obvious that my father had not called ahead of time to plan our stay with them. I was suddenly embarrassed to think we were imposing on them. Sylvia and Ted did not seem to mind, though, and I thought how lucky it was that this couple was less formal than most friends. I had previously overheard family members asking Dad to at least call before he came so they could get ready for us. I knew they were right—it was only considerate. My father most often went with the moment, without regard to how it may have impacted others. He did not see the harm in his spontaneous nature.

Sylvia invited us in and made us feel welcome while Alicia and I got reacquainted. Her room was upstairs, and Carrie and I would be staying with her. Jason was going to bunk with Forrest, and they seemed to hit it off. Since it had been so long since I'd seen them, I observed each family member, mentally noting how Alicia and Forrest had grown and changed.

Ted seemed a little odd to me. He spoke slowly with little fluctuation in his voice or expression in his face. It was very difficult to read his emotions. I could see his skin through his thin, brown hair. I would have to stop myself from looking to see if his scalp would wrinkle or move when he talked, to make sure to look in his eyes. He had always seemed laid-back and relaxed, almost to the point of depression, often sitting back with a cup of coffee glued to his hands. Sylvia was very different from Ted. She had been my mother's closest friend for years. She had a lot of spark and added energy to any room she was in. If I had a question or needed anything, I knew I could ask her.

Our visit only lasted a few days, however, before we were off to a new destination. This time it was Jason's turn to be in the front by the radio. We crossed the Columbia River and were heading up a large cliff with the view of a city and river below us. I leaned my head closer to the front seat.

"Where are we going next, Dad?" I asked my father. He seemed distracted and lost in thought.

"We're going to visit Sterling and Amanda's for a bit," he said. I wondered to myself if he happened to have called them and let them know we were coming, but I didn't ask. I also wondered what Gavin might look like now. I played a fun game in my mind. Would he be chunky with lots of acne? Would he be tall and too super-skinny? Would he be fun to hang around? Or perhaps nerdy or even a stick-in-the-mud? Growing more and more curious, I did my best to keep my voice and manner nonchalant.

"So, is Gavin going to be there?" I saw him glance back at me in the rearview mirror.

"I don't see why not," he answered in his sarcastic, teasing tone. "Why? Do you want to see him?" I looked away, and he said, "You *are* boy crazy, aren't you, Missy?"

I became embarrassed, but mostly angry with myself for even asking. I should have known my dad would tease me.

"No, Dad!" I protested. I wanted to act like I didn't care at all, but it came across too vehemently. "I just want to know if there will be someone to hang out with!" I made a face at him in the mirror. "I don't like boys!"

I knew I had just lied, but it was the only way to get the teasing to stop. I promised myself that even if Gavin was cute, I was not going to show any interest—least of all in front of my father. I felt awkward enough. I wasn't a kid anymore but I wasn't a young woman yet, as much as I wanted to be one. I was growing naturally more curious about boys every passing year, but I didn't know what to do about them. I had no desire to make out with one, as some of my friends had done. For me, when my time came, I wanted it to be special and romantic.

My style in clothes matched my attitude and confusion about life. I was drawn to the Kurt Cobain grunge look. For my birthday that summer, I got the military jacket that I requested from my mother. It was Army green, and I wore it even in ninety degree weather. I rather thought I looked like Alicia Silverstone in Aerosmith's video that had been released that summer. In the video, Silverstone wore flannel and torn jeans to give her a hard-edge appeal—the look I was going after in my army jacket. A little heatstroke was worth it, right?

I felt like I was a little bit like Silverstone in my grunge clothing, torn Levis, army coat and Stussi T-shirts. I wanted Doc Martin's but my mom could not afford them, so I wore brown Birkenstocks that my grandmother Lucy had given to me the summer before, even though they were too small and cramped my toes. In my eyes, Alicia Silverstone was cool because she could beat up boys in her video. It mirrored the internal struggle I was facing, of wanting to be wanted, and yet wanting to protect myself at the same time. Protect myself from what? I didn't know.

As we got closer to the coast, I could smell the salt water of the ocean nearby. I loved being near the beach; something about the ocean soothed me. Perhaps it was the rolling, consistent waves or the warm sand, massaging my feet.

My father drove through the small coastal area of Astoria and Seaside. Puget Sound was stunning and majestic to me anyway, but to see the large ships and yachts docked by salt water-stained Victorian buildings was so charming and unique. To me, there was magic about this incredible city, with its steep hills and spectacular views of the sea, and a history you could feel. Dad told us it was Lewis and Clark's final destination.

Taking our time and enjoying the scenery, we slowly pulled into a gravel driveway. It appeared that no one was home until we all got out of the car and walked to the back of the yellow house. I had not seen Amanda or Sterling in years. Amanda was in the yard, working on some wood that was being supported by some A-frames. She looked up in surprise to see all of us and called Sterling over.

My parents' friends looked the same to me, as if they hadn't aged at all. Amanda was charming and warm-spirited as always. I loved her soft German accent and her dimples when she smiled. She had a sweet disposition, and I never saw her upset about anything. Sterling was laid back in spirit and also a generous man. We hugged both of them, and then Amanda backed up to take a better look at the three of us.

"I am amazed at the difference just a few years makes!" she cried, looking us up and down. "I bet your mother is *so* proud of you." We nodded politely, and she seemed to sense the bit of tension in the air caused by her remark. We didn't like to talk about Mom when Dad was around. He was pretty negative and made cutting remarks about her.

"Well," she said quickly, "Gavin is inside. You can go in—just keep in mind it is a big mess. We are remodeling our home, and so *everything* is still a big mess." Just then Gavin appeared in the back door.

"Oh there you are!" she cried, ushering us over to Gavin. "Look who's here, Gavin! Here's your old train buddy—do you remember that, Jason? And doesn't Melissa look pretty?"

As much as I wanted to feel pretty, I didn't think I was attractive, especially because of my teeth. They were overcrowded and unruly, going in directions I wished they wouldn't. I wanted braces in the worst way. While Dad blamed Mom for not setting orthodontic appointments, Mom blamed Dad for not paying for them—but the bottom line is that I was left with a mouth that made me feel totally insecure about my appearance. I did not understand how Amanda could think I was a pretty girl, but her comments made me feel wonderful. She was the first lady I could remember besides my mother and Grandma Lucy to ever give me a compliment.

Gavin did not say anything at first. He just looked at me. I studied him back, and realized he looked even cuter than I had ever remembered. Not the stocky, little, brown-eyed boy anymore, Gavin was transforming into an athletic teenager. Something inside me started to melt at one look into his eyes. Quickly I thought back to the promise I made myself on the car ride—my resolve not to find him one bit attractive—or at least, I would not show it. Not to him or anyone else.

I did look away, but it took a moment, and I realized that keeping my promise would be more difficult than I previously thought.

Gavin invited us into their new house. They had been tearing it apart since they were completely remodeling the kitchen and bathroom on the main floor. They were also building a round stairway to get to Gavin's room on the second level. At the time, there was a ladder going up to his area of the house. I was deathly afraid of heights, and the ladder would be scary to climb. I sucked in my breath—it was worth the experience if I could get another look at Gavin.

Dad pitched in to help Sterling and Amanda on their kitchen remodel. I overheard my father offering Sterling his services in welding the round stairway. I knew then that we would be staying for at least a few days.

That night we all decided to go out for pizza for dinner. Once we were seated at the local pizzeria, I felt antsy and decided to ask my sister to go to the restroom with me. In the privacy of the ladies' room, I blurted out my feelings, confessing to Carrie that I thought Gavin was cute. Carrie's eyes got wide, and she started to laugh. Then a mischievous expression came over her face, and I was suddenly nervous that she might tease me openly, and reveal my very sacred feelings. *Why did I tell her my new secret?* What if she made me look stupid or embarrassed me? I was afraid of what would happen if she told Gavin my feelings. I begged her not to say anything, but privately I thought that I should appear very uninterested in him. That way, if my sister did tell him, I could play it off.

Carrie and I sat back down at the table just as the fresh pizza arrived. I felt a sudden and unexpected nudge on my shin. I glanced around and realized that Gavin must have accidentally hit me with his foot. Then it happened *again*. I looked at his face, and he was not smiling or giving any expression to acknowledge his flirting. Was he feeling the same feelings as me?

We went to a local mall, and my dad actually bought something for himself that time. He found a new pair of Nike shoes that fit just perfect, and some clothing that looked attractive on his tall frame. I was happy to see him wearing something different. I realized from the comments between the grown ups that it must be hard for him to find clothing that actually fit.

Amanda set up my dad on a date with a blonde coworker of hers. When they got back, there were apparently two very different sides to the story about what happened on their date. Picking up a small, whispered conversation, I took it that hers was not very complimentary toward my father. Nothing more was said, and I didn't worry about it any longer.

The next evening my father took all of us to see the movie, *So I Married An Axe Murderer*, with Mike Myers and Nancy Travis, about a man who marries someone who is not who he thinks she is. Apparently she marries, murders her husbands, and then changes her name and identity and moves on.

My dad thought it was hilarious. It wasn't rated R, but I could tell afterwards that it was a little disturbing to Amanda that Dad would take Carrie to see it. I really hadn't paid much attention to the movie at all, since I was sitting next to Gavin. I was in my own little world as he nudged my knee occasionally. The whole movie, I kept hoping he would put his arm around me. I didn't really expect that he would, especially with my father sitting right beside us. That would make him stupid, and he was anything but that.

After two more days, Dad and Sterling completed the stairway, and it was time for us to leave. I was sad to say good-bye to the pretty town and to Gavin, but as we were invited back next summer, I left thinking I would see him again on another trip with my father.

We made our way back down the coast and over to Portland to stay with Toni and her children. It had been nice to not have to deal with her so far this summer, but as we got closer, I knew I had to rectify the feelings of jealousy I had in my heart. I tried using the same technique I had been attempting with Robert—to look for the good in him. I did see some qualities in Toni that obviously made her attractive to my father.

Toni was pretty and very energetic. Wiry and semi-athletic, she could keep up with my dad's tremendous vigor. She was fairly spontaneous, like he was, and she had included him in her life and looked after him to the best of her ability. I tried to focus on these positive traits as we approached Portland. It didn't last long.

I would often wake in the morning to the sound of Toni yelling at her kids. Their response seemed to be bitterly angry and to become extremely withdrawn on the days she would pawn them off on other people. Then she tried all summer to convince Dad to spank her children as she did or to yell at them. He wouldn't do it. As the summer wore on, I couldn't help but see that my father was taking the higher road by showing fair and equal treatment to all of us. As much as I didn't want to, I had to give him some grudging respect.

Most of the summer passed without incident, except when Toni placed herself in competition with us when it came to Dad's money. I knew she didn't have a clue what our home life was like, and I was pretty sure she didn't care. She was too wrapped up in herself to realize that we relied on Dad to supply even our most basic needs, especially for school supplies. I had given up on designer clothing and was simply grateful for whatever items Dad might provide. Without his assistance, we would go back to school in last year's clothes and worn out shoes. We were wearing them now, but as Jason, Carrie, and I had all grown considerably taller during the summer, our entire wardrobe was several inches too small and full of holes. Jason couldn't get his Levi's to buckle, and the cuffs of his pant legs were so high, he looked like Erkyl. Of course, he smacked me when I told him so. I laughed, but I wasn't in any better shape.

Toward the end of the summer, we visited a cheap department store. I had asked Dad for a couple pairs of pants for me, Jason, and Carrie. I knew what kind I wanted—I had already tried them on and picked a couple of pairs. Jason was trying on his in the boy's dressing room, and I helped Carrie to decipher what size she ought to get now, getting some that were large on purpose, to be able to wear them for a while. Dad was holding onto my pants when I heard Toni come up with her cart.

"What the hell are you buying her those for, Keith?" I heard Toni ask. She must have seen the pants Dad was holding for me. "She's a brat!"

I felt like I had to go out there and defend myself.

"I'm not a brat," I tried to say to her, rounding the corner. "We just need a few things for schoo—"

"—She's a *brat*, and you shouldn't listen to her. She's spoiled, and she just takes advantage of you and your money. Don't you see that, Keith?"

I looked at Toni's cart, stuffed full of what she was buying for herself and her kids, compared to the two items in my dad's arms. I ran away, crying.

19

❧

attacked

After our summer adventures, being back in Spokane highlighted the reality that school would begin in only a few weeks. Because of Toni's interference, we didn't have all of the items we would normally have for school, and Jason and I were brainstorming what we could do to earn extra money. Even though money was tight, a small miracle had taken place that absolutely lifted my spirits. The house that I had seen in my daydreams had become reality! I had dreamed of a larger house, spacious enough for all of us to have our own space, with a fireplace and a lovely yard to play in.

I was surprised and delighted to find that our new home on Litchfield Street was everything I had pictured in my mind. It was a clean and spacious rancher, set on a rolling hill in a nice area of town. All of the neighbors were elderly, so it was mostly quiet during the day, although there were also two families that had children our ages. Our new backyard was spacious with a small hill in the back that looked great for sledding when winter came.

Now that we were back in our own place again, Robert seemed to be showing his true colors. In my experience, he was extraordinarily fussy about the smallest things, especially when it came to food. One morning, I witnessed him get wildly upset when a few crumbs from our toast got mixed in with the butter. Some foods were off limits in the kitchen, although it was never explained to us exactly which ones were forbidden to eat. I had begun to feel like the kitchen had land mines planted in it. I felt the need to grab, duck, and run, for I would not know if the food I grabbed was a prohibited one until I got "yelled" at. I never realized that a person who was deaf and did not speak out loud could have energy so strong that he could yell without making much noise. Dad had told us that he and Toni had broken up again, and he thought that this time it was over for good. I felt a small flutter of hope that maybe he would take us away from our home situation with Robert. However, he seemed tied to trucking as a job, and seemed to be dating a lot of women. I didn't like the details he would tell me about his dates. Was he teasing me or not?

Toward the end of the school year, I met a counselor who had big, beautiful eyes that seemed to see right through me. She was very kind and caring and she was always hanging around the cheerleaders as their advisor. Seemingly in tune with things that teenagers went through, she was easy to talk to about other challenges. Maybe she could explain some things to me and give me some really good advice on what to do with my dad and his conversations with me.

One day, after seeing her joking and laughing with the cheerleaders on stage, I decided I would get up the nerve to ask her. I went to her office after lunch and found her working on a stack of papers.

"Miss Jackson?" I asked hesitantly. "Are you busy?" I almost hoped she was because I had about lost my nerve.

"Well, hello, Melissa!" she said with a warm smile, brushing back her chocolate-brown hair. "I'm just doing paperwork, but it can wait." I was surprised and pleased that she remembered my name. Maybe this wouldn't be so bad. She pushed her pile of papers over to the side. "Go ahead and sit down. What can I help you with?"

"Well, I'm hoping you can give me some advice. You see, mm . . . my dad says things that I don't like. I don't know what to do about it."

"Really?" she asked, "like what?"

"Well," I began hesitantly again. I looked at her—could she handle it? She seemed interested. "Well, he tells me about the dates he goes on."

"Oh, really? And that makes you uncomfortable, Melissa? Lots of dads go on dates these days. Your parents are divorced I take it?" I nodded, and she went on. "There are a lot of kids with parents going through divorces, unfortunately, so there are a lot of dads dating. Probably most kids don't really enjoy hearing about their parents dating."

"Yeah," I said, "but I . . . I think this is different."

"Different how?" she asked. She tilted her head a little to the side to look me intently in the eyes. *Okay, here goes . . .*

"He tells me details," I said, opening up. "First about the girls he dates, and then about their body parts."

"Oh really?" she asked again, shifting a little in her chair this time. "Like what?"

"Well, like his date last week, and what he said about her." I went on to describe the details he had given me about Darcy's body. The counselor's eyebrows shot up. Okay, so she was as surprised as I hoped she would be. Maybe my father's descriptions were a little out of line.

"Oh my goodness," she said, appalled.

"And then he tells me about what they do on their dates," I went on, my voice almost in a whisper. I didn't want anyone outside the door to hear me.

"Oh, wow," she said. And then she added, a little hesitantly. "Like . . . ?"

"Like he'll say, 'Then Darcy and I went out for a couple of drinks, and she . . .'" I went on. "Sometimes he says stuff about how it used to be with him and my mom compared to what he does with his new girlfriends. It feels gross and it just makes me uncomfortable."

I couldn't believe how good it felt to get this all out! I had never told anyone about this—not even my mom, and I felt like now maybe someone could see what I was seeing. If it was as crazy as what I thought it was, maybe I could ask my dad to stop talking to me about those things. And if it really was normal, I would just have to figure out a way to deal with it.

"Well, yes, I guess that would make you feel uncomfortable." She looked at me carefully. "Honey, is your dad . . . is he molesting you?" At her question, my eyes got really wide. "Is he touching you in any way that makes you uncomfortable?"

"No!" I said, somewhat vehemently. But I was uncomfortable now and started to shut down. Of course my dad wasn't touching me. He wouldn't ever do that to me. I just wanted the conversations to stop. But maybe there was only a problem if he was actually molesting me. Maybe it wasn't a big deal for him to tell me these details. "No," I said, a little more softly. "I guess it's no big deal. I just didn't like the way he was talking to me."

"Well," she said, a little too brightly, seemingly relieved at my answer, "you let me know if there is anything I can ever do for you. I'm really glad you told me how you were feeling. Do you feel better now?"

"Sure," I lied—actually more unsure now than ever. I realized suddenly that if I pushed the issue too much, the school could call the authorities. All I was hoping was that this counselor could get him to stop, but I suddenly realized how quickly things could get out of hand.

"Well, thanks for your time," I said and walked out of her office. I felt cold and numb.

Looking back now, I can't believe that nothing ever came of that conversation. No advice was given and no one stepped in to help with that situation or take me out of the circumstances I was in. Instead, I was left thinking that I had to deal with whatever anyone said to me—that it was normal.

I began to surround myself with girlfriends as much as I could. I enjoyed their company and felt safer in the presence of girls and women. Then one sunny day my new friend, Kathy, invited me to come to her house after school. On the walk to her house, we decided to go to the park for something fun to do. We were halfway across the grassy area of the park, heading toward the swings, when I felt a heavy weight hit my back. It knocked me to the ground. Dazed, I looked up and saw Kathy running away and that I was surrounded by teenage girls. Fear exploded inside me as I saw their faces. They were intent on doing harm.

"Let me go!" I screamed. "I haven't done anything to you!" My heart was racing. I saw no escape.

"Your friend is wearing red," one of them said. *What the heck did red have to do with anything?* Then I realized that some of the territorial contention I had witnessed in middle school between the boys must also extend to some of the girls that hung out with them. A girl standing behind me spoke.

"Give us your ring," she said, in a voice that was used to being obeyed. I looked at my hand and saw the seashell ring my father had bought me on our summer vacation. That ring was more than just a gift from my father. It represented the peace I had felt on the beach under the stars and it gave me hope on my bleakest days that everything would work out. I must have been taking too long to decide

"Give us the ring or we'll smash your face in!" Dismayed, I took the ring off and gave it to her, not daring to look her in the eye. I was waiting for permission to leave when I felt a violent tug on my hair. The girls dragged me to the picnic bench and slammed my face into the metal slab. My head began throbbing, and for a moment I could not see. My adrenaline kicked in to an even higher gear, and I looked for escape. When my vision returned, I saw some light and along with it a boot heading toward my face. A sharp pain reverberated throughout my face and head. Then they punched and kicked my whole body with no mercy, using ring-filled fists and steel-toed boots. At some point, my arms came up to shield my head, but pain wracked my body, and I couldn't move. The blows continued, on and on until I lost all track of time.

"Stop!" A boy's voice sounded through the haze. I didn't know who it was, but his voice stopped their attack. One girl gave one more malicious kick, and then they left. Through swollen lids, I saw the legs of the girls, leaving with the boy, and I knew I was alone. I put my head down and began to cry, but it hurt too badly. I made myself stop. I couldn't move, and I was vulnerable to the world. What if the girls came back for me? I couldn't defend myself from anyone. I had never felt so alone in my life.

After a few moments, I knew I had to do something, anything. It hurt to move. I tried to open my swollen lids, and look around. Relief flooded me as I saw Kathy's figure running back to me.

"Melissa, we have to get you to the restaurant around the corner before those girls come back!" She was terrified. It took her a while to help me up. The walk was extremely difficult and seemed to take forever, even though she was rushing me. Every step brought fresh pain. Everything hurt, but my head was the worst. We finally reached a little Thai restaurant around the corner. The owner took one look at me and handed Kathy his phone. She called my mother, who rushed to pick us up. As soon as she saw me, she began to cry. Stuffing away the tears, she carefully helped me into her car and rushed me to the nearby hospital.

After endless x-rays, cleanings and bandaging, I was allowed to go home. When I went to the bathroom, I saw my face for the first time since the attack. It was swollen and bruising all over. My nose was twice its normal size and dark marks were appearing under my eyes. The instructions from the hospital were to lie down and rest for a few days so my fractured ribs could heal. They had been damaged from the steel-toe boots the girls were wearing.

For the hundredth time, I wondered why the girls attacked me. All I had been told was the red shirt excuse, but I knew there had to be another cause for that kind of violence. I had heard of gang initiations, and I wondered if that might have had something to do with it.

The landlady must have seen us come in, bandages and all, and she rushed over to find out what she could do for us. I had the feeling she just wanted to know all the juicy details. She seemed to know everyone's business and never hesitated to tell us all about all the other families in the neighborhood. I knew she also wouldn't hesitate to tell our neighbors what had happened to me, and I didn't want to be the subject of these conversations. I turned away and pretended to sleep. Mom, who was also very private, ushered her out quickly.

My mother called my father to let him know about the attack in the park. After only a few seconds, she handed me the phone.

"Who were those girls?" my father yelled. I had to hold the phone away from my ear—the sound of his yelling caused new ripples of pain in my head. "No one touches my daughter!" His voice got lower, but it was more menacing than before. "Let me know where they live, Melissa, and I will show them what it feels like to get attacked!"

I had never heard my father so angry before. I knew he was serious about making them feel the pain that they had caused me. "Dad, I don't know who they were. I've never seen them in my life and I don't have a clue where they live. They were older, probably in high school. I just don't know who they are or anything about them."

I tapped into my father's emotions and I knew without any doubt that if I had known where they lived and told him, he would have gotten in his car and driven up to Spokane as fast as he could. He would have taken care of the matter his way. I trembled from the violence I had already experienced that day. I was sad and I was angry with those girls for doing that to me—an innocent bystander in their stupid gang activities, or whatever it was that had provoked them—but I didn't want any more violence to happen that day. I didn't want anyone to have to experience what I had just been through.

Except for Dad's heavy breathing, there was silence on the phone line. There had been something in my father's voice—a violently desperate quality—that frightened me. It was like the time we were driving past the prison and dad had yelled, "You'll have me soon enough! But not yet!"

It was crazy, and at any other time I would have denied it, but that moment I had the most horrible *knowing* that if my father could have found those girls, he would have killed them all.

20

❦

a different way

Life seemed stable. We had lived in the Litchfield home for two years straight. I was able to stay at one middle school, Glover, for all of seven and eighth grade without having to transfer to another school. Making friends had become easier because of it, and it felt safer to devote energy and feelings into a friendship, knowing that I would not be moving away suddenly. But I was struggling with friendships that were sometimes shallow. One of my friends had secretly hooked up with the guy I liked. When I found out, I felt betrayed and once again I felt like I had no one to trust. I felt like the fish I had seen on my summer fishing trips with my dad. Those fish had floundered on dry land for a minute before my Dad or Jason killed them and gutted them. Since my attack, I had felt the same way—vulnerable and exposed, all of the time.

The sound of a whining tea kettle woke me up to a beautiful morning. The sunshine coming through the window warmed my face as I wiped the sleepiness from my eyes. As I walked from my bedroom into the kitchen, I could see my mother steeping her tea bag. She was dressed in Robert's T-shirt and her pajama bottoms. Seeing my mother in Robert's shirt in the morning created such a hopeless feeling within me. It was simply a physical object, but it struck a nerve. To me it was like seeing a jerk putting his letterman's jacket on your best friend in an act of ownership. That's how it felt, anyway—like Robert had claimed ownership.

The toast popped out and I could hear her buttering it, making the toast crackle as she spread the butter.

"Did you sleep well, Melissa?" my mother asked.

"Yeah," I replied sluggishly, "I just don't know what I want to do today." I didn't tell her out loud that I had one of two choices: either stay at home where I was a prisoner in my bedroom so Robert couldn't dominate my every movement, or I could leave for the day. My dilemma in leaving was that I did not have any nearby friends to hang out with. My classmates from eighth grade lived a few miles away, and I did not have a way to get out to their home. My brother and sister had developed neighborhood friends to spend their summer afternoons with while my mother was at work.

She took a wooden chair out at the table and sat down next to me. I saw her space off into a mental agenda. I decided to eat while I thought about my own options for the day. I got up and opened the cupboards, hoping to see some new choices for breakfast. Instead there was the usual two—bread or plain Cheerios.

I grabbed the generic box of Cheerios and poured them into my bowl. Between dripping spoonfuls of cereal, I attempted a conversation.

"What time do you go to work?" I asked, hoping beyond hope that she didn't have to go. That, of course, was wishful thinking.

"In an hour or so," she answered, still staring into her tea. I could tell she was looking forward to the day about as much as I was. Suddenly, she changed the subject and perked up.

"Are you looking forward to our Oregon coast trip in August?" she asked. "I think it will be the perfect time to go. The weather will be great!"

Like me, my mother tried to make herself look forward to the fruits of her labors.

"I can't wait!" I answered, getting into the spirit of it. "It will be so much fun!" . . . and I'll get to see Gavin. Thinking about him made my day a little brighter, but I could still hear mom's husband snoring—all the way from their bedroom into the kitchen. I knew I could not stand to spend a whole beautiful day wasted in my room. I liked listening to CDs and trying new makeup techniques to make me look more like the models in my Seventeen magazine, but this was a day to be enjoyed, not endured.

The other problem with staying in the house was that it became difficult to leave if I changed my mind. I would have to ask for permission in Robert's notebook before I could get his approval. Then my mother offered up a brilliant solution. Swimming! The Shadle Pool was just a mile away and I could walk there with my brother and sister, plus it didn't cost much. It was perfect. My mother finished with her breakfast and left the table to get ready for work. I poured the rest of my cereal down the drain.

In our bedroom, Carrie was just waking up. She looked so cute snuggled by her little Bunny Fu Fu and her long, blonde curly hair all ratted up from sleep. It was the same Bunny Fu Fu from that fateful Easter after my parents divorced, though it looked very different. Carrie had refused to let the stuffed animal get washed, and she took it everywhere (and I mean everywhere, like restrooms at gas stations). One evening when I was tired of seeing her dirty bunny, I decided it needed a bath in the washing machine. When it was through the wash, it looked so bright and new again! She would be so pleased. Then I tossed it in the dryer. A few hours later, Carrie screamed when she thought Bunny Fu Fu had been taken. I told her I had washed her pretty bunny and it was in the dryer. Carrie rushed to open the dryer door, and pulled out a pink, melted bundle of fur, somewhat, but not really, in the shape of Bunny Fu Fu. I was shocked to see her bunny in such poor condition, and I knew it was my fault. My sister cried all night, but eventually she got over the new shape of her bunny's fur and loved it just the same.

I looked through my old, white dresser for my swimsuit and an outfit to wear as I told Carrie my plans to go to Shadle Pool. Carrie had plans of her own to hang out at her best friend's Sadie's house. I gathered my gear and knocked on Jason's door before stepping in. His room was always ten degrees hotter than ours and smelled musky from his soiled socks. I shook his side, telling him we were going swimming for the day. He barked out an "Okay!" just to get me to leave him alone.

Mom was shuffling around the house for her keys, and anxiety filled my stomach. The moment she walked out the door, we were subject to whatever Robert told me and my siblings to do. My mother looked polished in her black slacks, shiny belt, and white blouse. She already had her Montgomery Ward's name tag attached.

"Well, I better get going now," she sighed under her breath. "Give me hugs."

As I hugged her, I instantly wished she could stay and protect us. When the summer days got hotter, so did Robert's anger. Just as you could feel the temperature rising, so it was with our home. We would start to tread a little lighter, watch our actions and what we ate a little more closely. You could never know what simple action would set the man off, and so we were constantly tense in anticipation of it. I tried in the past to prevent the episodes of his abuse and anger, but there was no common thread for every outbreak of violence. Once I ate the last slice of pizza that he was banking on for lunch the next day. I didn't have any idea, but as I gobbled it up, I suddenly saw Robert shoving my mother into the wall for *my* perceived selfishness.

Just as Robert's reign of dominance controlled the family, so did my mother's helplessness. Over the months, my mother's will decreased as Robert's temper increased, causing her to be in a paralysis of will. In her brown eyes, I could see sorrow for what had happened to her life. Where she used to guard us from her feelings, I could openly see shame and an overwhelming amount of fear. And if she left? What kind of future did she have if she was divorced from two men? Robert had convinced her no one else would have her, and in addition, he had conditioned her to take responsibility for the abuse he inflicted upon her and her children. As my mother remained trapped inside the abuse, I remained helpless to prevent it or change my environment. All I could do for the day was make a choice about where I wanted to be.

When people glimpsed what was happening and asked questions, I did not have the ability to express what I had witnessed. To me it seemed like progressive torture. Over their dating and marriage, Robert slowly broke her normal response until she no longer knew what normal response to give. My mother had become conditioned to second-guess every action until she had given up her confidence in conducting her own life and steering ours.

Once I called my mother to the carpet. I wanted to know, once and for all, why we were staying with this brute who dared to call himself a man.

"Why can't we just leave?" I asked her.

"Because he would find us and make things worse." I thought I had a solution to this problem.

"You could get a restraining order!"

She replied in such a whisper, that I almost didn't hear her. "That's just a piece of paper." Her voice seemed dead. "It does not stop him from hurting us."

I knew she was right. Robert could still be free to stalk my mother at work or attack her and it would be too late by the time the police arrived to save her from an attack. She was not safe unless he was in jail. The couple of times they had put Robert in jail, it was never long enough. I wanted to run away, out of the state, where he could not guess where we were, but two things stopped her. My mother needed her job to support us, and she also did not know what he might do to her own mother if we suddenly disappeared.

I gave my mother her hug good-bye, and watched her leave in her little blue Topaz for work. I felt blessed that Robert was still sleeping as I finished my preparations to go swimming. Carrie was dressed and Jason was ready to go with me. We all seemed to sense the same urgency, and we left at the same time, not mentioning out loud what we all knew—it was not safe to stay. We smiled at each other, knowing we were out of harm's way for one more day, and then Carrie bounced off to Sadie's as Jason and I set out for our swimming adventure.

The warm, sunny day had attracted a large crowd at the pool, and I was excited to be in the company of so many people. I was free to be fifteen.

After we got settled, I suddenly noticed that there was a ruckus in the corner of the pool near me. A pretty, brown-eyed girl stood in the water, her hands on her hips. She was thin and naturally toned, but the thing I noticed most was how she was speaking her mind to a guy in the corner of the swimming pool. Apparently, she had been practicing her stroke when the boy blocked her path and wouldn't let her pass. She was letting him know just what she thought about that, and his face turned a bright red, visible even beneath his lightly tanned skin. The tone she had used was stern, yet sarcastic. I had never heard a girl standing her ground like that before, and to me, it was entertaining and enlightening. I was enjoying her diatribe until she saw me observing her. I quickly turned away, pretending that I really hadn't been eavesdropping. I figured that my grin had probably given it away.

A few minutes later I noticed Jason speaking to a girl about his age who was standing next to the headstrong girl I had witnessed earlier. My brother pointed me out to the two girls, and they all began heading in my direction. Jason introduced me to them. The younger girl was named Summer, and her older sister's name was Heaven. I was a little intimidated at first, but Heaven was gentler with me than she had been with the boy. She told me she was just a year older than me, and that she was going to North Central High. She asked which high school I would be attending, and I laughed and said, "Your rival—Shadle Park High!" She laughed too.

It was easy to have a conversation with Heaven because I was anxious about starting high school, and she had many answers to my questions. I wanted to know if the rumor was true that seniors threw freshman into the garbage containers. I also wanted know about other critically important things, like what high school dances were like. Heaven and I exchanged information about our crushes until the lifeguards blew the whistle to warn us that there was only five more minutes of free swim left.

We exited the pool and continued our conversation in the locker rooms. We talked more about the boys in our lives. I talked a little about Gavin and she told me about her boyfriend, Dusty. Heaven then asked me if I was going to save myself for marriage. I pictured myself in a white dress and Gavin standing at the altar and said, "Sure."

Inside, I really did not have a firm answer for that question, since it was the first time anyone had ever asked my opinion on the subject. She went on to profess her intent of staying pure for her wedding day—that was going to be her special gift to her husband. I did not know why she thought it was such a "gift" since I had not seen the same care from the opposite sex in preserving their innocence. My dad never made comments about how special it was to remain abstinent until marriage. He actually expressed otherwise. My mother seemed to hold Heaven's views, but my father had told me details of their pre-marriage relationship that I would have preferred not to know. Heaven's point of view on things was intriguing to me. I wanted to stay friends. Instead of exchanging phone numbers, however, we arranged to hang out some more. I walked to her home with her as Summer went to our house with Jason.

Even though the walk was three miles, it did not seem long since I was fascinated by Heaven and our conversation along the way. She was stern in a way in that she was very black and white about her opinions, but her honesty was refreshing to me. She seemed just as interested in me as a friend as I was her, and that too was most enjoyable.

Heaven asked if I was going to church and what my beliefs were. I explained that I grew up Catholic, but that we did not attend any church now. She said she had plans to be picked up by a church leader later that evening for a youth group and asked if I would like to come. I had never heard of a youth group and was curious to find out what kinds of things happened at one. I was also excited to meet more girls who would be going to high school with me in the fall.

I was surprised when we finally got to her home. The outside of it was an old Victorian house that was neighbored by craftsman-styled bungalows. Her home sat right next to an appliance store called *Fred's* and her back yard was close to a Greek restaurant. Inside the house was the most shocking to me. In many places it had been torn down to the studs. The steps were just plywood and the bathroom had cardboard for sheetrock. It was a stark contrast to the heavy claw foot tub and the thick-paneled door with a fancy, glass knob. The living room had a television and an antique couch that was red and long. It was placed against the living room window.

The kitchen in her house was small and outdated. There were dirty dishes on every inch of the counter tops with flies buzzing around. Loud, hard rock music filtered down through the floorboards from upstairs. Heaven's forehead wrinkled a little, and she said that it was her older brother, Gabe, who was playing the music.

She asked me if I would like a snack, and at first I was hesitant because the mess in the kitchen made my stomach churn, but when I saw she had a cream pie in the fairly clean refrigerator, I could not object. The chocolate cream pie was wonderful. We did not get desserts like that at my house. If we did, they were gone before I could have a slice, or it was strictly forbidden to eat since it was bought by Robert or for Robert.

Even though Heaven's home was torn apart, it felt safe to be free from Robert's control, which is what I would have been under if I was home. Loud sounds thundered down the stairs, and Heaven's brother walked into the kitchen. He ruffled the top of my head.

"Who is this? And where did Summer go?" As Heaven explained the whole story to him, I could tell Gabe must be the caretaker of their house while their parents were at work.

After our pie, Heaven took me upstairs to her room, and pulled aside a green wool blanket so I could enter. Her wall was studs with cardboard tacked to it as well, but she had decorated the cardboard with drawings and posters. Inside her room there were two twin beds and above Heaven's bed there were dried flowers and a dance picture of her and her crush, Dustin. Her floor was simply rough planks of wood, covered with an oriental rug with lint balls on top. Like lots of teens I had met, she had piles of clothes in the corners of her room.

At the pool I had thrown my clothes over my swimsuit, so they were still a little wet. I asked her if she had something I could borrow to wear to youth group. Heaven was smaller than me, but I still hoped that something would fit.

She found some clothing that I liked, and I was surprised to see how many clothes she owned. Heaven's family appeared to have less money than mine, and yet she had a very large wardrobe.

"Where did you get all of these cute clothes?" I couldn't help but ask.

"Oh, there's a Goodwill close by here. I go over there fairly often. Have you ever been?" I shook my head. I had heard of it, but my mother did not take us to thrift stores for clothes, only department stores like Kmart or JCPenney. I was curious what you could buy there with little money.

"I'll take you there on another day. You have to pick carefully, but there's usually a couple of treasures every time I go." She laughed, swirling a skirt around. "As you can see, it adds up!" I had to agree.

By the time we were finished getting ready, I knew my mother would be home from work, so I called to tell her about going to Heaven's youth group. Mom had been working at Montgomery Ward as a full-time sales clerk in the children's department, and she had a fairly established daily routine. When she came home from work, she would grab a Dr. Pepper and watch television until it was time to make dinner. She would only detract from this schedule if she'd had a particularly long day, and then she would take a short nap before dinner. That didn't happen very often, because unless Carrie was around to watch the baby, Robert put all the responsibility for him back onto my mother as soon as she got home from working all day.

It was dusk now, and we heard a horn honk. A woman named Karen was there to pick us up for our activity. Karen drove an old VW station wagon that was yellow with rust in spots. She looked like she was in her later twenties, with shoulder-length hair and denim overalls. I was a little nervous to be traveling in a car with a woman I had just met, but I let go of my anxiety by telling myself it was okay since she went to church with Heaven, and Heaven didn't seem nervous at all.

During the twenty-minute drive to the valley, I found Karen to be young in spirit. She could relate to all the teenage issues that Heaven and I talked about and she even had great advice. I wondered why such a smart and lovely lady was still single. As she talked about her dating life, I could hear disappointment. She said she thought she might be expecting too much in a potential husband. To me, her requirements sounded reasonable. Karen wanted a husband who was employed and had the same religious beliefs as her. That couldn't be too hard, could it?

When we arrived at the church, I wasn't sure what to expect. The sign said, Four Square Church. The lot was graveled and there were two buildings. One was the main church, and the other was a one-level home. From outside, we could hear the steady beat of loud drums and a guitar warming up on some cords. It actually felt like a party atmosphere. This was not like any church I had been to.

As we walked in, both youth and adults welcomed us. Everyone was very friendly and asked me my name. Although it was a bit crowded in the main room, I found myself at ease from their warm welcome. Before long, we were sitting in the large white room with a projector aimed at the central wall with words to a song. A man walked up to the projector and introduced himself as Joe. He was the youth group counselor. He had a unique look that made it easy to remember him. His hair was almost white from lack of pigment, and he was extremely fair in skin tone. I had never seen a pastor or priest dressed like him. He looked like an Australian Outback guide. He seemed prepared to go on any adventurous outing that nature might offer us.

After Joe's introduction, the group of young adults quickly went into singing mode. They stood up from their chairs and sang along to the words on the projector while the band played the music. It was a new experience for me to see teens swaying, their arms upheld, as they whispered, "Thank you, Jesus!" and "I worship you, Lord!" with their eyes closed. I was unsure how to participate. Everyone was a new acquaintance to me, so I didn't feel like closing my eyes just yet. I also did not know why they were thanking the Lord. This was such a different environment from the church I went to back in Yakima, and even the one in Spokane. I had assumed this would be like our church, where you were expected to be extremely quiet, where only the clergy would speak, and sometimes that was in Latin. Suddenly I was in a church where they were freely worshiping without any rules of conduct. The more they swayed their arms, the more intense their worship looked. I had never known there was more than one style of worship. I was amazed, but didn't say anything to Heaven.

The youth pastor began his talk after the music faded. He talked about how we needed to be saved and baptized to go to heaven. I thought I had been baptized as a baby, but I sat there and wondered, *Am I saved?*

When I was dropped off at home later that evening, I greeted my mother as usual but then I paused.

"Am I saved, Mom?"

She looked a little amazed. "Yes, dear, why would you ask that?"

I explained that evening's events, and she then told me I had been baptized as a baby into the Catholic Church and that I even had a godmother.

It was my mother's sister, Kathy. I went to bed thinking of the day's events and Heaven's church. It seemed more modern, and so I thought it might have principles that were current with today's world. On the other hand, maybe religion wasn't supposed to be modern. The more I contemplated it, the more questions arose. It became a never-ending mass of questions, and I did not know where to get the answers.

Somehow, I thought that if I could find out the mysteries of faith, then I would have a direction to follow. Except for the smoking and his few rules, my father always said, "If it feels right, then it is right." This belief left me feeling guilty when I did something I thought my *mother* would find wrong. My mother, on the other hand, did not have many rules or guidelines to follow, except about "common sense and decency," as she said. I usually didn't know I had done something horribly wrong unless she brought it to my attention, and it usually was some black and white situation that I was supposed to understand but didn't. I felt like I needed some sort of road map, but I wanted it to be better than the ones my parents had. Theirs seemed to be missing some critical information.

The next day, I asked my mother if I could go another time with Heaven to her church. She did not oppose. Heaven's friendship and her youth group was a fun social activity, and it kept me busy for the remaining weeks of summer.

21

❧

mystified and bewildered

In the last eighteen months, my body had changed dramatically, and so had most of my classmates' bodies. Since I was year older than most of them, I had developed earlier, and that had often felt awkward to me. In addition, teen television, movies, and music videos all seemed to push the glory of sex. It was the topic of endless, whispered discussions at school. I listened, but I often felt stupid, like I was the only one who didn't know anything. And also the one who knew way too much.

At home it was the same, especially because I had two critically divergent messages taught to me by my parents concerning sexuality. My mother had grown up in the Catholic religion and strongly believed that sex was for marriage and marriage *only*, to the point that she wouldn't answer any questions or discuss anything else about it. My father, however, who was raised without religion, would always ridicule my mother for her beliefs. By this time, he had grown to care less and less about what anyone else thought, and his behavior and his words spoke volumes about his developing belief system and where he was coming from.

"Don't listen to your mom's prudish ways," Dad told me. "That's why we're not together anymore. She wouldn't . . . " and I would tune him out. "If it feels good, do it," he said over and over.

But I had completely drowned it out. I couldn't stand to listen to him talk about my mother like that. It was hard enough that I struggled because I couldn't talk to her, couldn't get her to open up and talk to me about anything real or intimate. She commented on the weather, school schedules, or superficial happenings at her work, but that was about it. Most of the time, she lived in her own little world, and my tentative questions made her turn cold, change the subject, or walk away.

Since my father was more open about discussing sex, I would some-times turn to him for the answers. Within only a few seconds of asking him a question, however, I would get a sick feeling in the pit of my stomach. My father talked openly about sexuality, but completely without rever-ence, respect, or dignity—for himself or anyone of the opposite sex. I had learned early not to repeat to my friends the things my father told me. He spit out body parts and functions as effortlessly as ordering a hamburger and fries. I couldn't carry on a conversation that way, and I didn't share his views on the topic, so I stopped asking him questions as well.

A natural shyness developed within me when it came to this myste-rious topic of sexuality. I remained curious, but I felt so bewildered and uncomfortable with the little knowledge I had. Surely there was some-thing more natural and healthy than what both my parents thought? I knew there must be people who saw sex not as bad, sick, and wrong, but genuinely beautiful. Several of the movies I saw seemed to carry my dad's irreverent point of view, but there were other movies that made a relation-ship between a man and woman seem like maybe it could be pleasurable and playful but also romantic and . . . safe. The thought of someone loving me, holding me, actually caring about me, seemed almost magical, and too good to be true.

Sometimes, Dad's way sounded more appealing—that this life was just a free-for-all, and we would not be accountable at the end of it. This was a complete contradiction to my mom's beliefs. Still strongly attached to her Catholic beliefs, my mother felt that we would be punished for every wrongdoing. These two strong but divergent viewpoints left me very con-fused about which parent was right. The two could not be combined to make my own beliefs.

Sometimes, when I felt guilty about a choice I had made, like how I treated a friend at school, or when I had snuck a piece of cake from the kitchen without Robert's permission, I would decide that my father's "reli-gion" was correct to help live with my remorse. The choice made me happy at the time, so according to my dad's rules it was fine.

One evening my mother and Robert left to go out with some friends.

The three of us children were left alone for a few hours. With Robert gone, the house felt peaceful and safe. I thought about all the foods that were forbidden to eat. And then there was the bottle of wine that had sat in the back of the refrigerator for months . . . It was pink and clearly an off-limits item. The pink color was so pretty that I wanted to know what it would taste like. Every time I opened the refrigerator it awakened my curiosity of what flavors it held. Did it taste like candy? Or maybe it was creamy like a strawberry shake?

Tonight, with Mom and Robert out of the picture, I prepared to do something I had never done before. My heart pounded as I opened up the refrigerator door and saw the bottle of wine alone in the corner of the nearly empty fridge. It was now mine to taste.

Ripping off the foil felt like opening a Christmas present. There was a cork lodged tightly in the neck of the bottle, and I didn't know how I was going to remove it. Just then I remembered the wine opener in my mother's utensil drawer. I twisted the metal into the cork and pulled the lever. It was all mine.

I decided to use a wine glass to make the presentation even more enticing. I poured the pale pink wine in and looked at the sparkle. The glass was glamorous and I felt like an adult. I lifted the cup to my mouth, being sure to stick my pinkie out like a movie star would do. The first taste was bitter. *How could this be?* It looked too beautiful to taste this awful. I thought my taste buds might have been off, so I took another drink. It was still bitter, but this time I felt a warm sensation in my throat. I took a few more drinks, finishing the wine I had poured into the glass.

Sheer disappointment filled me. Now I had an opened bottle of wine that I would have to explain to my mother when she returned. I couldn't think of a good excuse. *I might as well drink some more if I'm going to get into trouble*, I thought. I poured another glass, then a third. When I was on my fourth glass the phone rang.

It was my father. I was so glad to hear his voice. I blurted out my secret—that I had opened the bottle of forbidden wine and now I was going to get into trouble. He laughed, and was light-hearted in his tone. He promised me that I would not get into trouble if I simply followed his instructions. I was to take the bottle of wine and add some water to it from the sink. Then I was to put the cork back into the bottle and wrap it again with the foil I had torn off earlier. After I assembled the cork and foil, I was to place it back into the corner of the refrigerator and not say a word.

"They will never know you touched it," my father said.

Feeling relieved, I did just what he said to do when I got off the phone. After the wine was back into the corner of the refrigerator precisely how I had found it, and the wine glass back up in the cupboard, I ran back to my room and lay down.

"What were you doing?" asked Carrie as she looked at me. "Did you sneak some of the 'forbidden food'?" Her voice was low and full of drama, and we giggled. Living in that house, we had to find humor anywhere we could so we wouldn't go crazy.

"No," I said and looked at her with a sloppy grin. "Worse. I tasted the wine that was in the fridge!"

"You, what?" Carrie asked. Her eyes were wide and full of fear. "He'll kill you, Melissa!"

"I fixed it," I said confidently. I didn't tell her what Dad told me. It didn't feel right to pass that on to her. "Just don't say a word to Mom." Carrie agreed.

Once my head hit the pillow, the room began to spin. The spinning was getting faster, and I tried to bury my head into my pillow face down. It did not help. Now every sound was making my head dizzy. I heard the front door open and keys being tossed onto the end table. Mom and Robert were back earlier than we had expected. *I hope they don't suddenly have the urge for a drink of wine right now.*

My mother came into our room to check on us. I told her I was feeling sick, but that I would be all right. Then she left my room to see if Jason was asleep in his bed. I listened carefully as she walked into her and Robert's room. I was safe from their wrath for now. My father was right. They never did notice the watered-down wine.

For a while after that, I began to think my father might be right about doing whatever felt good. Dad had brought up a good point. We were not attending any churches, so how did my mother know for sure that she had correct beliefs? Knowing I could drink whatever I wanted, do whatever I wanted—that seemed far more appealing. Wasn't that what being happy was all about? I could live life freely from that perspective.

Then something within my heart said, *Use caution.* I had been assisted by that voice before. I decided to reserve further judgment and to gather more information. I wasn't done with this lesson yet, obviously.

The next time Dad came to the house, it was our usual routine. I knew he was coming before he got there. He parked his truck, played with us, stayed over in Jason's room, bought us food for our cupboards, and took us to the Flying J truck stop for lunch before he left town.

This is where we had to hear the sexual comments about every woman in sight. Every single female was under scrutiny. Anyone waiting on us, or assisting us, or standing near us was subject to sexual conversation, sexual comments, and sexual analysis. Then quite suddenly, when we were done eating, Dad's mood would shift. The party was over.

Carrie, Jason, and I hated it when this happened. It was becoming a repeated, confusing pattern. Dad would suddenly act like he wouldn't be able to eat for a month because he had spent all his money on us. We didn't know how his finances were, but he always said he paid too much in child support. I could see it on Carrie's and Jason's stricken faces that they thought the same as me—we're not worth providing for. *We're not worth it.* When he left, we all breathed a big sigh of relief. We were grateful because we wouldn't have to witness his anger for another few months—until he came back again, to build us up and then destroy us.

22

❧

cinderella

As we pulled out of the driveway to leave for our trip, I looked back at our house. I was glad to see that the plywood sign with blue spray paint spelling "Kittens for Free" was finally down. The board was the size of a twin bed! I was so embarrassed when Robert put the tacky sign in the front of the house by the large window. This was the nicest neighborhood we had ever lived in, and I didn't like our house looking ghetto or redneck.

My mom's car was not dependable, so she had rented a white minivan. To me, it felt like Cinderella's carriage. It represented a safer, better, more financially stable life. It smelled like a new car, and it was so clean! Even better, it was taking me to see my Prince Charming—Gavin. My heart galloped rapidly every time I thought of him. I had constant daydreams about getting my first real kiss. He was the only guy in my life that appealed to me. My girlfriends had all described the wonder and glory of what it was like to kiss a boy. I hoped I would soon find out for myself.

The road from Spokane to the coast seemed to have doubled since last summer. I had spent an entire year wondering what girls Gavin was dating, and if he had found someone serious since I had seen him last. We had exchanged a phone call and a couple of letters, but I could tell that my feelings for him were not reciprocated. He was a year older than me, so at sixteen he was definitely old enough to date. Somehow, my mother must've guessed what was on my mind. At one point on our drive, she turned around to look at me. I was dreamily staring out the window.

"I think he probably has a girlfriend by now, Melissa." Startled, I looked at her, and then looked back out the window. I knew he probably did, but what if he had dumped her when he found out that I was on my way to visit? My wishful thinking played out a large number of make-believe stories during the long trek. I sensed my mother's excitement too. It had been years since Mom had seen Amanda and Sterling, and I knew this trip would be good for her.

We made a stop at a gas station once we finally reached their coastal town. Even though I knew I could remember how to get there, my mother called for directions. She didn't trust that I would be able to find the way without getting the family lost. Since Robert was in the van with us, I didn't question it much. Whatever I could do to keep the vacation going smoothly without flaring tempers was best for all of us.

Soon we were coming up the drive to their home. Without giving us time to stop the van and open the doors, Amanda and Sterling rushed out with warm, welcoming hugs, smiles, and exclamations. As happy as I was to see them, I couldn't stop the surge of disappointment that Gavin wasn't there to greet me. Amanda told me her son was out at the beach with a friend. Worse still, she did not give me a clue if the friend he was with was a girl or a guy.

Pulling out the luggage, we dragged it into the house and began deciding on sleeping arrangements. As we were talking, Gavin suddenly came in the door with his new girlfriend in tow. I said my hellos, keeping my face bright and cheery, even though my heart felt like it was made of stone. I told myself not to let this hurt me; he had just been my friend all these years, and nothing had changed between us. Deep down, however, I wanted so much for his feelings to mirror the intensity of mine. I had even turned down a couple of guys wanting to go out with me so I would be free before coming here. My naïve heart had assumed he might do the same for me. I quickly shoved those feelings away and was polite to Cindy, his girlfriend, but I was sure my burning cheeks said a lot more. His girlfriend watched me stiffly, suspicion reflected in her eyes. I excused myself to my room to get unpacked, and Gavin followed me, taking me aside for a moment.

"Are you disappointed that I have a girlfriend?" he asked, his eyes intent on mine. I had to look away.

"No, it doesn't bother me at all," I replied with forced cheerfulness. I was determined to overlook his girlfriend as an obstacle, and instead, I decided I would try to be friends with her.

Cindy stayed for dinner and afterwards while the adults stayed at the table to visit, the rest of us went upstairs to hang out. On my way up the stairs, I noticed that Robert was signing stiffly. He seemed a little irritated and uncomfortable, and I realized that he was used to having my mother to himself and not having to share her attention much. Gavin's friend, Cindy appeared to be feeling similar feelings. As Jason and Gavin started to play video games, I attempted to engage her in conversation. Perhaps by getting to know her, I could see what it was about her that appealed to Gavin and it would make it easier for me to like her and handle this time together.

I found Cindy to be very reserved with me, almost cold, and she answered my questions with as little response as necessary. When I could see that the conversation wasn't offering much for either of us, I decided to go for a walk and enjoy the beautiful weather on the coast. Carrie asked to come with me. Soon we were approaching a nearby school, and seeing a playground, we decided to swing and enjoy the cool breeze. Suddenly I heard someone walking behind us and turned to face Gavin. He was alone.

"Hey, are you mad?" Gavin asked. Once again his eyes searched my face intently, but this time I didn't have to lie.

"No, I was just bored." My earlier disappointment was gone, and I was feeling almost neutral about the situation. The breeze on my face and the lingering sun were warming any coldness I had felt earlier. If Gavin liked Cindy, it was absolutely fine with me. My life was not over. I would simply find someone else to like, whether on vacation, or back home. Gavin seemed to pick up on the fact that I was losing interest in him.

"Will you please come back for a little bit?" he asked. I looked deep into his eyes for the first time since he brought Cindy back home with him. I thought about the fact that all year I had been looking forward to being around him again. I couldn't help how my heart started pounding.

"Okay," I said, smiling. We followed him back to the house. Gavin included all of us in the rest of the evening's games and activities, and I liked how he treated my brother and sister. Before long, it was getting late and Cindy had to go home. As I was cleaning up, I felt her piercing gaze on my back, and a sudden surge of compassion went through me. Of course she would feel insecure, knowing that another girl was staying the night at Gavin's house. No wonder she was reluctant to leave.

Not long after Cindy went home, Gavin became more playful and started flirting with me. I had missed him, but it only slightly assuaged my guilt for flirting back. The younger kids put on the Disney movie, *Aladdin*, and then everyone settled down in the room together to go to sleep.

Carrie and Jason drifted off quickly, but it was hard for me to go to sleep that night. I glanced over at Gavin, and noticed that he was still awake.

"Hey, why do you have a girlfriend?" I whispered. He was quiet for a moment.

"Well," he whispered back finally, "you don't live here." I felt a warm feeling go through me, and I suddenly remembered why I had felt such an attraction for him. Unlike most people, Gavin seemed to read me easily. Because of that, I knew he could also play with my emotions just that easily, but my fear slipped away as his whispers turned into a soft, tender kiss.

My lips felt like jelly, and I felt the flutters in my stomach just as my friends had told me I would. I smiled in the dark when we broke apart to sleep in our own separate areas. Quiet within my thoughts, I transitioned between elation and remorse, knowing I had kissed Cindy's boyfriend. From Gavin's quietness afterwards, I knew that he felt some remorse as well.

The next morning dawned bright and sunny, like my heart, which felt lighter than it had in years. After breakfast, I asked my mother if we could move to Seaside. I couldn't help thinking about Gavin's comment, and that if I were around, perhaps things could work out for us. My mother actually said she might consider moving, and my heart swelled with joy. Later in the day, I partnered with Amanda to help find information that might assist my mother really want to make the change. I suddenly had something new to wish for, and felt elated at the prospect. Suddenly there was a knock at the door, and Cindy came in, announcing she was there to hang out with Gavin. My heart was filled with guilt and jealousy mixed with daydreams about moving.

For the rest of the afternoon, I realized that while I had become accustomed to hiding my true feelings, Gavin wasn't nearly as skilled at it. We all spent a slightly uncomfortable afternoon together, and I wasn't surprised to find that Cindy didn't come the next day. Gavin and I didn't have an opportunity to kiss again, and in a way I was grateful. That kiss had been special, and I certainly wasn't ready for anything more.

All too soon, it was time to go back home. I hated the thought of leaving. I could tell from Robert's signed comments to my mother that he wasn't keen on the idea of moving. I knew in my heart that every mile that took us closer to Spokane would make it easier for my mom to get back into her settled routine and forget about moving to Seaside altogether. I sighed, already missing the fresh breeze and the beautiful scenery. I missed Amanda's loving conversations and the way my heart skipped whenever Gavin was in the same room with me. I knew that life would go on, and eventually I would get over it. I always did.

Still, a strange foreboding filled me, and as much as I wanted to blame it on the changing scenery or on the simple fact that we were headed back to Spokane, something didn't feel right. I put my head down and tried to picture Gavin's face, to remember his tender kiss, but I couldn't shake the dark feeling that something was wrong. Something in my life was about to change forever.

We drove back home to our house on Litchfield Street and Mom was disappointed when she had to return the minivan and drive our old car back home. I felt kind of like my Cinderella carriage had turned into a pumpkin and that it had smashed. I'd had a wonderful summer, for the most part—so why did I feel like I was under a dark cloud?

I started classes at Shadle Park High School. Amanda had mailed a thick yellow envelope of information about moving to Astoria. My mother did not seem eager to look into the move any longer, and she didn't even tell Amanda that we were going to stay in Spokane. I was embarrassed that she just dropped the subject and left Amanda in the dark.

One night, just before bed, our father called. He got on the phone with me and at first all he did was make small talk. But I could tell something was wrong.

"What's going on, Dad?" I asked him. "You know you can't hide anything from me." I could tell by the hesitation on the phone that he was struggling, but I was not prepared for what he said next.

"I want to kill myself, Melissa," he said. My blood turned cold.

"Dad, why would you say that?" I asked him, trying to break out of shock. I needed to be calm so I could talk some sense into him.

"I would be better off in prison than I am now, honey, because they would feed me and give me dental care. I wouldn't have to make child support payments. I just can't make it anymore." I began to cry now. Once again, I was responsible for making someone in my life miserable. It was my fault my father had to make child support payments. Worse still, he was going to kill himself over it.

"Dad, this is not the answer," I said, crying. "We need you. Things will get better, I promise." We talked for a little while longer, and I reminded him of all the great memories we had created. I told him about my special place with him and Carrie and Jason on the beach, under the stars.

"I knew then, Dad, that there is always a better day, if we choose it. It's a matter of choosing it. Can't you choose it? Can't you choose one more day of living, and give it another try? For me? Please, Daddy, please!"

He didn't promise but he said he would call me later that week. I hung up the phone, and went to my room crying. My mother had overheard me and she came in and asked what happened. I told her what Dad had said, and she looked angry. I heard her call him back and ask him why he would say such a thing to me. Of course I couldn't hear what his response was, but when she hung up the phone she came back and told me that he was not serious. I looked into her face, searching for the truth. I saw that she, at least, really felt he was not serious, so I thanked her and turned over to go to sleep. Mom left the door ajar as I was falling asleep.

23

❧

bait 'n switch

Dad seemed to get past his temporary depression, but I paid attention to his phone calls the next several times we talked and watched him carefully when he came to visit.

I went to youth group with Heaven and Karen a few more times that summer. I found their Four Square church entertaining and interesting. Instead of seeking answers from my mother, I was now asking Pastor Joe. It was giving me some direction when otherwise I would have remained in the dark. What was hard for me was that for some of my questions, even Pastor Joe did not seem to have the answers.

Before long I was going to my first day of class as a freshman at Shadle Park High School. I was nervous about the change, even though I had gone to an orientation earlier. Some faces were still familiar in the crowed halls. Science was one of my favorite classes, second only to English, the last class of my day. Fascinated to discover how other people lived through stories, I loved English. Fascinated to discover how things worked, I enjoyed science. I thought perhaps my love of science was passed down through my mother's side, since my uncles where chemists and engineers. Then again, my grandmother, Frances, had been a world traveler and served in the Peace Corps. When she would open up to tell a story, she would do it skillfully, and I felt like I was really in a distant land, experiencing what she went through.

In my sixth-period English class, I paid attention, sometimes obsessively. It was there that I became acquainted with a young man named Sean. I had no strong feelings when I first saw him, no idea that this person would affect my life in such a dramatic fashion.

The first time I saw him, Sean was joking and laughing with some other guys in the front row of seats. In spite of myself, I enjoyed hearing his wisecrack remarks. While he was not extremely handsome, he was easy on the eyes. As I got to know him, his sense of humor added to his appeal. Sean was about 5′6″ and very lean because of his passion for rollerblading. I found out that in order to pay for his expensive gear, he worked a paper route in the neighborhood by the high school. Instead of riding a bike, he would rollerblade in the streets, throwing the papers on the doorsteps at dawn and doing amazing tricks on the sidewalks.

Sean also appeared to have a passion for the latest technologies. Pagers had just come out and were all the rage. He was the first kid to own one at our school. Rumors flew that he was a drug dealer, since no one could understand how he was able to have that much money when he wasn't even sixteen. He didn't seem to mind the rumors and didn't rush out to reveal himself as a paperboy.

Over the next few weeks, Sean and I struck up a friendship and began to talk after class. I enjoyed being his friend and left it at that. One day, he asked me to the Homecoming Dance. I was flattered that he had asked me, but I was not prepared for how my friends would react.

"Melissa, no!" exclaimed April. Gretchen looked at me, horrified.

"What?" I asked them. "I think he's kinda cute."

"That's not what I'm talking about," said April. "He *is* kinda cute, I guess, but that's not the problem."

"He's been in trouble, Melissa!" whispered Gretchen, looking around to make sure no one heard her. "He's been in trouble with the police."

"What for?" I asked. I couldn't imagine this friendly, funny guy in any trouble with the law. Gretchen looked around again and then whispered in my ear.

"He vandalized someone's car . . . and . . . he got in trouble for assault, though no one seems to know why." I wondered if that was another rumor, like the stupid, unfounded gossip about drug dealing.

"How do you know it's true?" I asked. They couldn't tell me, except that they knew he had served time in a detention facility.

"Well, I don't think it's a big deal. Besides, it's just one dance." I laughed. "It's not like I'm going to the marry the guy or anything!" I thought about how young my mom was when she married. I knew that she hadn't dated much before she met my dad. I had always figured I would be dating a lot so I could have plenty of experience and knowledge of guys before I trusted one enough to marry him.

Since my friends were so worried, I agreed to spend all my time with Sean in a public place with lots of friends so I would be safe.

The night of Homecoming, April, Gretchen, and I all met up with our dates at the football field to see the game, and then later we went back to the high school for the dance. The combination of the scent of fall leaves and Sean's cologne was romantic. So far, Sean had been a complete gentleman. He had opened my door and paid for the dance tickets. I did not tell anyone, but I wouldn't have been able to attend the game or the dance if I'd had to pay for the tickets myself. My family could not afford extras like that. Sean's gentlemanly behavior was becoming more appealing, and his reputation was starting to fade from my thoughts.

Soon after the dance, I found myself spending time with him in the late afternoons after school. Heaven was another friend who was not thrilled with my association with Sean. She too had heard about his character through her younger sister, Summer. She warned me that he was not liked by many people and that she was afraid for my safety. She'd been having some problems with Dusty, her old boyfriend, and I thought perhaps she was jealous that I had a boyfriend. After all, he had not even kissed me and had only been courteous and gentlemanly. I ignored her advice and kept dating Sean. I felt happy and confident about our relationship.

Things were starting to turn for the worse at home, however, and I felt the tension and stress in my mother's relationship with Robert. For some reason, money was getting tighter, even though my mother was still working full time at Montgomery Wards. I had seen the signs too many times before and was a little worried that we might have another move on the horizon. I pushed it out of my mind and did my best to ignore what I was experiencing at home. I stayed busy. Luckily for me, I did not feel the financial pinch personally; Sean was treating me to dinner and to the movies often. We had lived in the Litchfield home for a few years, and we all loved it there. Surely my mother would handle the situation. I knew she loved that house as much as I did.

One day on the bus ride home, I suddenly knew what was coming. It hit me before my bus stopped at the corner on Litchfield. I walked into the house, not speaking to Carrie or Jason, and I went right to my bed. They couldn't let this happen. Not again.

That night, dinner was tense. I avoided eye contact with anyone.

Then the fateful news came, we where moving back to Grandma Frances's house.

How could you do this to me? I wanted to shout at my mother. Moreover, I wanted to shout expletives at Robert, who did nothing, not one thing, to contribute to our household. I did not want to change high schools when I had just started at Shadle Park High. I had just mastered my locker combination, I knew the layout of my classes, I had new friends and a sweet boyfriend. Life had just gotten comfortable.

24

❧

the hunt for Toni

During my freshman year of high school in 1995, my father was working for a local trucking company out of Spokane so I was starting to see him more often. He would still show up out of the blue, but somehow I always knew he was coming. Sometimes I mentioned these feelings to Jason, Carrie, or my mom, but most of the time I was the only one who knew he was on his way.

Even though Dad and Toni had broken up a few years before, I could tell from my dad's constant questioning that he really wanted to find her again. Actually, from his recent behavior, I could tell he was *obsessed* about finding her.

At one point I thought I might have seen her, so when he popped unexpectedly into town I mentioned it to him. My father's eyes got big and intense.

"Where!" he cried. "Show me!" I wasn't expecting this intensity. He drove us all quickly down to the middle of town and I pointed to the spot I thought I might have seen her when I was on the bus. He looked around and threw up his hands, giving the expression that it was useless. I had not been aware of his continuously strong feelings for her until I realized that he was hunting her down. It was obvious that my father felt he *had* to find Toni. *Was it to profess his love for her? To get back together with her?* I wasn't sure why, but it seemed just a little creepy to me, more than just the fact that I did not care for her. After he gave up, we drove even farther into town.

My father had asked us if we would like to go swimming with him and spend the night. Dad's company had put him up in a room at the Ridpath Hotel, nearly smack in the center of downtown Spokane. He had never stayed there before, and I teased him about it.

"Moving up, aren't you, Dad?" I asked. Trucking companies didn't usually spring for upper-scale hotels. The Ridpath was a ritzy hotel with an elegant bar and a prestigious reputation. It had a pool for us to go swimming, which was wonderful for us because it was the middle of January and so cold outside. We hadn't been swimming in five months, and it felt heavenly.

On the few other occasions that his companies had put him up in Spokane (usually at a Super 8 or some other discount lodging), we had loved it. Each time we had spent the night with him in his hotel room and it had been like a little mini-vacation for us. That night, however, we had only come to use the pool and hang out with Dad for a while. Each of us had previous engagements with friends for the evening, so we would not be staying the night. It was different when Dad would come and spend the night in Jason's room. Now that I was fifteen, to spend the night in a hotel bed with my dad seemed a little weird to me. He only had one queen-sized bed, so the other drawback was that one of us would have had to sleep on the floor.

After we finished swimming, my father dropped us off at home and then he went back to the hotel for dinner and a drink. I thought it was really strange that he didn't call before he left in the morning. I wondered if he was upset with us because we chose not to stay the night with him.

A few months later, my father brought a woman with him to meet us. Her name was Julie Winningham. I noticed right away that she was rough like Toni. Although she was pretty, her face was kind of leathery. Like a lot of Dad's friends who were smokers and drinkers, she had hardened, chiseled features. She also had a nervous temperament. Her demeanor and behavior reminded me of a girl in my English class who had just gotten kicked out of school for doing drugs, and for an instant I was suspicious. But I knew my father would never develop a serious relationship with a woman that did drugs. "No drugs" was one of his only rules.

Julie had shorter hair that she feathered back, and it was dark blonde. She had pretty, hazel eyes, and she was thin, of course. All of my dad's girlfriends were slim. Julie wore simple jeans and a T-shirt with no frills. I didn't take her too seriously, although I could tell my Dad did. The way he looked at her was usually tender and somewhat protective. He watched her like a hawk—every time she went to the restroom or to get something from the car, his eyes followed her. I didn't get attached. I knew better. Something about her didn't seem right for Dad. I could tell in one visit that it wasn't a healthy relationship, but he never saw what I could see. The one good thing I could see about Julie was that maybe she would help my dad to get over Toni . . . once and for all.

25

intuition

One day as I was leaving for school, I turned to my mother. "I think Dad is on his way here."

She turned and looked at me, shaking her head. "He just called last week and said he'll be in California, dear. Don't get your hopes up. I don't see how he can make it up here to Spokane."

I did not tell my mother the truth—that I wasn't really hoping for him to come. In fact, it was actually quite the opposite. My stomach had been doing nervous jumps all morning, and my insides felt edgy and anxious. It was too familiar and too uncomfortable.

"Mom, I can feel it. He'll be here." I spoke in a matter-of-fact way. The feeling had been building for a few days, until it felt like I was suffering from a form of paranoia. Just yesterday afternoon I had begun looking out my window every few minutes, watching for my father's car or truck to park in front of my home. This growing, deep-seated anxiety was so strong, it had prompted me to tell my mother.

As I prepared to walk out the door, I stopped to give her a hug. "He will be here very soon."

"We'll see," she responded. Her tone reflected how skeptical she was. If I hadn't been feeling so serious, it would have made me laugh. This was the fourth or fifth time we'd had this conversation, and every time I told her, she was skeptical until the second she answered the door and my dad was standing on her porch.

During the entire time it took me to walk to school, I started to ponder why I would have these intense feelings in my belly and then my chest when my dad was about to visit. I used to call it the *knowing*, but then if I described it to people, they freaked out on me. I wondered if any of my friends felt on edge or even a little frightened of their fathers. If they did, they sure knew how to suppress their feelings well.

Maybe I'm weird, I thought. *I should get over these sensations and this fear.* I had begun to doubt the state of my mental health, especially since I had experienced these uncomfortable feelings around my father since I was a young child. *Am I secretly adopted? What is wrong with me?*

I tried to sort through my strange emotions, but I only felt more tense and unsettled, especially since I could not find a logical explanation. I was feeling the same way I had felt that day on the couch in our old home. If I were to act on my emotions, I would run and hide until his visit was complete, but I was sure I would only question myself when it was over, and that it would make people question my sanity. I felt strangely alone. I didn't know anyone in the world who had experienced this kind of thing.

I wondered if I would ever grow out of this peculiar phase and want to be close to my dad. Recently, I had watched a movie where a bride was dancing with her father. The thought of me dancing with my father made my stomach turn in disgust. *This is crazy!* I thought. *I am abnormal.*

Once I got to school, I let go of my deep thoughts as my friends greeted me. I pretended to let go of the *knowing*—the warning—and started to walk with my friends through the halls to our homeroom.

The next morning, I woke up, eager to leave the house early. I was almost ready to head out the door when I heard a big rig coming down our street. There were a few of those in our neighborhood. It could be anyone, I told myself. Then our doorbell rang, and my stomach dropped. It was far too early for it to be any of our friends.

I heard my mother open the door and be greeted by a large, joking laugh.

"Hey!" said my father with a huge amount of excited energy, "are the kids still asleep? I wanted to surprise them!"

"They're getting ready for school," my mother said. I heard Jason's door being thrown open with a thud and Carrie jumping out of the bathroom and running to him. Forcing myself to breathe normally, I stayed in my room for as long as I could until I knew he would begin asking where I was.

Just pretend everything is fine, I told myself as I took one more deep breath and went to the living room.

"I told you Dad was coming!" I turned to my mother. "You never believe me." She turned and looked at me, just like last time and said, "Well, now I will pay more attention."

She smiled. I could tell it was a relief for her when Dad came to town. He would mitigate the stress of caring for us, at least for a few days. On top of entertaining us, I think she was grateful to him for providing the things we needed and filling the cupboards with food that would last for at least a week after his departure. But this visit was a little different.

"I'm just in town briefly," he said somberly. "I'm headed off to the Midwest, so I wanted to take the kids to school this morning." Everyone else was disappointed, but I was secretly relieved. My sister was still attached to my dad's leg, holding on to it. She wouldn't let go.

Once it was time to go to school, I glanced quickly at Jason and Carrie. They both seemed quite comfortable around Dad, and this made me wonder how I could move past my feelings. I hurried to finish getting myself together for the day and then I caught a glimpse of my father's huge, green semi-truck, parked in front of our home. I realized that I would be getting dropped off for school in a semi, and it embarrassed me. The truck was huge, loud, and grass green. While several of my peers loved anything that made them stand out, I just wanted to quietly fit in. I wanted to be normal. Anything that made me stand out made me uncomfortable. This morning I was going to be with my big dad, in his big truck, and all I could feel from the pit of my stomach was big trouble. *What the heck was wrong with me?*

One by one, we kissed Mom good-bye. She was already dressed in her work attire and jacket and ready to leave too. I watched as my father opened the truck cab door. With him standing next to the truck, it made both of them appear normal sized. He had to help Carrie up the chrome foot-rails and into the back of the semi cabin, and when I stood at the foot-rail and peered up, it appeared to be impossibly high. It felt as though I was climbing a ladder to a second floor. In a moment I was up in the cabin as well. Jason needed no assistance and was soon in the passenger seat and ready to go.

As we rumbled down the street, I kept quiet while Carrie and Jason chatted with Dad excitedly. I was hoping to be able to get my license in less than a year, so I had been paying attention when Mom drove us somewhere or I got a ride with a friend. I looked at all the knobs and buttons in the truck with confusion. *How does he drive this thing?* I thought. Jason was checking out all the bells and whistles, too. Then he opened up Dad's glove box while my father was looking at the road.

"Dad!" he exclaimed angrily. "Why do you have these?" Dad quickly turned his attention to Jason, who was holding a carton of Camel cigarettes in his hand. With the shiny foil pulled apart slightly, we could tell some had been used, and there were still some remaining. "I thought we aren't supposed to smoke! Are you smoking?" he demanded. Dad looked a little caught off-guard.

"No son," he explained, "those belong to a friend of mine. I keep them in here for when they ride with me." Jason appeared to be a little skeptical, but he gave Dad the benefit of the doubt.

In the meantime, I realized I had an agenda that Dad might be able to help with. He had helped us out of a jam before.

"Dad, we have to move again."

"What?" he cried, angrily. "Where to this time?"

"Back to Grandma Frances's house," said Carrie. Her eyes were troubled, and Dad caught the sound of her voice. We were all deeply saddened, but Dad got angry.

"What the hell is that man's problem?" he blurted out. "Does he do anything in that house at all? Does he pay any of the bills? What kind of man did your mother marry?" We were silent. He was voicing the same feelings we had but never spoke out loud. To the question about the kind of man Robert was, I wanted to blurt out, *The kind that throws Mom into the wall every time he gets mad!*

I waited, holding my breath, for Dad to say he would help us out, do anything so that we didn't have to move. Instead he said, "Well, I've given them enough money to build a castle. I pay child support every month to keep you out of messes like these. I've been an enabler, but not this time. Laura made her bed, and she'll have to lie in it! Maybe it will be good for that idiot she married to have to go back to her mamma's with his tail between his legs." He muttered something else that I was glad I couldn't hear, but I saw Jason glance up at him sharply, then out the window.

I was devastated. This was what my father was supposed to do—help us out when we were in trouble. He was supposed to . . . save us! I knew I was being dramatic, but I didn't care. I felt like my whole world was crumbling. I finally had friends and felt safe at my school, and now we were going to have to move. Once again, it was up to me to find a way to survive the mess that my parents had created. I knew it wasn't my dad's fault that we had to move again, but I wanted to blame him.

We stopped and picked up treats for Jason and Carrie, and soon enough we were at their schools. We dropped Jason off at the middle school first, and he gave Dad a big hug before he ran to class. Then it was Carrie's turn.

"I love you, Dad," said Carrie, giving him a great big squeeze and a chocolate-donut kiss. "When are you coming back?"

"I don't know, sweetie," he replied. "Whenever I can, I will be up here." I saw a sudden sadness in my dad's eyes as he looked at her, and the anger in my heart melted for a moment. I hoped my dad wasn't depressed and suicidal again. Maybe that was why he had quietly asked me to go to breakfast with him. *I had better be careful what I say and how I say it,* I thought. Carrie was off and running to make it in time before the bell.

Now that the large, musky-smelling truck was empty, I could have sat up in the passenger seat, but I didn't feel quite as at ease as Jason. I decided to stay where I was, in the back on the sleeper bed. The mattress did not have a sheet on it, just a thin pillow and an old gray silky sleeping bag that had slid off to the corner. On the walls were compartments that had the trucker's staples: NoDoz and other pills to stay awake, toothpaste, a toothbrush, some gel, and some dirty clothes. The cabin in this truck, like the others, didn't seem clean or warm, just a dark corner. I had heard my dad refer to it as a coffin, and the name seemed to fit. I wondered if other truckers called their sleeper cabs coffins too. Moreover, I wondered how my father could even rest back here, since the mattress was very hard. I zipped my jacket up and folded my arms to ward off the chill I felt.

As he rounded a corner, I almost lost my balance. I moved the flat-looking pillow out of the way to get more comfortable and have more room for my hands to balance myself. As I did so, my hand hit something hard, and it scared me at first. Looking more closely, I saw that it was a roll of duct tape. *Men and their duct tape,* I thought, bringing to mind Heaven's dad and all his home fix-it projects covered in duct tape. I knew Dad used it constantly in his work, but I thought it was odd to have duct tape under his pillow. I brushed the thought aside. My stomach was still jumpy, and this was the first time I'd been alone with my dad in quite some time. I was a little nervous, but he was the only man who could fix my home life.

My father started to make small talk with me, and my tension eased as he talked about his family and how everyone was doing. We stopped at the light in front of my school. I looked out the front passenger-side window to see everyone going to class and part of me wished that I had made some kind of an excuse to be there instead of going to breakfast with my father alone. The light turned green, and my father started to turn right to head downtown. He was talking about Grandpa Roy and the antics Grandpa was up to now. As he turned sharply, everything in the cabin moved and shifted almost violently, and I had a hard time sitting straight.

"Ouch!" I exclaimed. The heavy roll of duct tape had fallen off the mattress and hit my leg, just above the ankle. I smoothed the skin where it had hit, and then picked up the roll.

"Oh," said my father, as he saw what I was making noises about. "Just hand it to me." I did so, and he was silent for a time. I realized I must have been lost in my own thoughts because I couldn't remember what he was telling me before he stopped talking . . .

We pulled into Denny's and found a side parking place large enough to park. I was relieved to get out of the semi and be around other people. The cold air felt good, though I hoped we were on the downward slope of winter. Spring always gave me hope. We sat inside in a booth by a window, and after my father's prerequisite flirting with the waitress, our conversation turned to what he wanted to share with me.

"Melissa, I want to buy some property in Astoria, Oregon." I looked at him with wide eyes. He knew how I loved the coast and my summers we had spent there. I was pretty sure he knew I had a crush on Gavin. Was he teasing me? Was he telling me this so I would move there with him? "I have plans, Melissa," he said. "Big plans."

"Like what, Dad?" I asked him.

"I want to build a home there."

"That's really cool," I said, but I wasn't sure he was serious.

Our topic changed to the fact that I was turning sixteen that summer and I wanted to get my driver's license. My father laughed and told me stories of having to teach my mother how to drive when she was an adult.

"You are not much like your mother, are you, Melissa?" I shook my head, remembering how just the day before Robert had thrown my mother into a door. In my mind, I saw her crumple to the floor. I loved my mother with my whole heart, but I *never* wanted to be like that.

"I think I'll buy you a red Pontiac Grand Am," my father said and watched for my reaction.

I was shocked. *My own car!* Suddenly all thoughts of my problems at home faded away. With my own car, I wouldn't have to transfer schools. I could stay at Shadle for as long as it took for Dad to build his dream house. I could take Jason and Carrie away from Robert and the horrid little basement we had to share with him. *We would have freedom.* As we talked, the thought of being able to drive was thrilling, although a red Pontiac was not my personal taste for a car. At first I thought that if Dad was going to spend money on my first car, I wanted to pick one that fit my style. The more I thought about it, though, the more I realized that I didn't really care. I looked at all of the vehicles in the parking lot, and the freedom they represented for their owners. I realized that a car was a car! If a Pontiac was what my father wanted to provide, a Pontiac it would be.

Just outside of our window, my father and I spotted a beige car pulling into the restaurant parking lot. A man in a suit got out, removed a piece of wheeled luggage, and placed it by the passenger door. Then another car pulled up. Another suited man got out and brought an identical piece of wheeled luggage out. Without a word, the two men traded their baggage, got into their vehicles, and drove away. *What the heck?*

I was puzzled, and my father studied my face intently as our breakfast arrived. I found that I wasn't hungry, so I just picked at my food.

"Melissa, not everything is what it appears to be." I looked at him, wondering if he knew why the men were trading their suitcases. "I have something to tell you," he added, "and it's really important." His tone was suddenly very serious, and the look in his eyes mirrored it. My stomach dropped again, but this time even harder and deeper. *What was wrong?* I had to look away from his piercing eyes. I wanted to sink into the vinyl bench as deep as I could to avoid this feeling.

"What do you have to tell me?" I asked after a long, uncomfortable silence.

"I can't tell you, sweetie," he said, looking down for the first time since we had started the conversation. Emotion after emotion crossed his face, and I could tell he was having some sort of battle in his own mind. Despite the rock in the pit of my stomach, I was morbidly curious. I thought about all the things my father willingly told me that I had finally realized most fathers generally did *not* tell their children. What could he possibly not tell me?

"What, Dad?" I asked, gently. I thought of his admission of contemplating suicide a few months ago. I thought I shouldn't sweep this under the rug. What if I was the only person he could talk to? "What is it?"

I was not prepared for what came out of his mouth next.

"If . . . if I tell you, you will tell the police." I sat in stunned silence while the rest of the world disappeared. I felt like I was in the middle of a movie. *The police? Did he steal something?* I had once overheard my grandpa yelling at my dad about stealing something. The uneasiness in my stomach was expanding rapidly, filling every cavity. I could hardly breathe, and I suddenly felt like I was going to vomit.

"I need to tell you," my father began, "I need to tell somebody or I will go crazy. I am not what you think I am, Melissa. You see—"

"*GET OUT OF THERE!*" It was the voice.

"Dad!" I practically shouted, stopping him abruptly, "I've got to go to the bathroom! I think I'm going to be sick!" I slid out of my seat and practically ran down the thinly carpeted aisle to the women's room. My stomach felt as if it was cramping with food poisoning, but I had not eaten more than a bite. I leaned over the toilet, willing myself to breathe.

I hated vomiting, but I wanted to purge. Purge what? I hadn't eaten anything. Realization dawned. I wanted to purge the emotions I was feeling. It wasn't about me; it was my dad. It was why I could feel him when he was coming to visit. Whatever was going on with him at that moment was the reason for the warning in my mind.

Finally breathing, finally feeling logical about the whole thing, I turned around and sat down, my knees still weak. Everything about that conversation seemed surreal to me. I had to stop being dramatic. I had to stop feeling. I had opened up to his feelings because I was worried about preventing him from suicide, but now I had to shut down all feeling. I looked at the yellow stall wall and started to read the doodles and graffiti to collect myself—to get out of myself and into someone else's life for a moment.

"Jodi loves Ben."

"Alisa is the witch that stole my guy. She's going to wish she hadn't."

"Marissa and Kenny 4-ever."

And finally, "If you are reading this, you need to get a life."

Yes, I need to get a life. I felt the nausea subside greatly. I took a breath and stepped out of the stall, pretending that everything was okay. I washed my hands for a long time and looked at myself in the mirror. There was still a little fear in my eyes, but I suddenly felt a beautiful peace wash over me. Something had shifted, and whatever happened now, I could handle it. I knew this peace. Everything was going to be all right.

Back at the booth, my father hadn't eaten a lot either. His half-eaten meal was in front of him, but he was looking out the window again, watching some pretty women walk by. His cup was filled with some new brew, so I knew it would be a few more minutes before we left.

I sat down, a little hesitantly, but he smiled at me, and started talking about Astoria again. I tried not to breathe an audible sigh of relief.

"Do you remember my girlfriend, Julie Winningham?" he asked, his eyes sparkling once again.

"Of course," I said, getting more eager about Astoria in spite of myself. I did my best to erase from my mind all of the personal comments he had made to me about Julie. "You introduced us, remember?"

"That's right. Well, we're getting engaged. We're going to be married, and I want us to settle down—buy that property in Astoria and build a home together." I stared at him. My dad had worked a hundred jobs it seemed, and I knew he had lots of skills, but I had mostly ever known him as a trucker. I couldn't imagine him settling down and staying in one place again. Still, the thought was appealing in its own way. Could I actually get away from Robert and move to Astoria, the most beautiful place on earth?

"You and the kids could move in with us," my father said, his tone a little dreamy. *If it could be reality . . . If it really could happen . . .* I wanted him to be in a place that was stable, and maybe in a relationship that was stable.

The waitress handed my father the check and he flirted back, making a comment that made me blush.

He'll never change.

When he dropped me off at the high school, I turned to wave good-bye and then ran to third period. I knew in my heart that I had narrowly avoided something frightening and perhaps even dangerous. I had no idea that would be the last time I would ever see him outside of a prison wall.

26

∾⟡∾

confession

On my way home from school, I didn't notice a single blossom erupting all around me in the abundant fruit trees of Spokane. Normally I would have taken in the resplendent color and been joyful with the newness of spring. I had always felt more vibrant and alive with the promise that accompanied the beginning of my favorite season. Today, however, it was all I could do to make it home. After the bus dropped me off, I had to will one foot to follow the other the entire, agonizing way home.

For once, I wanted nothing more than to lie on the uncomfortable cot in the cool darkness of the basement where no one could see me as my eyes filled with tears and hopelessness. The familiar, musty blackness of the basement greeted me, matching the cold darkness of fear that engulfed me. Warily, I glanced around, wondering if my uncle was here yet. He had moved into the basement when we moved out last time, and now we were all down here, squished in together. He was nowhere to be seen, and I sunk into my cot, exhausted and ready to let the tears run their course again.

If only I had listened to my heart. If only I had listened to the voice that told me to walk away from Sean that day.

For the millionth time, I played out the events of that fateful afternoon in my mind. How often had we hung out and nothing had ever happened? All we had ever done was kiss after a special date here and there, before we had gotten to my doorstep or his. When he had started to kiss me that afternoon, I had never expected that he would force me—force himself on me. In my swirling mind, the chaos repeated itself over and over. The change that had come over him, the shrouding of his eyes, the way he pushed me down and wouldn't listen to my screams or my cries. The way he had become a monster, and I couldn't make him stop.

It had made me nauseated just thinking about it again. I never wanted to see him, ever. I hated the face that had suddenly become full of concern once the monster was gone, suddenly pretending to care about the pain he had just caused—the violation, the physical pain, the breach of trust. *"How could you do that to me?"* I had screamed at him.

At school, our friends knew something was wrong, but they didn't know what. I wouldn't speak of it, wouldn't speak to him. Sean kept passing me notes, trying to make up. He wanted me back, he said. He was sorry he had hurt me, he said. I had no one to talk to. I couldn't tell my mother. She would be appalled with my behavior, I was sure of it. I couldn't tell my father, either. He would crack some wise comment, to the effect that it was "about time," and that I would feel better about it after a while. *Yeah, right.* I couldn't tell my friends. Who would believe me? He had been my boyfriend, after all—that wasn't rape, right? I had heard similar conversations in the hallways before, and I wasn't about to make myself the brunt of school gossip and innuendo.

On the day it happened, I had come home and showered for hours, scrubbing every whit of my body, not caring that the water had gone cold. I scrubbed until it felt like every inch of my skin was raw, but I couldn't scrub it clean enough. No matter what I did, I still felt dirty, used, useless. My insides hurt, and I wanted to throw up and couldn't.

Like my swirling thoughts, the nausea had never gone away. And then it became even worse when I realized it was evidence of the growing body inside of me.

And what was I going to do with this baby? I had finally had to break down and talk to Sean. I'd had to tell someone, and he was just as responsible for this situation as I was. Maybe even more responsible. I knew I shouldn't have been alone with him after school. I should have listened to the *knowing* that had told me he was capable of this, but I had trusted him and his gentlemanly ways. I had *bragged* about him! Now I was furious with him, and what he had done, not just to my body, but to my life.

I had never envisioned my first time being anything like that. After attending Four Square with Heaven, I had learned that my body really was a gift. *A gift I had wanted to freely give to the man I loved, when it was time.* Sean had taken that gift from me. I wanted to shout it to the rooftops and have the cops come take him away, but I didn't think anyone would believe me. Sean had even said as much to me. On the way out the door, when he could tell I was still upset—maybe upset enough to tell someone, he had made it clear that no one would believe me. I was alone.

Then, after I told Sean I was pregnant, this time he made it clear that he wanted absolutely nothing to do with this baby. He kept seeking me out at school and at home. He kept asking how I was going to do it—get rid of the baby. That was all he could talk about. He was obsessed with it. I didn't feel like I could respond. I hadn't ever believed I would be pregnant as a freshman in high school. I hadn't even imagined being pregnant in college. I really wanted to make something different with my life. That's why I was taking three buses to get to school and then back every day, spending three hours of every day on the bus. I wanted to continue my education and not have to switch schools. I wanted to be somebody!

My thoughts spiraled downward. I realized that, actually, that was part of the reason why I had begun accepting rides from Sean. After months of taking the bus for three hours and running from stop to stop to get there on time, it was easier to accept a ride. And it was also a lot more enjoyable to hang out with Sean and do homework and watch TV at his place than to come back to Grandma's crowded house where it felt like there was no room for me. I wasn't brave enough to transfer to a new high school in the middle of the year, and I wasn't content to continue taking the bus home from school. *Maybe I'm not meant to graduate. Maybe I have to scrape a life out of what is given to me like the rest of my family.* That was a sobering thought. Jason and Carrie were struggling in school, and I was worried what it would take for them to survive—to reach my grade, finally.

I shook my head. I couldn't deal with it. Since we had moved so far from Shadle, it took all the energy I had just to get to school and back. Especially now that Sean and I had broken up. Now I was back to taking all the buses necessary. I didn't want to think of the responsibility of this baby growing inside me. As much as I always wanted to help Carrie and Jason, I couldn't put one more expectation on myself. I assisted with homework as much as I could when they needed it, but the thought of one more responsibility . . .

My head sunk farther into my pillow. I was so tired. How could anyone be this incredibly weary? I drifted off—dreaming of a place where I could have my own room, where I wasn't carrying a baby inside me, where I was free to go to school and the bus came to my front door, filled with people who wanted to be my friends . . .

From the dimming light, I realized I must have slept for quite a while. I woke to the noise of Carrie's small feet running down the stairs. Usually she was quieter, but perhaps she was excited. The noise was different from Jason's loud, boyish clomps and Mom's measured steps. It was especially different from Robert's heavy footfalls. I thought of all the times I would pretend to be asleep when he came down the stairs, just feet from me . . . The times I would pray he wouldn't stand over me, watching, looking, using his hands to sign in a language that was so confusing and unfamiliar yet uncannily easy to read because of the agenda in his eyes.

As I listened, I turned to see if I could catch a glimpse of Carrie's face through the gaps in the sheets. All of a sudden, I felt an intense rush of fear from her me wash over me, even as she ran to her area of the basement. I couldn't see her, but I felt her confusion and fear, and then I heard her begin to sob. *Had a neighbor or friend been mean to her? Was she in trouble for something?* Despite the whirling nausea and my strong desire to stay still on the cot, I rose to go to her.

Suddenly the light from the doorway at the top of the stairs cast a shadow halfway down, and I heard the almost imperceptible footfalls of my mother on the stairs. This time they weren't measured but hesitant.

"Kids?" she called quietly, then a little louder. "Kids?" I heard shuffling in Jason's corner—he must have come in while I was sleeping. Carrie's sobs had quieted and there was an expectant stillness in the air. "I have something to tell you all."

Jason stepped out of his corner and into the lighted stairway, looking up at Mom. He cocked his head, as he always did when something seemed out of place, and I felt the hair on the back of my neck begin to rise . . . Something wasn't right.

"Your dad's in jail," Mom said simply. Then she started to head back up the stairs. *What? What the heck?* She continued up another step, and I realized this was my mom's way of avoiding another conversation. But she needed to talk to us. I had to know more, and obviously so did Jason.

"Mom, wait," he said, before she reached the top of the stairs. "Dad's in jail? For what?" There was a long pause.

"For murder," she said. The disgust in her voice was unmistakable, and so was the unspoken message, *Don't ask any more questions. Don't mess with*

Mom. This time we didn't stop her as she made her way up the last few steps and walked away.

Jason and I looked at each other, our eyes filled with fear and a million unanswered questions. We parted, retreating to our separate corners. We could not help each other through this one, not yet. Neither of us had any strength to go assist Carrie. I suddenly realized she must have overheard a conversation or news broadcast about Dad.

I was in a state of shock. How was that even possible? Had he been in a fight with another man? My father was more than perfectly capable of killing another man, this I knew. I had heard about other men who killed when they were overcome with rage and adrenaline. My father was so strong and powerful, he did not need to be angry to kill.

Abruptly, I saw a vision of my dad strangling a cat with his bare hands. The cat was wide-eyed and clawing at him, trying to get free. Suddenly the vision shifted. The cat disappeared, and in its place was a woman, eyes bulging in fear, clawing at my father's hands which were grasped tightly around her throat. I crumbled to my knees in shock and pain, willing the vision to leave. I crawled onto my cot, and everything went blissfully black.

We never talked about it again. The next morning, when we woke up, we were expected to go to school. Not a single word was spoken about my father.

The next morning, I was on my way to school on the bus. That was the hard part about taking the bus for hours a day. I had too much time to be alone with my thoughts, and I still hadn't been able to come to terms with it. Murder. I had wanted to be in denial about it, but I couldn't. Part of me was still in shock, but I had so many questions, and I would not find my answers at home.

Sean found me at school, and I was sure he was going to ask again what I was going to do about the baby. When he saw my face, he softened.

"Melissa, what's up?" he asked. I looked into his eyes and couldn't believe he was showing me genuine concern. I wanted to hug him. I wanted to hit him. I wanted him to go away.

"I can't talk right now," I said. Truthfully, I did have a few minutes, but I knew that I if I started talking I would lose my composure in a hallway of Shadle, and the whole school would know in a matter of minutes.

I couldn't let that happen. I felt like everyone must know anyway. Everywhere I looked, it seemed like there were eyes full of accusation and knowledge that I didn't even have. "I'll tell you if you meet me after school by the city bus stop." I walked away, uncertain if that was a smart thing to do.

Sean met me near the corner of the school where the city buses came. I lived too far from Shadle now to take the regular bus.

"Hey, why don't you get in the car so we can talk, and I can run you home. You'll get there hours faster." I stared at him for a moment, like he was crazy.

"I won't hurt you, Melissa, I promise," he said. "I just want to know what's going on." He opened the passenger side. I paused for one more moment, and then I got in. It had been all I could do all day long to stay strong, and now I had someone who seemed to care about me.

"My dad is in jail, Sean. For murder!" I told him how things had transpired at my house the night before—what was said and what wasn't. "I have a gut feeling that he . . . that he strangled someone."

"Well, let's go downtown and look at newspapers. No one will know who you are.

We walked into the large library, and I felt very small. As angry as I was with Sean, I was grateful to have someone beside me. Sean did the talking, and a librarian led us over to the newspaper section.

There was not a lot in the newspaper, especially in Spokane. However, Vancouver's paper had more in it. My dad had been arrested in Arizona but brought to Vancouver and placed in the Clark County Jail. He had confessed to murder.

When I read " . . . for the murder of Julie Winningham," tears blinded my eyes. What had happened? How could he have murdered his girlfriend—someone he loved, someone that he had wanted to settle down with and build a house with? Sean had to finish reading the article out loud for me. As he read on, there was some additional information I didn't understand and some information I understood all too well and wished I didn't have to hear. She had been strangled, and her nude body had been disposed of by throwing it over an embankment alongside state Highway 14. Sean continued reading, and there were some comments from Julie's sister. She stated that my dad was a monster and should be killed. I made Sean stop.

"This lady just said that my dad deserves to be dead!" I cried. "That's a horrible thing to say!" I couldn't believe it, and then the truth of it set in.

I realized what I would be feeling if someone had done this to my sweet sister. Julie's sister had suffered a horrific loss, and logically, it was my father that was responsible for all that pain. My dad was alive, but her sister was gone forever, and my father had confessed to doing it with his own hands.

On March 24, 1995, my father wrote the following letter to my uncle, six days before he was taken into custody. I would not see that letter or even know of its existence for quite some time. He wrote a similar letter to me and my siblings. I would not know of that letter for years. My father regretted writing the letters. He knew my mother would never show our letter to the police. Uncle Luke, however, showed it to my grandfather, and together they agreed to hand it over to the police. Very quickly, the results of that letter began to ripple into the lives of hundreds of people.

> Hi Luke,
>
> It seems my luck has run out. I will never be able to enjoy life on the outside again. I got into a bad situation and got caught up in a bad emotion. I killed a woman in my truck during an argument. With all the evidence against me, it truly looks like I am the black sheep of the family. The court will appoint me an attorney and there will be a trial. I am sure they will kill me for this. I am sorry that I turned out this way. I have been a killer for five years and have killed 8 women. Assaulted more. I guess I haven't learned anything.
>
> Dad always worried about me because what I have gone through with the divorce, finances, etc. I have been taking it out on different people. We pay so much of child support. As I saw it, I was hoping they would catch me. I took 48 sleeping pills last night and I woke up well rested. The night before I took two bottles of pills to no avail. They will arrest me today.
> Keith

Before I heard the news from my mother that late spring night, I had believed that my father would remove me from my dysfunctional mess at home. What was there left to hold onto? I was angry that he had abandoned us, but even angrier that he would think that it was acceptable to rape and murder people. It was too close on the heels of my own rape, and I was furious with him, though I kept my feelings deep inside, not voicing them to anyone. Who was my father? I thought I knew the man, but it was evident to me that my father was a total stranger.

27

⚜

dragon slayer

While my father was in Clark County Jail, I found myself outside of the loop, not knowing what was happening with him. There were two unspoken rules:

1. Don't talk about it.
2. Don't ask questions, either.

Everything I knew came from what was in the newspapers, and there wasn't much. When I happened to be in the area of the downtown library, I would look for articles in the daily papers, but I didn't know how to conduct any sort of formal research. I thought my father was just going to serve time for Julie's murder and then it would be over. I thought it might turn around somehow. Whether I would admit it to myself or not, what I was searching for were clues that my father didn't murder her in cold blood. I didn't want to believe that it was blatant homicide.

Considering the circumstances, I honestly thought very little about what was going on with my dad. Survival was all I could focus on. Getting to and from school, completing homework, and finishing out my freshmen year.

The biggest issue on my mind wasn't my dad, it was my pregnancy. I was in a constant state of fear. How much time did I have before people could tell I was pregnant? I was afraid of other people's judgments. I could hear the words *slut* and *stupid pregnant teenager*. How many times had I heard people pass that judgment? How many times had I passed it, when I never thought I would be in this predicament? I was in fear of telling my mother. What would she do? Would she kick me out of the house? Would she hate me? Would she believe those things about me?

A natural effect of being pregnant was wildly fluctuating hormones and fragile emotions. I cried all the time, for reasons I couldn't explain in words, and sometimes for no reason at all. I definitely had stressors at home. I also had stressors at school with how Sean was treating me. He was extremely unhappy that I hadn't made a final decision on the pregnancy, so he would show me where it hurt the most. In front of my friends, he had yelled at me and called me a bitch. My earlier resolve to completely sever ties with him had crumbled when I found out I was pregnant. Not having anyone else to talk to, or to give me a ride home so I could sleep in the afternoons, I had been afraid to leave him. I was putting up with behavior I would have never believed possible. But every day, I stayed with him anyway, and the pressure from him to get an abortion was growing stronger and stronger.

From what Sean and his parents had told me, I only had a limited amount of time to make whatever decision I was going to make: another six or seven weeks, to be exact. If I was going to get an abortion, it had to be in the first trimester. My brain was in a constant state of war. Sean's parents urging the abortion didn't help.

I had always done research when I had a problem. I would find out as much information as possible on any issue, so that I could make a wise, informed decision. In this case, I felt so uneducated about my entire pregnancy. I knew that there were some resources out there, but I didn't know where to go, and I didn't want anyone seeing me either. We didn't have a computer, so I was going to have to put myself out there in order to discover some information. I knew I had to make a decision, and I had to make it fast. All of a sudden, I realized that I had been waiting for someone that I trusted to show up and to show me the way to go.

The next morning I rose at 5:00 AM. My body could have easily slept for another four or five hours, but I showered and got ready for school while the house was quiet and the bathroom was empty. Having four females and three males sharing one bathroom was often a trial, so I avoided it by being the first one up each morning.

I caught my first bus of the day, and then got off at my first stop. I had to walk for some time through a neighborhood in between the stops. I passed apartment complexes and the county library to reach the corner of Division and Hawthorne where I would take the next bus. I was so grateful it was spring and that the huge mounds of snow I had trudged through in my sneakers just weeks ago were all gone. I was already exhausted.

I checked my watch, making sure I had left enough of a cushion to catch up to the bus on Division Street. Since Shadle High was almost in the center of downtown, I would get off at Welsley, 40 E&W to take another bus east for twenty-five more minutes. Then I would finally arrive for the day at school, a few minutes before the bell rang.

Initially, my decision to bus to Shadle had been liberating in some aspects. I had quickly learned to be independent and to rely on myself. I was the one in charge of finding the correct schedule, and it was all on my shoulders to catch the buses on time. It cost me seventy-five cents each day to ride the bus, so it taught me to prepare ahead of time. I would babysit, scrounge for cash, and do odd jobs as needed. I felt confident because I had overcome all of these obstacles and continued to make it to school.

Today, however, I felt isolated and alone on the morning commute. I hadn't minded before that there was no one my age who took this route. The buses were primarily filled with college students, business professionals, and an occasional elderly or poverty-stricken person. This morning I was feeling abandoned and angry. I felt like my mother didn't care about the circumstances I was in. Anger with my father also simmered beneath the surface. My hero was behind bars along with all the dreams he had shared with me—a car for me, a house in Astoria, a future—he had thrown it all away.

The whole ride was quiet. Most of the students were doing homework or reviewing test questions. How I longed to be in college with them. I dreamed of the better life a higher education could bring. All the way to school, I daydreamed of this better life, without the limitations of pregnancy. First I imagined getting a car. That would mean I could participate in after-school sports and clubs. I had actually made it on the volleyball team, but I'd had to quit when I realized that by the time practice was over, there wouldn't be time to catch all the necessary buses to get home. Besides, I had no money to buy the uniforms. A car would provide a more flexible schedule and enable me to get a job to pay for my extracurricular activities.

As the bus rounded a corner, I daydreamed of getting braces. My horribly crooked teeth had kept me from a real smile most of my life. I was so self-conscious of my teeth that I only curved my lips a bit to smile, and I never showed a true grin. It was also necessary to monitor my laughter carefully, in case a rebellious smile slipped beyond its strict bounds. With straight teeth, I would be able to laugh and smile whenever I wanted. That daydream left me with a joyful and lovely feeling.

As I caught the final bus to school, I knew it was time to think about reality. I had to face my decision with the baby and with Sean. I ran through scenarios of how I could escape the situation I was facing, but I didn't see any answers. At that moment, I felt I was in the worst possible situation any girl my age could ever be faced with: pregnancy, living in an impoverished, abusive home, in an abusive relationship, with a father in jail for murder. These thoughts made me want to cry, but I saved my tears for nighttime in my pillow.

My options were few and my future looked bleak. I was not yet sixteen and would not be able to afford a child without a job. Everywhere I turned, I heard the fact that pregnant teens were less likely to finish high school. Obtaining my diploma was my only hope of getting out of poverty; it was my main goal.

Once again, I realized that I had been waiting for someone to rescue me—a hero, a knight in shining armor—someone to slay my dragons and allay my fears. Someone to fix everything and make it all right.

That day, I set an appointment with Planned Parenthood, the first of several.

"I'll take you to your appointments if you agree to get an abortion," Sean said when I told him.

"Sean, I told you, I haven't decided," I said firmly. "I need to understand what all my options are. I'm going there today to find out more information so I can make a wise, well-informed decision." He looked at me for a long time, without saying anything. I didn't care. I would find a way to get there, and I would make my own decision. He seemed to sense my independent spirit, and it changed his mind.

"I'll take you," he said. I then realized he probably meant to use the time there and back to pressure me further. I was grateful for the rides, but I felt as though I was stuck between choosing bad over worse.

As he dropped me off he said, "Remember, I'll pay for your procedure." *Some knight in shining armor.*

Without a word, I walked inside.

No knight had come. There was no soldier to fight my battles, slay my dragons, kiss away my fears, and chase the demons away from inside my head. Once again I didn't have anyone to talk to. Like my baby kittens on the clothesline, I felt suspended in mid-air, beaten back by life.

But today . . . today I would don the armor myself. I would raise my sword and face the demons in my mind. Today . . . I would become educated.

28

❧

the oppressor

While attending one of my Planned Parenthood appointments, I saw the outline of the baby through the ultrasound machine. I remember thinking that even though it resembled the shape of a peanut, it was a cute, living creature. For the first time, I allowed myself not to think of the life inside me as an unwanted obstacle, but as a human being. My heart softened, and I felt love overturn fear.

That feeling lasted until I arrived home. Walking down the steps to my "room," where I had to pull a string to turn the lights on, where I used shoe boxes for a dresser and an old, green army cot for a bed, I tried to picture a sleeping infant. It would not work; it would not be fair to the child. My initial thought was that my decision would have to be for an abortion, and it was not the answer I wanted. That night I cried for three hours straight, quietly into my pillow. I poured my heart out. I didn't come up for dinner, but Mom, Robert, and Grandma didn't seem to notice. Carrie and Jason knew something was wrong, and likely thought it had to do with my father. I let them think that. It was so much easier that way.

After that night, I started to play with thoughts of giving the child up for adoption. Sean would not hear of it, but I had some say in the matter, and I told him so. I began to realize that in that scenario, I would be stuck with spending the daytime hours with either Sean or Robert for months on end, and for however long it took after the baby was born. That thought was the most terrifying of all.

I was sick to death of Sean's badgering. He tormented me every day, trying to get me to accept his way of "getting rid of the problem." He called

me names, told me I was getting fat, and that he hated looking at my changing body. In a way, I was glad because it also meant that physically he left me
alone, which was what I wanted. I'd had no desire for intimacy since the rape.
I only stayed with Sean to have some kind of listening ear and support.

The school year had ended in a nightmare. Glad to have survived, I
didn't know how I would make it through the next month. I had only two
weeks left to decide what to do with the baby, or it would be too late.

One afternoon, Sean picked me up from my grandmother's to take me
to Planned Parenthood. I was going there regularly so they could monitor
my health. I hadn't seen a doctor since I was a little kid, except for when I was
hospitalized after the attack the previous year. Sean's mom had invited me
over for dinner. Afterwards, his parents went out for a drink with friends,
and Sean and I decided to watch a movie on TV. I sighed, knowing that soon
enough it would be time to go home. Wrapped in a familiar catch-22, I didn't
want to go home, but I didn't want to be at Sean's, either. I lost myself in the
only place I was comfortable for the moment, and that was escaping into the
movie—into someone else's life for a little while.

As we watched the program, Sean kept looking at my belly. Finally,
I pulled my knees up to my chest. I pulled my oversized sweatshirt down
over them, pretending I was just trying to keep warm.

When the program was over, Sean got up and motioned me to the
door off to the side of the room.

"Melissa, come here for a minute," he demanded. I was puzzled. I knew
it was his bedroom, and I didn't want to go in there. He hadn't looked like
he desired me for weeks, so I had been feeling safe with him. "Come here,
just for a minute," he repeated. I did what he asked, and came over to the
door. The door itself opened inward, into his room.

"I have an idea!" he exclaimed. "Stand inside here with your back to
the wall," he said, motioning behind the door.

"What's your idea?" I asked, still puzzled.

"You'll see," he said. As I stood behind the door, he suddenly slammed
it into me from the other side, causing the knob to hit my stomach with
incredible force. I cried out in pain, and crumpled to the floor. What was
he trying to do to me?

"Stand up again, Melissa," he ordered.

No way! I wouldn't let him hurt me again. I backed away from the door and rose a little, looking around wildly for something to protect myself with. As soon as I had straightened, he punched my stomach with his fist. I thought the first blow had been agonizing, but part of the force of it had been taken by my foot. This time, I felt the full force of his blow, and I dropped once more to the floor, writhing in pain.

"Sean, stop!" I screamed, struggling to breathe from the force of the punch. "This is not the way to solve this! Please, stop!" He looked at me for a moment, and then he reached behind me, grabbing a baseball bat from out of his closet. I curled up into a ball, crying. I had flashbacks of the attack at the park. That had been total strangers. Now here was someone who had professed to care about me, trying to kill me.

"Get up!" Sean screamed.

"No!" I cried. He kicked my arms out of the way. Down came the bat. I curled again in self-preservation. I didn't know how I was going to survive this. I was certain the baby wouldn't, which was obviously his clear intent. The bat came down again.

"Get up, you bitch!" he screamed. "Get UP!" Again and again, he struck me with the bat, as close to the gut as he could get. Abruptly, there came the sound of a car pulling up. Lights flashed across the driveway. Before his parents could come in the house, he hit me one more time. "Shut up!" he menaced, "and don't you dare make a noise, you hear me?" I nodded, painfully. I would have done whatever he asked in that moment.

He got up and left the room. A few minutes later, he came back. I was still curled in a fetal position, tears silently staining my cheeks.

"Let's go," he said. We walked out to his car in the darkness, and he took me home. I thought I had hated him before. Now I detested him, and myself, for getting into that situation.

Sean knew I was in fear of my mother's response to my pregnancy. He was aware that I had nowhere to turn. Realizing that I had not revealed the rape to anyone, he was aware that I would never tell another soul about tonight. He was a bully, an abuser, and tonight he had gotten his own way once again through force. I stumbled down the stairs, in the dark, not daring to turn on the light. The next morning I told Jason and Carrie I had the flu, and everyone left me alone while I slept and recovered from my beating. As soon as the last person was gone from the basement, I sobbed into my pillow. I not only cried for myself, I cried for the baby that could never be.

29

❧❧❧

lovely daffodils

At twelve weeks pregnant, just before my sixteenth birthday, Sean drove me in his parent's car to Planned Parenthood. I felt tense and uneasy at the final decision. Sean was pleased and so were his parents, but all I could do was cry inside. At my arrival, the attendants gave me two pills and a small Dixie cup for water. I had always had difficulty swallowing pills, so I did not take the medication. Then I changed into a hospital gown and was escorted into a small, square room.

I lay on the examining table and looked up at the ceiling, as hate filled every fiber of my being. I hated Sean. I wanted him to leave the room. I really wanted to hit him and punch him in the face for all the torment I was feeling. There was a mobile hanging to my right that had the outlines of birds. The birds floated with the breeze in the room and I kept my gaze fixated on it. I refused to look at Sean when I felt the pressure and pain from the machine tearing into my body. I cried out, and it frightened the attendants. The pills they had given me were supposed to reduce the pain. I hadn't known that the procedure would be physically painful, and they hadn't known I didn't take the medication.

When the procedure was complete, Sean drove me to his home. The plan was for me to stay there and regain color in my face before my mother saw me. The opposing emotions of grief and relief fought for dominance in my heart. I was grieving for the child I would never know. I was also relieved that I could finally leave Sean and never look back. Soon other thoughts came—I would now be able to finish high school and have a chance at a normal life. I could go to dances, graduate, and go to college.

These thoughts were supposed to make me happy, but my grief consumed me. I would have to let myself just feel for a while. And in the meantime, though I didn't really know God, I begged for His forgiveness.

A few days later, when my body was sufficiently healed to be up and about, Sean invited me over to spend time together.

"We're through, Sean." I informed him. "I don't ever want to see you again." Sean didn't agree. He wanted to stay together and tried being the gentleman again. That had earned him my trust twice before. To gain resolve, I remembered the rape, the treatment in front of my friends, and the attack against my body and the baby. I stood my ground firmly.

Sean's parting words were demeaning and cruel. He made me feel that my body was no longer sacred, that I was already used, and that no one would ever want me. It took me some time to get over the continued grief and pain, but after a few weeks, I knew I could do it. Still, I desperately wanted my mother's healing touch, her love, her affection, and her under-standing.

Two weeks after the abortion, I knew I needed to tell my mother. I had grown up in those two weeks, and had faced some of my worst fears. I had known I would tell her for quite some time—even before the proce-dure—but I didn't want her to feel like *she* had to make my choice for me. That wouldn't have been fair. I had wanted to shield her from the pain of the rape and the assault.

Tonight we were alone in the kitchen, and it was quiet.

"Mom," I said quietly. "I need you to know something important." She looked at me expectantly and waited.

"I just want you to know that I had an abortion. I was raped and I didn't know what else to do." My mother gave me a look that I will never forget. *Please, don't tell me anymore,* it said. So I didn't.

For the next week or so, I completely avoided my mother. I was afraid she was ashamed of me, unable to believe she had such a trampy disgrace for a daughter. What she didn't know, what nobody knew, is that I kept praying to God that He would forgive me for what I'd done, even though I couldn't seem to forgive myself. My heart felt tied into knots all the time, and I could barely breathe. I dove into food and found myself gorging on tremendous amounts of it. It gave me comfort for brief periods of time, but it didn't feel good for long because soon I would feel even worse for having eaten so much, for not taking care of my body.

I woke up one morning soon after that and for the first time in my life, I contemplated suicide. What was my life worth? Sean had said no man would want me. My home life situation had deteriorated; I was afraid for my siblings constantly—at home and in the world. I had finally opened up to my mother and all I had felt was her disgust and disappointment. My dad could never help me again. I had no one to talk to or lean on. My body was still weak, and I felt more alone than I ever had in my life.

When I realized I was contemplating the end of my life, I snapped out of it for an instant. It was only long enough to pray to the God who was such a mystery to me. The formal prayers of my youth felt cold and distant. The praise-filled prayers of the Four Square church felt beyond what I was capable of. I uttered a simple but sincere prayer, straight from my heart.

Dear God, please help me. I have nowhere to turn except to you. If you know who I am, if I'm supposed to be here for any reason, please let me know.

Exhausted, I fell back to sleep. When I awoke, I felt like I had been in the most delicious dream. It was filled with so much joy—like I had never known before. I felt peace and comfort and the most amazing, unconditional love I had ever experienced. I reveled in the feeling, half awake, half asleep. When I finally woke fully, still in my darkened basement corner, I felt the humiliation, shame, and despair begin crashing in on me again.

You are better than this . . . You are more than this . . . It was a lovely, deep and wide voice that brought with it the feelings and beautiful *knowings* of love that I had experienced in my dream.

"You know me?" I whispered—afraid to ask. Afraid not to ask.

Yes.

I lay in my cot and basked in the healing warmth. I was loved.

Later that day, our mother informed us that our cousin was getting married in Seattle. My aunt Clara had arranged to pay for Jason, Carrie, and me to board a Greyhound bus to visit them for several weeks over the summer. I was excited and filled with hope at the prospect of getting away, but I felt I had to resolve some things within myself before I could go. Somehow I knew I had to learn from my recent experiences or my life would continue the way it had always gone. I was unhappy with the results, and I was determined to make new choices.

I thought about what I had done that had created my issues with Sean. I realized the most important thing was that I hadn't listened to the warning voice of my friends or the intuition in my heart. I promised myself I would do that from now on. The second most important thing was that I had placed myself twice in a precarious position because I chose the easy way out. Sean had been an easy way out of the long bus rides home and the long bus rides to the Planned Parenthood appointments. Had I listened to my intuition in the first place, I would not have been raped, not been with child, and certainly not been available for his subsequent physical, mental and emotional abuse.

I took a long, hard look at myself. Then I looked at what my mother had created in her life by taking the easy way out. It was easier to ignore the phone calls than to confront my father about having affairs. It was easier to stay with Robert than to face the unknown terror of leaving him and what he might do to us. Because of that, she had buried her head in the sand, refused to look at options, friends, and resources that could get her out of her situation. I had followed in her footsteps. My life would go the way hers had gone—or worse—unless I learned to "cowboy up," to take what would sometimes be a more strenuous path, but what would be *my* path, nonetheless. And while it might be full of unknowns, it would be free of abuse. I decided at that minute that I would no longer be lazy about taking care of myself.

That night, under the stars, I took a walk in my front yard and listened to "Daffodil Lament" by The Cranberries. The song mirrored the feelings I was experiencing about my dad, about Sean, and about Robert.

That night I resolved to look for the lovely things in my life, just like the song said. More important, I learned to be the captain of my own soul. I did not fully know what that meant, but I was determined to find out.

30

✥

bliss & agony

One day, shortly before my siblings and I left for Seattle, I headed to the downtown library on the bus. I had overheard a couple of cryptic conversations at home and had read a few things in a newspaper before it was swept quickly from the house.

It was time to find out what was going on in my own family. I was tired of feeling like I was always flying blind. Entering the large library, I hesitated, almost losing my nerve. I didn't know much about what I was doing, but I decided that it was worth a try. I was too afraid to ask for help, fearful that someone would want to know who I was, and why I was looking. It took me a couple of hours, but I found what I was looking for.

I was shocked to learn that my father had confessed to the murder of Taunja Bennett, and seven other murders that included his fiancée, Julie. *No way!* I thought. *They've already captured the killers and they are behind bars!* A very big part of me wanted to believe that my father was just being crazy. He had never killed Taunja Bennett, someone else had killed Julie, and he was trying to take the fall for that, too. A small, but rational part of me knew that this was really not the case.

Something floated to my consciousness, unbidden. I remembered when I stayed with my dad the very last time we were in Portland. We drove by a tavern and dad mentioned that he liked to play pool there. He made an off-color remark about the bar woman, and something about other uses for his stick. Later, while we were camping, he told a story about sitting on his and Toni's porch:

"One day, I saw a cat walking by . . . " he said, mischievously. "I watched the cat. I caught the cat. And then I killed it." He had paused for effect. "Then I saw a woman jogging by . . . I watched the woman. I caught the woman . . . and then . . . "

He didn't finish. We all cried, "Oooh, gross, Dad! Sick!"

At the memory of that story, I began to tremble uncontrollably, dropping the copy of the newspaper I held I my hands. *I thought it was a campfire story! I thought it wasn't real!* Because of that memory, I was driven to do more research into the Taunja Bennett case. I only felt marginally better. She had not been jogging by Dad's and Toni's house. But she had met him at the tavern he had pointed out to us. It sparked another memory. I remembered I had seen a small spatter of blood on the ceiling of Toni's front room. I thought that it was weird, so when I came home, I told my mother about it. Other things my dad had told me ripped through my mind. Other stories, the duct tape in his sleeper, under his pillow . . .

Suddenly, I didn't want to know a single other detail. I didn't want to know who my father's victims were, how he had met them, or what had happened to them. It was like a switch went off in my brain. I walked out of the library, cold and numb. I didn't remember how I got home. I was done dealing with my father's murders. I had to be, or I would go crazy.

The trip to Seattle on the Greyhound bus was surprisingly short. It brought back happy memories of when Jason, Carrie, and I were creating new adventures in our alfalfa field. On the trip, we looked out for one another, honored each other, and enjoyed each other's company. Once again, though not the oldest, Jason captained this adventure and watched over us with a careful eye. Most people were nice, but there were a few unseemly characters on different legs of the journey that tried to strike up a conversation with pretty little Carrie, or with me. Jason, who sat between us, let them know we were not available to talk.

I found out that Carrie and her friends had collected some newspaper clippings of our father, his confessions and his crimes. Whenever she had something new, she shared it with Jason, so between the three of us, we had about the same amount of knowledge. It wasn't much, but at least we weren't completely ignorant. That felt especially good because we were about to arrive smack-dab in the middle of our father's family.

We arrived in time for the preparations for Susan's wedding. My cousin was ten years older than me and happily in love with her beau, Tom. Her mother, Clara, my other aunt, Anne, and Susan herself all spent the next few days bustling around in preparation. There was a great deal of excited anticipation in the air, and the adults attempted to include us in as many of the preparations as possible, not wanting us to feel left out. They had no idea that we were blissfully happy just to be in their presence. Here, we did not have to find ways to escape or survive. If we looked uncomfortable, it was because our home life was so different from theirs, and from long habit we were still trying to figure out the rules. It took us a few days to just relax.

Although no one mentioned my father, I could feel their anger at my father's actions, their shame for his dishonoring our family. I could also feel great sadness that he would never be free to be a father, enjoy family holidays, or give me away when it was time for my own wedding.

My aunts, Clara and Anne, were such strong women who had control of their lives. I watched them carefully. Through their example I came to realize that I could be just as strong as they were. Surrounded by their love, I felt like I was absorbing their strength as well. Aunt Clara knew I enjoyed hairstyling, and she even let me cut her hair. I knew she was scared, but she didn't show it. She gave me perfume as a gift for my services. My aunts made me feel that I had talents—that I was a contribution and not a burden.

My uncles were Jesperson men. They were so strong and easy going that I wasn't sure if they were angry over my father's actions. They did not talk about their feelings so I didn't think they had any. I found out later that they had basically written my father off. He had brought so much pain that it was better to pretend that he didn't exist.

My grandfather was the surprising anomaly. When he came up for the wedding, he cried all the time, and I thought it was strange to see this old, western tough-guy breaking down. It caused tears to come from me as well because I was really sad—but I didn't know how to let my sadness out. Each day I stuffed my emotions down, except when it was safe to be vulnerable enough to cry. In other words, I had to be alone to do it. When my grandfather hugged me, I felt this huge coat of love surround me. I also felt his pain, which was overwhelming in its magnitude and in my inability to do anything about it.

All in all, they said little or nothing about my father, except my cousin Kristie. While in town for the wedding, I was staying in her room and we talked one night for a while. She could tell that I was not myself, and like everyone else, she assumed that it had to do with the shocking news of my father. It was easier to pretend this was the case, although I could tell I was still suffering from the loss of my child. I was mentally, physically, and emotionally exhausted. I felt fragile and tender . . . and still broken. I'm sure for other people, it was like being in the presence of a zombie. For many days I felt like I *was* the walking dead.

Hesitantly, Kristie broached the subject with me. Unlike my own family, Kristie's and Susan's families had talked somewhat openly about my father—before we arrived, at least.

"Did you know that Susan used to call your dad 'Mean Uncle Keith'?" Kristie asked thoughtfully. "She said it was because he would tease her all the time. He teased her about her hair, about how she looked. It was like he enjoyed torturing her." She paused and cocked her head to one side, as if puzzled. "What I remember is a lot of people being furious with him for stupid things, then the next thing I knew, he would be doing something *really* nice for someone—you know, going *way* out of his way to do it. Melissa, was it like that for you?"

I nodded but found I couldn't speak much about it. My zombie form didn't talk much about the Jekyll and Hyde experiences I had had with my dad. When we shifted the conversation to other things, like the wedding, I found it easier to talk. It was also easier to breathe.

Before the wedding, I had the opportunity to spend a little one-on-one time with Susan. She chatted nonstop about the wedding and her sweetheart. For whatever reason, it was surprisingly healing to see that life hadn't stopped just because Dad was in jail. Things were still moving forward all around us; lives and relationships still moved ahead. Maybe I could, too, if I could figure out how.

Susan showed me her beautiful, elaborate wedding dress and her shoes, as well as her veil and all of the small intricacies of her attire.

"What are you going to wear to the wedding, Melissa?" she asked, turning the conversation kindly to me. My face fell. The last dress I had gotten was when Mom got married, and that was ages ago. When I had attempted to try it on, it had been way too small, especially after my recent experiences. Instead, I had put two of my nicest school items together to form some kind of an outfit. It wasn't fancy, but it was all I had.

"That will be wonderful!" Susan assured me when I showed her, and I smiled. She must have mentioned something to her mother because Clara took the three of us shopping the next day for suitable wedding attire. She bought me a beautiful burgundy shift that tied in the back, and some matching white shoes. It was a special treat to have something new and lovely, and it spoke of hope.

The wedding was absolutely stunning, and it was delightful to be around so many of our family members whom we had felt estranged from for so long. No one mentioned my father; it was as if he didn't exist. Susan and David left for their honeymoon, ecstatically happy. I was such a romantic; I was glad for Susan to have her happily ever after.

A few days after the wedding, things had settled down considerably, and there wasn't the same frenetic pace we had experienced before. We were now staying with Aunt Anne in Bellevue, planning a few more fun excursions around the area. At breakfast, she looked carefully at Jason and me. Carrie had eaten like a jackrabbit, and, as usual, had run off to play. She didn't feel the same desperate need for food that Jason and I had often felt. We noticed that Anne and the rest of the family had made sure we always had access to good meals while we were there. My aunt Anne was also loving and affectionate to us, and it was delightful to be in her presence. I found her studying us today, though, and it made me a little nervous.

"I've been thinking about your father," said Anne. "He's in the Clark County Jail in Vancouver. What would you think about going to see him today?" she asked. Jason dropped his fork but picked it up again quickly. We glanced at each other, a little protective of our feelings. This was the most openly we had talked about Dad with a grown up—ever. We shrugged at about the same time.

"Sure," I said.

"It might do us all some good to have some answers," she said quietly.

On the two-hour drive down, Anne had discussed with us some of the rules of the jail. Although they were understandable, some of them caught me off guard. For example, girls couldn't wear underwire bras. That made sense to me, but I only owned one bra, and of course it was underwire. I wondered if I was really supposed to go, but I spoke to my aunt, and we handled it.

When we arrived, we found that the Clark County facility was not friendly, though I hadn't expected it to be. We learned that years prior, the notorious child killer, Wesley Allan Dodd, had been arrested and booked into the same facility as my father. Dodd was later hanged for his crimes at the Walla Walla prison.

We were ushered into a room that was lined with booths between glass walls. My heart beat heavily in my chest. I hadn't seen my dad in several months, since the day of our conversation at breakfast. I didn't know what to expect. Jason was nervous as well.

The door on the other side of the glass wall opened, and an officer came in first, leading a whole line of inmates dressed in orange jump suits. My father, always easy to spot with his build, sat down in a chair and we walked over to sit across from him. The telephone at each station was the only way to communicate, so it was necessary to speak one at a time. Anne went first.

"Why, Keith?" she asked him, attempting to keep her cool in front of us. "Why are you here?" I think more than any of Dad's brothers and sisters, Anne still held some vestige of hope that her brother wasn't capable of such atrocities. She was demanding an explanation and fighting back tears. At some point during their conversation, I think she wanted him to wake up to what he had done. He looked at us, and it was the first time he had shown any remorse, I think. According to his letters to the media before and after his arrest, he didn't seem to care about how his aftermath affected any of us. He only seemed obsessed with was his reputation as a killer.

Anne pulled the phone away from her ear and looked at us. It was obvious she didn't get the answers she was hoping for, but she seemed to have gotten some closure.

As my dad talked to her on the phone, from time to time he would look at me and Jason. I was still getting over the shock of seeing my own father in a prison jumpsuit. He looked like a felon—in our eyes it made it real, and it made it horrible.

I was filled with shame. I didn't know anyone who had a dad in prison, much less for murder. *Serial murder.* I let that ring through my head for the first time. My father was a serial murderer. He himself had admitted it. I didn't know all the details, but I knew enough. Flashes of my rape and the other physical abuse I had endured filled my mind. *My dad did those things to women and then choked the life out of them?* I remembered how he would fling animals to the ground after he killed them, as if they were nothing but garbage. He had done that with his victim's bodies, not bothering to clothe them or honor them in any way—not even his girlfriend—just tossed them naked down embankments like other people did with their old tires.

I began to cry. I could tell Anne and my father thought I was crying for him, but I wasn't. I was angry with him. I felt alone. It seemed like I had been dealt a really unfair hand. I was crying for myself. Despite all I had been through and survived, this was the first time I had felt sorry for myself. I didn't like it. In the past, I had almost always felt hope for a brighter future. Suddenly I remembered the feeling and experiences I'd had when I prayed on my little cot. I spoke another prayer in my heart to be able to make it through this, to be able to learn from it and to create something different from the sheer and utter hopelessness I was experiencing now.

It was my turn to pick up the phone. I didn't know what to say.

"I'm so sorry, Melissa," my father said, and I saw tears in his eyes. Were they real? "I really let you down," he went on. "I wish I could make things different for you. We're not going to have those fun summers together anymore. I'm going to be here for a long, long time. I'm sorry." I stared at him. My anger, my sadness, and my shame for what he had done all boiled within me.

"What am I going to do, Dad?" I cried, the tears streaming down my face. "You took away our lives together. You were supposed to get us away from our stepfather. What am I supposed to do?" As the oldest child, his leaving had put me in charge of Jason and Carrie. Mom was unable to protect them, and that made me even angrier. Some teenagers thought they were invincible, but I had learned that year just how breakable I really was. How was I supposed to look out for my siblings?

"I'm sorry I'm not going to be there to help," was all he could say. I looked at him through my tears. I loved that man and I hated him. I hated what he had done to all of us.

Jason got on the phone for a short time. He asked his questions and mostly listened to my father. Abruptly the guards said it was time to go and all communication was cut off. For a moment, there was only body language and eye contact, then Jason and I had to look away as the guards led my father out.

There goes my life, was all I could think. That thought seemed to scoop out a big, black hole deep inside me. I was abandoned and alone. I was back to being the zombie. The real world wasn't real to me anymore. I didn't feel like I was in my own life. I felt like my body was there, but my soul was living somewhere else.

On the way home, Anne mentioned that the jail was going to be expanding. Its capacity was listed at 461, but it generally had 462 inmates going in and out—except for my dad. The only place he would be going to once he left here was straight to prison. And we wondered, if like Wesley Allan Dodd, he had something else in store for him. Because it was safe, because we were with Anne, Jason and I cried for most of the way back to Seattle.

31

❧

song of hope

On my way back home, we took a side trip to Yakima to see family and a few old friends. Gavin happened to be there at the time visiting his family, too. From his behavior, it seemed like he still liked me. He promised to keep in touch, but he had promised that two summers in a row. I didn't bet on it. I didn't bet on anyone liking me because I didn't feel like I deserved it. I wanted it, badly, desperately, but I wondered if what Sean had told me was true.

"No one else will ever want you, Melissa," he had said ruthlessly. "You're used goods now." Sean's words rang often in my head. I had finally had to give up on guys. I'd decided that all I wanted to do was go to school and make a better life for myself. If I was successful, surely someone would want me. All I knew was, I was determined for life to change.

When I got home that summer, I discovered that I had more courage to speak out about our circumstances and living conditions.

"What are we still doing here?" I asked my mother when we returned to Grandma Frances's. After weeks of freedom, it was incredibly crowded for all of us. While Grandma and Uncle Bart lived upstairs, Mom, Robert, me, Jason, Carrie, Uncle Lewis, and my half brother, Benjamin, were all crammed downstairs in the tiny hole of a basement.

In my Aunt Anne's home, I had observed that my cousins didn't have to wonder how they were going to get clothing; it was just provided. They didn't have to worry about where they where going to live; they had a warm and clean home, food in their cupboards, and regular vacations. I knew it was not healthy to compare, but this wasn't about comparing—this was about surviving versus thriving. I would not be able to thrive unless I understood the choices that created a thriving life. I observed choices that my aunt made. Although it was hard work, she chose to be a day care provider so she would be available when her children got home from school. Her paycheck paid the bills, and when she struggled at times, she chose to keep moving forward with faith that things would work out. For a little while, I resented my cousins for having a safe home. Then I realized it didn't do anyone any good to live in squalor, and their example gave me hope that I, too, could somehow have a healthy and loving lifestyle. Our housing situation seemed like the most important step in that endeavor. It was a very big deal to me, so for quite some time I had been looking for opportunities for progress, similar to what I had done before we found our Litchfield home.

For me, living in that tiny house felt like a military torture device—it felt as if the world was testing my ability to survive. I never knew how many months, or even years, I would have to endure this round of basement living. Maybe if I knew how long I would have to endure, it might not have been so awful.

"So, how long do you think we have to live here?" I asked my mother, shortly after we had returned home.

"However long it takes to find a home," she said resignedly, "one that we can afford."

One day I found some literature that Habitat for Humanity was building some homes nearby. I didn't understand the entire concept, but from everything I read and saw, I felt like our family would fit the bill. I was surprised and pleased when my mother agreed to look into it. The downside, Mom said, was that there was an enormous waiting list. She doubted it would work.

"Well, if it doesn't work, what other options do we have?" I asked.

"Not many," she said with gloomy acquiescence. "I don't see a lot of opportunities for us. Life is really hard, Melissa. It gives you tough breaks, and you get what you get."

"Mom, you know we can't stay here forever," I pleaded. "Don't give up. Look at what it's doing to Jason and Carrie. They're never here." She looked at me as though I had stomped on her foot and then she turned away.

I went downstairs in a haze, and I felt the dark energy start to spread again. I decided to turn to someone I did not know very well, and I abruptly kneeled down beside my cot, my knees carrying my weight on the cool, hard cement. The few times that I had earnestly prayed, I had been given sudden strength to endure another day. In my heart, I knew He had answered my prayers, though not always in the way I had expected. I had wanted my problems to go *poof* and disappear, but instead, I was given peace and the feeling that my burdens had been lifted a little.

Now I was again in need of a divine source to relieve my feelings of powerlessness. We had only been home for a short while, and my hope was already starting to dissipate. I needed the strength to keep enduring because my will to keep going was fading fast. I thought about all the kids at my school that drank and the ones that did drugs. It would be so easy to slip into that lifestyle. I was preparing to go to a whole new school, and I knew I was floundering.

God, I feel so alone right now. Is there something I did wrong, or missed? Is this a punishment? I'm not sure I can go through any more right now. I need your help. When will this all be over? What is the lesson that I'm missing?

Hot tears were running down my cheeks. I remembered a scripture that was read during youth group of the woman who secretly touched Jesus' garment. He instantly knew it and turned to ask who had touched his clothing. The woman admitted it was her. In this moment, I fully understood why that woman would reach out just to touch the edge of His garment. If she could just grasp something so small, so brief, then maybe she could have hope again.

Please, God, let this be over soon. Please help us to have hope in our lives, something to look forward to. Let me feel joy again. Amen.

I quickly wiped my tears away, embarrassed for having a breakdown and showing emotion, even though no one was around to see it. I did not like feeling vulnerable and weak, and I was glad that none of my family had come downstairs in my moment of despair. I laid down on my cot and wrapped my sleeping bag around me. I thought about what it would feel like to live in a new home. I thought about clean, bright walls and new carpet and appliances. I thought about not being embarrassed to ask my friends to stay the night or to visit, and I thought about what it would be like for me to feel normal.

I pictured how I would decorate my very own room. I could feel the lightness and joy of living in what felt like light. A feeling of something greater in me started to pull through the despair. The more I pictured this bright new home, the more I believed that it was mine and that I would have it in a matter of days! I *knew* that God was arranging this gift to me in every new minute that passed. I felt freedom to put in all the details that would make this home special and real to me. The more I decorated this home, the more I believed it was mine. In my daydreaming, I imagined how it would feel to walk across clean carpet that had been untouched. I reveled in the freedom to take a long shower without taking from someone else. I believed this was the beginning to the answer to my prayer because I felt this blessing was on its way.

As the days passed, I would add more details to my visionary home. Then one afternoon, I arrived home and was asked to have a seat in Grandma Frances's tiny living room. The air was filled with frantic energy, and my mother and grandmother were busy cleaning all around us. Jason, Carrie, Jonathan, and I were all in one place, which felt rather foreign. I had hardly seen Jason or Carrie since our return from Seattle. We had all been living separate lives, and now, without explanation, we stared at each other, wondering what the big news was.

The bell rang, and the four of us looked to the door in anticipation. Three people walked into our already crowed living room. A man and two women, all dressed professionally, grabbed chairs from the table to join in our circle. My mother and Robert sat next to each other nervously. The strangers looked over at the younger ones in the room. One woman smiled.

"Do you know why we are here?" she asked.

"No," we answered in unison, our curiosity peaked.

"We are from Habitat for Humanity," she said, and my heart leaped inside my chest! "We want to take a look around at your home and determine if you will be receiving a new home!" The other two broke out into smiles at our excited reactions, and the woman went on.

"Now, there are seven members in your family, correct?"

"No, only six," Jason and I chimed in quickly. I wondered how she could make that kind of mistake when we were all present for the meeting. I experienced a small pang of fear. *What if having less than seven in our family would disqualify us for a new home?*

"Yes, seven is correct," my mother said. I looked at her as if she were a liar. Jason was upset too. My mother pointed at her belly and said, "One on the way."

My initial fear that she wasn't telling the truth turned into something else entirely. How could my mother continue to be intimate with a man who hurt her like Robert did? I couldn't believe it. I put my head down so these people could not see my feelings of humiliation and despair.

"Have you ever heard of birth control?" cried Jason. He stormed out of the house. My mother appeared shocked at his outrage but did not say a word about it. The most important thing, apparently, was for the Habitat for Humanity people to see the entire family together. It had been a huge undertaking to have all of us present at one time.

I watched as the Habitat for Humanity people went downstairs. I felt embarrassment creep up as they saw my cot and my shoeboxes. I had to tell myself over and over, that they had to see how we lived in order to make their assessment. *This is a blessing. Surely, this is a blessing.* I had to keep telling that to myself over and over. It was the first time someone had witnessed my living conditions, and it made me very nervous. I *never* invited anyone into the basement. *Ever.*

We said good-bye and watched them leave in their nice suits and their clean, pristine car.

"Do you think we'll get chosen?" I asked my mom, not doing anything to disguise my rising excitement.

"Honey," she sighed, "there are a lot of people on their list. I really don't think so."

She had to be wrong. I knew she was wrong because the minute they told me who they were, I felt this was the answer to my prayers for a home. Somehow, I knew that God would not allow this dream to be taken away from me.

"I know we're going to get it!" I cried. "I know it!"

"How do you know that for a fact?" she asked.

"It's a strong feeling," I said. "There is no doubt." I thought again of the woman touching the hem of His robe. *There is no doubt.*

32

❦

sacred trust

A phenomenon had happened over the last six months. Between finding the fortitude to escape my abuser and feeling the peace of getting away for several weeks, I found that I was not as afraid to speak my mind anymore. I think it was hard on my mother because I wouldn't treat topics like they were taboo. She still did, especially when I spoke openly to her of the abuse she was suffering at Robert's hands. She pointed out that it was not nearly so bad anymore, and I told her I thought that was only because of Grandma and Uncle Bart being around all the time. Despite the fact that he didn't throw her into walls here, his often furious signing and the angry looks on his face when we were out, or when there were no other adults around spoke volumes about the rage he held inside.

We had all learned to read Robert, even if we didn't know sign language. My siblings and I could tell that he was starting to boil when his signing would escalate in pace. Robert's grunts would get louder, sounding like high-pitched gawks. Once it reached that level, anything could happen—and too often in the past, it had. When he got that way, my mother would try to reason with the irate man, and it was like shoveling snow during a blizzard. It was useless. I could not understand why she would try to appease him when his requests where most often absurd or trivial. In my opinion, he was like a giant, overweight toddler throwing a fit. The only time Robert's anger seemed to decrease was after he physically assaulted my mom.

My refusal to put up with the abuse seemed to spark something in Robert. I found he was stealing my diaries and reading them! This only infuriated me more. I tried different hiding places, and he kept finding them in my private things. I got the feeling that he was reading to see if I mentioned anything about him, so once I did mention something on purpose. I absolutely spoke my mind to protect my siblings. If he was going to continually invade my privacy, I was going to let him have it.

I decided to illustrate in my journal a situation my family had experienced with him. I wanted him to see how petty, selfish, and cruel he was. I also wanted to make sure he left my siblings and me alone. I wrote:

I cannot understand why my mother puts up with Robert's abusive behavior. I am sick of him pushing her around and throwing her into walls for no reason! In addition, he has stepped out of bounds where my sister is concerned, and if he ever does it again, I will not hesitate to call the cops.

When we were supposed to be traveling to Colorado to meet his two sons, we stopped at a park near Boise, Idaho for some dinner. Pressed for time, we decided to eat inside the station wagon with the doors wide open to invite in some fresh air. It was a much-needed break from being on the road for six hours! Carrie and I first got out of the station wagon to walk around and stretch. Then she decided she wanted to have part of the meal. The fast food bag was sitting in the center of the console, between my mother's seat and Robert's passenger seat. Carrie reached over Robert to grab a sandwich, and he bit her arm! I saw the look on her face as she pulled it out and burst into tears.

Mom looked over at Robert and signed, "What did you do?" He then told her in his angry, fast-paced signing that Carrie had reached across his lap for the food and it was rude. Mom inspected Carrie's wound, and it was horrible! Robert bit the soft, fleshy area so hard, Carrie couldn't stop crying. Her arm was already turning black and blue, and blood oozed where his bite had broken through the skin! I wanted to hit him. Everyone except Robert got back into the station wagon, and Mom drove back to the Albertson's in Boise where we had picked up our dinner. She said she needed to use the phone and told us to sit in the car and wait for her. Our vacation was over. I was relieved that we would not have to make the long car trip to see Robert's family. To me, he has never been a stepfather but a dictator and abuser.

Somehow, Mom was not as convinced as I was. She got back into the station wagon after her call, and turned around in the dusk to return to the park where we had left Robert! While sitting in the station wagon, Carrie and watched as my mother tried to negotiate with the irate man. She gave in to his demands and soon Robert was sitting in our car again and we were headed home. I couldn't believe it! I know I wouldn't have brought him back to hurt us again.

Robert had better not ever, ever, ever touch my sister again! And if he touches me or Jason, the same thing applies. I can't control how my mother feels, but I can protect my brother and sister, and I won't hesitate to do so. I will make sure he goes to jail.

What I did not add in my journal was what happened when Robert got back in the car. I had wrapped my arms around my little sister, and we looked at each other with fear. The monster was back in our car again. All we could think was, *What else will happen?* Would we *ever* be safe? We had no idea at the time that there were people and resources who could have helped us get out of our abusive situation. We thought we had to endure whatever Robert dished out. Sometimes it would appear that my mother wanted to do the right thing for us, like leaving Robert, but every time she tried, she would reconsider her stance and return to him. She was as reliable in this as Old Faithful, and I grew angrier every time she went back to him. Jason, I knew, was having the hardest time. He couldn't handle seeing what was going on with mom, and as he got bigger, I worried that sometime he might get in between Robert and her. What would happen then?

I was a little worried about writing that about Robert, knowing that it was just a matter of time before he read it. When he got angry at us, he took it out on my mother, and I did everything I could to avoid that. Still, I thought, he was trying to hide the fact he was reading my journal. I had confronted him about it in front of my mom, and he wouldn't openly admit that he had been reading it. Because of that, I felt like it was safe.

In the beginning, I had tried several times to reach out to Robert, but I no longer had any compassion toward him. Appeasing him had only helped him become the dictator he was now, and he was not worth the pain he generously dished out. And to read my journal! Not only was that a huge violation of my privacy, he had taken away the only tool I had to release the feelings of frustration, resentment, pain, anger, sadness, and abandonment I was feeling during that time. Robert kept going through my things and reading my journal until I finally stopped journaling altogether. Still, I never stopped thinking and feeling that the abusive behavior he exhibited toward my mother was simply unacceptable.

33

❧❦❧

bloody sunday

From the time of his arrest, my dad seemed determined to haunt everyone, including us, with his callous behavior toward his victims and with details of the crimes he had committed. During his many letter-writing campaigns to reporters and website authors, he sometimes referred to his victims as "piles of garbage." Apparently he had been learning about the legal system from the inside, and he was doing everything he could to discredit his confessions, to mislead prosecutors, and to avoid the death penalty. While I could understand survival techniques, some things that my father wrote were so twisted, it made me sick. When I heard that he had offered a "Self-Start Serial Killer Kit," at first I was confused, but only because I wasn't familiar with websites and I didn't understand the implications. Once I read the words he had published, however, I was beside myself with horror.

I always knew that my father had a bizarre sense of humor, but when I read Julie's name included in the description—that he could write something so cold and callous about the woman he had told me he wanted to build a life with—it floored me. Despite my father's generous qualities, he absolutely lacked boundaries, and he lacked compassion. I wasn't aware of everything that my father had been through as a child, but he and I had once commiserated on how difficult it could be to fit into society. Somehow along the way, on a deep level he had forgotten what it was like to be the one who was hurt. He had become desensitized and beyond feeling.

I felt an intense amount of shame and embarrassment about my father's behavior and the media circus he was creating with the press. Because we lived far enough away from Yakima, Portland, and most of Dad's stomping grounds, not too many people knew that he was my father. After the things I had been seeing and reading about, I began to have an intense fear of being connected with him. Jason and Carrie were experiencing some of the same feelings.

People like to compliment one another on positive family traits. "Like father, like son" for example. Then there are ones that can be construed negatively, such as, "The apple doesn't fall far from the tree." Every time I heard someone talk about family traits, I began to experience sheer panic. I didn't want to be compared to my father or my mother. I avoided any questions like, "Who is your father?" or, "So what does your dad do for a living?" I certainly wasn't going to mention self-starter kits for serial murderers. I longed for that father that I had once been proud of. Becoming more and more introverted every day, I worried that I might end up like some people I had seen who had become so afraid of other people: alone, reclusive, shut away from the world.

Worse than that, however, was the responsibility I took for my father's actions. My dad did not feel any regret, remorse, compassion or shame for what he had done. He didn't take any emotional accountability; he had no conscience. It was a big joke to him.

He was my father! He had committed those horrible, heinous crimes. Unconsciously, I took on the responsibility that he refused to take on. As the oldest in the family, I felt that if he wouldn't bear the shame and remorse, someone had to. Without realizing it, I took the blame.

In August of 1995, I chose to go to Mead High School. I was sick of busing all the way to Shadle, and I was firm in my resolve to have nothing to do with Sean. Despite my nervousness, my first day at Mead was wonderful. The pressure I had put on myself the previous year to wake up at 5 AM was gone! I slept in to a normal time, and caught the school bus like everyone else in my neighborhood. My classes were easy to find, people were friendly, and I felt my life improving. I suddenly didn't care that I was sixteen and without a car or driver's license yet.

On the bus ride home, I met a girl who was new to the area. Her name was Tania, and she had beautiful eyes and lovely brown hair. Naturally willowy and lithe, her most appealing feature was an open, engaging smile.

We sat next to each other and struck up an instant friendship. Tania asked me if I would like to try some of her lip gloss. I looked at her necklace and saw a dozen, colorful tubes of flavored lip gloss hanging around her neck. I smiled. *A girl after my own heart!* Tania had almost all the flavors available to collect and she had more at home.

The next day we sat together on the way to school, chatting like we had been lifelong friends. We were disappointed to find out we didn't have many of the same classes, but we didn't let that get in our way. Tania began inviting me to her house quite often, and we found we had enough in common to form a tight friendship, and enough divergent interests to keep it intriguing.

I never invited Tania to my home, and she never asked to see it. There were a lot of unspoken things between us, and she seemed to honor that space inside me. Her home life had been rough in a different way, and so we felt a connection in our friendship. Every day, I grew to trust her more and more. Tania grounded me. I finally felt back in my own body, back in reality, and ready to move forward with my life.

From time to time, I would tell Tania something that was happening with me. She never broke any of her promises, or any of the trust I had in her. She kept my secrets safe.

Tania's mother had recently gone through a divorce. She was suffering from depression, but she made sure she was present for Tania. She began to be there for me as well, like a second mom. I loved my mother, and didn't need a replacement, but Lynne was like the balm that my mother was not in a position to be: Lynne had a safe and secure home.

It was around this time that my father started sending me letters. I had not opened up to anyone at my new school about my father, not even Tania. Within short order, however, I told her, and it felt so good to have someone that I could trust and confide in. She knew I was ashamed of my father, and she didn't pressure me to talk about him. When one of his letters came, though, it was nice to share them with her because I needed to have a sounding board. Sometimes Dad's letters would sound like a normal letter from a father to a daughter. Sometimes they were really weird, and I liked it when Tania validated what I was feeling, without me having to ask her.

One day, I read a letter to her, and it seemed quite off to me, but in a way I couldn't have put into words. I had grown up with my dad's inappropriate behavior and his lack of boundaries, and I wasn't always sure where they should be. I read the words " . . . your mother was never good in bed," and I glanced up to see a strange look on Tania's face.

"I *cannot* believe your father would tell you this kind of stuff, Mel!" she said, her eyes wide with incredulity. She slapped her knees loudly. "That's it! Your father is *officially twisted*! Hey, wanna go get some ice cream? My mom bought some really yummy stuff yesterday."

That's what I loved about her! Tania could take my peculiar life and make it funny. She created a safe space where we could talk about the things that bothered me and then move on. We didn't have to waste time or energy on melodramatics, pity, or even pretending. She made me feel . . . normal.

In the fall of 1995, Tania and I heard on the news that based on specific information given to authorities by my father, a Nebraska highway patrol-man found what was left of a woman's body. Angela Subrize was found in the tall grass near the tiny town of Gothenberg, Nebraska, located near the South Platte River. Authorities believed the remains had been decompos-ing there since January, and a tattoo of Tweety Bird, still visible on one of her ankles, was one of the only identifying marks that remained. We found out that Wyoming prosecutors were planning to seek the death penalty.

Tania was there for me as I cried.

My father had ulterior motives, as usual. In November of the same year, he waived all of his rights and was transferred to Oregon, where he entered a no-contest plea before Multnomah County Presiding Judge Donald H. Londer for the murder of Taunja Bennett. Judge Londer sentenced him to life in prison, with a minimum of thirty years before being eligible for parole. I did not know that this is what my father wanted. Prison time in Oregon meant it would be expensive to extradite him to other states for prosecution, and the clincher—it made potential death penalties in other states less likely.

In the meantime, there was still the murder of twenty-three-year-old Laurie Ann Pentland. My father had written letters as the Happy Face Killer after Pentland's murder, claiming responsibility for her death. He was given another life-in-prison sentence in Oregon, with a thirty-year minimum term before parole and was to serve consecutive sentences. He would never leave prison because if he somehow lived through his first two sentences in Oregon, he would be transferred to Washington State Peni-tentiary to serve his other life sentence there.

All I understood were two things. The first was that my father's sentencing meant that the people who were innocent would finally get out of jail. I wondered about the woman, Pavlinac, who had set herself and her boyfriend up. Would she be safe? Had either of them learned anything in the process? I would never know.

The second thing I realized was that as my father was given life-sentences in prison, I was sentenced to a life without a father. Gone were the child support payments. Gone were the weekly phone calls because all calls from prison had to be made collect, and none of us could afford them. I now had a permanently absent father, in another state where it was easy to forget he existed.

⟨⟩

Thanksgiving was very hard that year. Part of it was that I didn't like having an abundance of food for only one day and then having to struggle the rest of the year. Also, we didn't feel much like a family lately. Jason and Carrie were always gone, and I couldn't blame them. So was I, as often as I could. That holiday weekend, I spent as much time away from the reminders of what my father had created and the mess that my life was at home. When I was away, I felt more at peace, like life was *friendly*. Because of the trust Tania and I had built, I began trusting other people, too.

Tania and I had a made another friend, Stephanie. She was a junior that year at Mead, and had invited me over a few times to her house. I really, really loved her mom. She was a warm and nurturing kind of woman who had an enormous love for her children.

Once I entered Stephanie's immaculate home, it reminded me of my friend, Katie's home. There was something almost tangibly peaceful and loving about that place. I felt it often at Tania's too, and it was intriguing to me. Stephanie had invited me for a sleepover, and I was grateful for a place to go where I felt so loved and comfortable. I almost felt as at home there as I did at Tania's house.

On Sunday morning we were having breakfast in the kitchen. It was my favorite place in Stephanie's house because there were always multiple things going on at once. We were cooking breakfast, watching TV, talking about crushes, taking questionnaires out of teen magazines, and having a great time. All of a sudden, I was shocked to see my father's face appear on the screen. It was a national news program, and they were doing an exposé on my father, "The Happy Face Killer." They reported that on that day, Sunday, November 27, 1995, after serving more than four years in prison for a crime they didn't commit, Laverne Pavlinac and John Sosnovske were being released from prison. The entire show was on the original crime, on Pavlinac and Sosnovske, and on my father.

Fascinated, Stephanie and her mother stopped what they were doing to watch the coverage. I was so embarrassed and humiliated. I thought they *knew*. I began to tremble. The secrets I kept in the dark hole deep inside me—all the shame and guilt—had been called out by the national news anchor. They were going to ask me about him . . . they were going to judge me, based on my father.

Stifling a cry, I ran away down the hall, blinded by my tears. Stubbing my toe on the door frame, I hurdled into Stephanie's room and collapsed onto her bed. I wanted to die, right there, to sink into the bedclothes and never come out again.

"Melissa, what is it? What happened? Are you okay?" Their tender, worried questions made me cry even harder. I crumbled in their arms, awash in the pain of it. I felt like my worst fears were coming true. It took several minutes for me to calm down, and for them to get the story out of me because they really *didn't* know. Even though our last names were the same, they had no idea that the serial killer they were watching on television was my father. I was so afraid that Stephanie and her mother wouldn't welcome me over to their home anymore. I had only just gotten to know Stephanie, but I really liked her, and her approval meant the world to me.

Once I was calm, and they assured me I would always be loved and welcomed there, Stephanie and I had a long talk. I told her about my dad from my perspective, and how hard the whole year had been. She was baffled as to why I had kept it a secret from her. Stephanie then shared with me a very personal and traumatic experience she and her family had suffered, and we realized that we were able to relate to each other's pain. We were also able to relate to the desire to move beyond it into a better life. From that point on, Stephanie became a very sincere and valuable friend to me. We never discussed my father again, but now I had two friends who knew me—knew my past and knew about my father—and still loved me. The shame never left, but with Stephanie and Tania beside me, it lessened considerably.

34

❧

a new home for new holes

The corner lot had weeds that looked frozen and stone hard. It was difficult to picture that contractors would soon be putting in our foundation for the Habitat for Humanity home we were approved for. I had pictured this home for months in my mind, and now I could see what the address would be. As we had driven through the neighborhood, I observed the surrounding homes. I was a little concerned about how we might be received by our neighbors.

Most of the homes were tiny and in need of care. Several had "fixer-upper" cars lined up in the yard, waiting for repairs that would never come; tall grass was growing through the spokes of the tires. Discarded trash had blown into the bushes by the sidewalks. On one side of our lot, there was what appeared to be a commercial property with a barbed-wire fence and a boxy building.

I kept looking for something to bring a hint of welcome, and then I found one. The neighbor across the street owned a small, cute home that appeared new. My mother saw me looking at the home.

"That's a Habitat for Humanity home, too." It gave me a point of reference on what our home would look like, although my mom explained that hers was just a two bedroom and ours would be a four. That was a relief. The existing Habitat home appeared to be the same size of our Nordin home. That had been just two bedrooms, and there were more of us now. I did not relish the idea of living in such tight quarters again.

My mother was staring at the lot, trying to picture our new home.

"I think country blue would be a good color with white trim, although our neighbor will have to agree."

"Our neighbor has to agree?" I asked.

"We're getting a duplex since the lot is so big," she explained. I was just happy to have a new home regardless of the color it would be. Maybe having a duplex would keep Robert from making a huge ruckus when he was angry.

We drove off, feeling satisfied that this dream was truly becoming a reality. Now as a family, we were actually united in something; we were united in hope. Every one of us was eager to leave the cramped basement for good.

The months got warmer, and soon it was the great housewarming day. The staff from Habitat for Humanity and all the volunteers came to congratulate us. When I walked in, I saw a large "Welcome Home Smith Family" on an easel. I overlooked being classified as a member of the Smith family to feel the clean, stiff carpet under my feet. It was surreal to be standing in a home that just months ago did not exist.

Jason, Carrie, Benjamin, and I all ran to claim our rooms. My sister and I would have to share one. Jason got his very own, and Benjamin and our new baby half brother, Christian, got the very back room, closest to mom and Robert's master bedroom. Jason had not lived at home permanently since Robert had thrown him across the yard during an argument. We all hoped this was a new beginning, and that Jason would stay with us so we could be a real family again.

The kitchen was new and bright white, with shining appliances that still had yellow energy-saving stickers on them. The home was just as I imagined! All the walls were perfect and without a single nail hole. I could not wait for everyone to leave so I could move my belongings in and celebrate our new beginning. A lady handed my mother her key with an enormous smile. We had a home of our own now!

I could turn the light off and on with a switch instead of a string and I had a closet for my clothes instead of the shoe boxes. I savored that beautiful moment. I gave thanks to the God I was just beginning to know but who I felt that I had loved forever. I knew from that moment on that whatever I desired could come to be, if I just believed. My visionary home now in solid form, I felt powerful and in control of my destiny for the first time.

That feeling of power and control did not last long, but had inherent lessons in it. It did not take long for Robert to dominate the new home. Within three months, he was dictating even the smallest details of how the home was run. Since it was a one-story home, he had a view of the whole house at all times, including a full view of the kitchen. Since all of the bedroom doors faced the living room, Robert could even monitor our movements when we left the bedrooms.

Within three months, violence in our new home had escalated. Mom had stayed home with baby Christian as long as she could, and then she had Carrie or Robert watch him when she went back to work. One evening, Robert brutally hurt my mom when he got mad at me for eating some leftovers. He left while she went to the hospital, and I thought he was leaving permanently. My mom changed the locks and promised he was out of our lives for good. A few days later, however, Robert showed up at our door with new keys that my mother had given him.

Not long after that, Robert and my brother had an argument in our new house. Jason grabbed a baseball bat, ready to swing at Robert if he tried to attack him while he was leaving out the front door. My brother was gone again.

When my mother came home from work, she discovered that Jason had moved out. She went to Robert to investigate the day's events. Trying to be the peacemaker backfired on her. Robert suddenly snapped and shoved my mother into the new wall. As she got up, I saw the sheetrock crumble where her back had landed. As soon as she was on her two feet once more, Robert shoved her again by the open front door. This time she flew backwards on the cement stairs outside, and screamed in abject pain as her head hit the cement. She lay there for a minute, and when she got up, I saw that her hand was bleeding, and the back of her head appeared to have split open. I was frozen with fear, not daring to confront Robert, but aching to help my mother. I had seen what happened when anyone tried to protect my mother, and Jason had taken the only baseball bat.

After Robert left, I ushered all of the children into the car as Mom slowly drove to the hospital for treatment. That night we stayed at my grandmother's home. In the morning my mother filed a police report and obtained a restraining order against Robert. I complained to my mother that I wanted to go back to my own room and I did not want to stay another night with Grandma Frances again. She agreed and little Christian, Jonathan, Carrie, my mother, and I pulled up to the blue house and saw that Robert was gone and that all of our personal things were still there. My mother, fearful that Robert would return, changed the locks on the front door once again.

I could sense my mother's fear about sleeping alone in our home. She did not feel confident she could protect us if Robert were to return. Inside, I knew she was right, but I was not about to let Robert intimidate me away from my new bedroom. I had survived two years in a basement to get that bedroom, and I was not going to abandon it that easily. We had a right to the house.

It had gotten dark one night and everyone was starting to get ready for bed. I looked through my dresser drawer and saw that I had only a top to my PJ's and the bottoms were missing somewhere. I shrugged the worry off and decided just to sleep in the top since Robert was not in the house. After saying our good nights, the house fell silent. I was having a hard time going to sleep with the assault still replaying in my head over and over again. Then I heard a noise in the living room. It sounded like tapping on the window. Just as I was starting to wonder what that noise was, I heard a banging on my window above my bed. Startled, I jumped off my bed and ran to my mother, who was already up and in the hallway.

"What is that noise. Mom?"

"It's Robert," she whispered, "but he cannot get in. He'll just try to keep us up by banging on the windows." I did not believe that Robert would be content to simply bang on windows.

"Should I call the police?" I asked as the warning came up inside me.

"No, we will be all right."

The voice of warning sounded again. *Do it anyway!* I picked up the white telephone on the side table in the living room and dialed 9-1-1. An operator answered, and I gave her my name, telling her that my stepfather was trying to break into the house. She had just asked for my address when I heard a large *crash*. Robert was now standing over the broken front door, glaring at me. I screamed.

"He broke through the door! Please help me now!"

"What is your address?" the operator persisted, but Robert had charged at me and pushed me over as he ripped the phone off the cord. He headed to the back of the house.

There was nothing more I could do except hope that the police were on their way. When I got up, I witnessed Robert attacking my mother in the hallway. I flew at him, hitting him on the back, but he appeared to not feel a thing as he rampaged against my mother. I was afraid she was going to die, and then I, Carrie, Benjamin, and baby Christian would be next. In mortal fear, I grabbed my half brothers and my sister and we ran across the street to a neighbor's house. I banged desperately on their doors, but no one would answer.

Sirens sounded around the corner, and police cars screamed to a stop, surrounding our home. I was standing on the corner in my PJ top and underwear with my three siblings, watching as four policemen tried to get Robert out of the house. Robert was attacking the officers, and they had to contain him. Once I saw Robert being escorted into the police car in handcuffs, I wanted to run to my mother, but I was deathly afraid of what I might find. Would she still be alive? Four policemen on Robert—my mother against Robert, all alone. I felt guilty for leaving my mother there while she was being attacked. I felt like I had abandoned her.

Carefully, I walked my siblings over to the house, embarrassed to be in just my underwear and PJ top. Inside an officer was holding my crying mother, rocking her consolingly as her face was beginning to swell beyond recognition. Another officer began to question me.

"Can you tell me what happened?" he asked, his tone compassionate and caring.

I nodded and then proceeded to share the story. The officer assured me that Robert would be spending some time in jail for assaulting an officer and my mother, and for violating his restraining order. Robert would also get charges for ripping the phone off the hook while I was on the line with 9-1-1. The officers kindly assured my family that we could sleep in peace for a few nights. Before leaving, they took photographs of my mother's injuries. I was amazed that she did not have to go back to the hospital. I eventually learned that she had refused medical care. She was exhausted and just wanted to stay home.

Later in the week, there was a hearing for Robert. It must have gone in our favor, since he was away from the home for a while. Every night I slept in peace, knowing he could not touch our family. I wanted the protection of a father, but mine was serving time for serial murder.

Within three months, Robert somehow came back into our lives and moved back into our home. Being more fearful now of Robert, I stayed at my friend Tania's house every chance I could.

Tania's house felt safe and more like home than my own house did. Tania's mother treated me like her own child, and welcomed me into her home. I was free to eat her dinners and sleep over any night I needed to. Most nights in the summer, I stayed with Tania. Over time we became as close as sisters.

35

⁂

redemption

That summer I turned seventeen years old. My home life was hell, but my mother did everything she could to keep our little rag-tag family together. Quietly, privately, on my birthday, she gave me $50. I knew what she must have sacrificed to save and scrape that together. For the first time in years, I shed tears in front of my mother.

We had connected for a few, intimate moments, and I couldn't help it; I asked her to leave Robert for good. She was afraid to leave him. Afraid of going without his limited money to help with the bills, afraid of what he might do to us if we left or forced him out.

One day when I happened to be in our new home and not at Tania's, I was in the front room playing with my half brother, Christian. He was a beautiful boy, always peaceful and happy. He loved people, and his eyes would always light up when I walked into the room to play with him. I had been wondering why he didn't seem to make the babbling sounds that Benjamin had. I had mentioned it to my mother, and she said that all babies develop a little differently. She told me some time line differences between me, Jason, and Carrie. I shrugged. It made sense. Christian would definitely have a different personality than his brother, I thought. Mom was doing dishes in the kitchen, and suddenly there was a loud banging noise as she dropped a pot and it clattered into the sink. I had been startled and felt my heart pound loudly in my chest. I looked over at Christian, expecting him to start to cry. Shocked, I saw that he hadn't been affected by the noise. He hadn't responded at all—he was just happy playing with his toy.

"Mom, I think you had better get Christian's hearing checked." She took him in a few days later for testing, and we found out that Christian was deaf.

During the following school year, I spent more and more time at Tania's—sometimes four or five days of the week, sometimes more. I felt safe there. I was beginning to be able to break out of survival mode and into moving forward. I had plans and dreams, and I kept focused on getting my diploma to further those dreams. But one thing kept getting in my way, no matter how I tried to get past it. I awoke at night in cold sweats, plagued with nightmares. I cried during the day when no one was looking for no reason.

Even though more than two years had passed since the rape and the abortion, I could not get over it. I could not forgive myself for having made that choice. It didn't help that my mother's son, my half brother, was two months younger than my child would have been. Every time I looked at him, it was a reminder of the life that would never be. My self-incrimination haunted me always, day and night. I needed help. I was beginning to have sleep deprivation and was having trouble eating. I had lost weight and at first everyone said how good I looked, but it was becoming apparent this wasn't healthy. I was lacking the desire to live.

Tania was the only person who knew anything about the abortion. She knew it plagued me, but she didn't know how bad until I finally confessed that I had written my father to ask his advice.

"You did what?" she cried in dismay, her eyes wild with pain for me. "Melissa, you know he's not right in the head! How could you do that to yourself?"

"I need my daddy," I cried, my eyes filling with tears. "I just need my daddy." Tania hugged me for a moment, sharing my pain with me. She knew I didn't have a therapist—my family couldn't afford one. I couldn't talk to my mom; I'd already tried that and she totally avoided the subject. Tania was the only one I could turn to, and since she was my same age, she didn't always know what to say, though she did her best.

What neither of us knew was that I would really need her to get past this next hurdle—the one my father threw at me.

A few days later, I received a letter in the mail from the prison in Salem, Oregon. I was happy that my father would write me so quickly, and I was so relieved that I had finally shared this burden with someone I loved and had trusted, once upon a time. It would be like old times, and I would relish his advice. He had to see that I was hurting and desperately needed his love and care. I toyed back and forth with the idea of reading it by myself, or keeping in the tradition of having Tania read it to me, in case anything deserved to be censored. Finally, I decided to wait and share it with her that evening.

Tania's room boasted a trundle bed that fit under hers, but it was always out; it had practically become part of the permanent décor, since I lived there more often than I did at home now. We bounced on our beds and she opened up the letter.

"Dear Melissa," she began, her eyes twinkling as she was reading ahead to figure out ways to make my father's letter full of light humor. She stopped still, frozen. Nothing moved but her eyes, rapidly scanning the letter and going wide with shock.

"What is it?" I cried, wondering if something horrible had happened to my father inside the Salem Penitentiary. He had alluded to some of the very dangerous elements in there, and how every so often some tough guy or another wanted to mess with him. "Has my dad been hurt?" I began to get up so I could sit beside her and find out the news. She held up her hand to stop me, not taking her eyes from the paper. Her hand was firm, *Go no further.* She finished the one side, and flipped to the other side. After scanning that, she looked up at me, not one trace of humor in her normally merry eyes.

"You will *never* read this letter," she said firmly.

"Aw, c'mon," I said. "It can't be that bad." I really wanted to hear those kind and loving words, and I was disappointed—actually getting a little frustrated that she wouldn't hand over the letter. It can't be any worse than the other stuff you've read me, Tania. Please let me see it."

"No." Her voice was quiet now, but had an edge of steel to it.

"Tania!" I said, now cranky. She was acting like the close sister she had become. And like a sibling, she was annoying me. Obviously she was feeling the same way because she blurted out what came next.

"Okay, Melissa, if that's what you really want, but I'm not reading it to you." She flung down the letter and angry tears filled her eyes. At first I thought I had hurt her feelings. Then I realized that the tears were actually for me, not for her.

I stared at the letter, then looked at her, and then back to the letter again.

"What does it say?" I whispered. She looked at me, and the tears spilled down her cheeks.

"He says that you are a murderer, too, and that you deserve to be locked up in a cell right next to him."

36

⚜

bitter sweet

In the spring of 1998, after more than two years, Wyoming was finally able to extradite my father for the murder of Angela Subrize. He was always in the news as he continuously caused legal and media chaos. I heard some bits and pieces here and there, mostly that my dad was taunting the authorities, that he kept changing his story, and that he was making a laughing stock of the legal system. I could tell he was enjoying it, and it made me sick. It was another way that he was toying with his prey—the only prey he had now.

Finally, some kind of deal was worked out, and he pled guilty to the murder of Angela Subrize in Wyoming. Laramie County prosecutors had to agree to not seek the death penalty against him. On June 3, 1998, District Judge Nicholas Kalokathis sentenced my father to life in prison and ordered it to run consecutive to the two life sentences in Oregon and the life sentence in Washington. He was returned to Oregon.

I didn't know what that meant, so I went again to a library to find articles about what was going on. I told a librarian I was a college student, working on a summer quarter project, and I asked her to read that part of the article so she could explain to me what all those consecutive sentences meant. She read through the whole thing quickly, her face screwed up in concentration. After a few minutes, she looked at me, and then glanced around to see if anyone was within hearing distance. Satisfied, she leaned forward to whisper to me.

"What this means is that Keith Jesperson will *never* leave prison. Whether it is in one rat hole or another, that sick bastard will die in prison, and get what he deserves." I was careful to keep my face a mask as she looked at me. "If it were me," she added, "I'd rather undergo the death penalty than to live that many years with the knowledge of what I had done."

The year of my high school graduation was the light at the end of the tunnel for me. I would soon be in charge of my own life and my own choices. Over the last two years of high school, I saw my siblings dropping out of school and I vowed to continue to the last day, graduation. I was delighted to hear that my father's family from Yakima would drive over to Spokane to watch the ceremony. To feel their support was a reward for the determination I had needed to endure each day of classes. There were moments when I wondered if I should quit and find a full time job so I could support myself in a different environment. Deep down, though, I knew that I was making a wise choice and that quitting high school would have caused more complications than enduring the difficult days.

The summer after my graduation, I found a job on the north side of town at a beauty supply house. The job became flexible with my college classes in the fall. I had decided to attend a local community college that offered general studies while I worked for my cosmetology license for Washington State. During high school, I had found that I had a talent and passion for coloring and designing my friends' dance up-do's. Over time, I thought I might want to receive a bachelor's degree, so my general studies classes were equally important to me.

Since I was mostly on my own, I found that my intuition and that my connection to God helped me in numerous situations. Seeming coincidences, which I called miracles, began to happen on a daily basis as I met certain people at the right time and the right place to further a goal, to serve someone in need, or to find joy in the moment. I also learned great lessons in the warnings that would come. For example, one night when I was out with someone I considered a true friend and mentor in the salon business, I did not heed the warning, and I lost self-respect and a friend in one night. Another time I listened, and right away, and it saved me from another horrible situation on what started to be a fine, beautiful morning.

Spokane had developed beautiful walkways from the outskirts of town, all the way into town. They were referred to as the Centennial Trails. People often walked, biked, and rollerbladed on them. Sometimes they were frequented by people with other agendas, however, one of whom I met one early morning when I was on my way to work. Still living at Mom and Robert's, I was headed downtown to an upscale department store that I had begun working at. I still didn't have a car or a license, but I loved my job, and I loved how I was feeling there.

As I hurried along the trails, a man came out of nowhere and fell into step with me. Within a few minutes, he began a conversation with me, and my warning signs went off. In the conversation, the man would make a comment, and I felt the distinct prompting to agree with him, instead of arguing. He had my father's energy, and flashbacks of the times he would get angry about money came into my mind. I remembered that by agreeing with my father, I placated him until he could settle down.

Now as this guy was talking to me, I knew he was trying to goad me into an argument so I would react. He *wanted* me to react, to fight. Agreeing with him was buying me more time.

"You're right," I said. "You are so totally right. You're great."

As we neared a bend, the guy started pushing me to the side with his shoulder. I knew right around that corner was a lot of greenery, underbrush and trees. If he was able to push me in there, I would be in trouble. I whispered a fervent prayer, all the while I was agreeing with this man, throwing him off just a little.

All of a sudden, from around the corner, appeared a new man, a stranger. Due to my prompting, I spoke.

"Brad!" I cried and latched onto the stranger going in the opposite direction as if I knew him from long ago. "Oh my goodness, how are you?"

"I'm not—" he began, but I cut him off with more deliberately bright and friendly talk, and when we were far enough away, I explained the situation and thanked him profusely for not blowing my cover and for coming along at just the right time. I knew that my prayers and intuition had paid off.

College was a wonderful experience. The feeling of some control over my life drove me out of a slight depression. The world was now mine and everything was finally within my reach. There was only one thing holding me down—I was living in my mother's home, where Robert still resided.

To really be free, I knew I had to find my own place. I brought the idea to Tania that we should look around for an apartment to rent together, and she agreed. In the fall we found a cheap place in the Historic Brown's Addition area of town. While looking at the two-bedroom apartment, Tania and I fell in love with the old charm appeal it had. The hardwood floors and fireplace were stunningly beautiful. Tania thought the built-in hutch would be perfect for her place settings since we would not have any furniture when we first moved in. We felt ready to make our own rules and manage our own lives. The freedom was thrilling.

After moving in, I enjoyed some time of freedom on my own. In my striving to be independent on a tiny budget, I got into some problems that I didn't know how to deal with. After floundering for a time, I realized that the first step was to take accountability and clean up the mess I had created with my finances and my relationships. Taking accountability became a blessing! I saw that when I did not take accountability for my life, I created chaos. When I did take accountability, then I was free from my excuses and I was empowered.

For the first time, I realized the ripple effect I had as a person. I recognized that my ripple was either positive or negative in its effect on others. Negative ripples came from not caring about others or not caring to know about others. My father wanted to avoid going to prison, so he killed, not caring what that meant for his victims, their families, or his family. My mother wanted security, financial help, and safety from the unknown, so she stayed with Robert, not caring to know how this affected her children. Sean had wanted to satisfy his sexual urges, so not caring about who he was hurting, he took what was not given to him. The self-serving desires of those I cared about had cost me a lot. In my own financial fiasco, I had been utterly self-serving. It had affected other people and my relationships. I resolved that from moment forward it was time to be something different from what I was taught.

I received an email from Gavin. Since that first summer when my father drove us to the coast, we had been making regular summer reunions. Each summer my feelings for him had grown stronger. I had believed that we would eventfully get married, especially since our time together the previous summer, when we discussed the possibility of me moving down to San Francisco with him. When Gavin graduated, he enlisted into the Air Force and was stationed at Travis AFB. Two days before I was to fly out to see him, he informed me he had a new girlfriend but that he still wanted me to come out. I was crushed. I flew out and met his girlfriend, but the ensuing drama didn't work for me, so I quickly flew home again. It was the last time I saw him.

Prior to our last summer together, I had always placed him on a pedestal, thinking there would never be anyone better for me. After a while, I realized that Gavin had been a gift to me. Summer after summer, his friendship and the prospect of seeing him gave me hope in an otherwise dark and dreary world. He had been my first love, my teenage crush. He knew me at a time when I was young and immature. Releasing him gave me permission to grow up and to grow into adulthood. Now I was free to stand on my own, without a crutch. I was also now available for someone wonderful to enter my life.

While I was in college and working at a pizza joint, I met a cook who worked there. Zach made me laugh. Eventually we became the best of friends and began dating. He treated me like a queen, and from him I learned that I could have a man in my life who treated me with kindness, gentleness, respect, and openness. He and I could talk for hours, and even after we broke up, I knew that he had laid a foundation for me—that every man I included in my life would have to walk a little taller because finally I knew what I could expect in a healthy relationship.

37

great expectations

Lying under a blanket of glorious stars, I looked up into the magnificent brilliance of the night sky and smiled a cheesy-wide smile, crooked teeth and all. Of course no one could see me, but I was happy! I still had goals I had set, and challenges to overcome, but for the first time in my life, I could look back on the past year or two and point out how many triumphs and blessings I had, rather than all the tragedies and losses I had experienced. Though I was naturally optimistic, I had found so much more than optimism or hope. I had found faith. Faith in myself, faith in other people, and faith in the One who created this amazing universe. I felt so alive, so connected to everything. It was a beautiful and empowered place to come from, and I wanted to be able to put it in a bag and take it with me. Even the hardest lessons I had learned in the last year were still lessons. I had learned so much, and now I felt that I was truly ready for a life that was powerful, passionate, more honest, more fun, and more real than I had ever experienced. Then I thought about how fun it would be to have a relationship to share in this new life I had created.

I relaxed even further into the grass and closed my eyes. I pictured in my mind someone that would be a good fit for me. Suddenly, images of a world traveler floated into my mind and then slowly out. A large map of the world unfolded, and Europe was highlighted. Then I saw him—a man with a strong, solid build and blond hair. I knew he was finishing or had already completed his college degree, that he would be an excellent provider, and that he was compassionate, loving, interesting, and had a great sense of humor. I could see our laughing silhouettes dancing in the moonlight. This man was very, very real, and I knew that he existed. I let go and trusted that he would come into my life at the perfect time. I said a prayer of gratitude and then I let it all go. The when's, where's, how's, and why's didn't matter. I decided I would let God handle it. That wonderfully familiar feeling of peace washed over me, and I sighed in the sweetness of the spring grass.

Two weeks later, I got a call from my friend Rebecca. In my last year of college, she and I had become very close. She was full of spark and joy. Rebecca came from a large Mormon family and she was one of the younger children. Her outlook was always positive, even though her family had gone through some tremendous trials with health and money. I had even felt comfortable enough around Rebecca that I had invited her to my home often, knowing she would never judge my home furnishings or lack of material things.

"So, do you wanna go to a church dance with me?" she asked. If she could have looked through the phone, she would have seen my puzzled expression.

"Umm, do Mormons dance?" I asked.

"Of course we do!" she laughed. "Just like you would at a party. The only difference is that we think we can have a great time without getting wasted." She was teasing me. I had an occasional Corona, but I was not into consciousness-altering agents. I liked to be in full control of my faculties at all times. In my opinion, it was too dangerous not to be.

I was obviously pretty ignorant in my knowledge of her beliefs and did not know what to expect. Only because I did not have other plans for the weekend, I agreed to go with Rebecca once we both finished up work.

The dance was at a church building out in a rural part of town. I was amazed how packed the building was with people my age. The DJ was playing the most popular songs of the time, which surprised me. It really *was* like a normal party I was used to, but without alcohol, which sat well with me. When I was a few years younger, I had experimented a little with the bar scene, but I didn't enjoy the dense energy or people's excuses to completely lose their boundaries. I had always felt tense and on guard. This dance was different, and I was trying to figure out exactly why. It wasn't just the alcohol.

The gym area had been decorated with balloons and streamers. Always the observer, I watched as people mingled. Most of them appeared to know each other. Suddenly out of the corner of my eye, I spotted a guy sitting toward the back of the room on the edge of the stage. I could tell he was looking at me, but whenever I would glance in his direction, he would look away.

I felt a little self-conscious, wondering if I looked out of place. *If he was attracted, wouldn't he ask me to dance?* I found myself wishing he would. He certainly was one of the hottest guys I had ever seen, and I noticed he got a lot of female attention, though he didn't seem to be welcoming it. *Bad sign. Either taken or not into female companionship,* I thought. I lost interest. Suddenly Rebecca, the gregarious social butterfly that I had come with, flitted away, and I found myself alone in the crowd.

I looked around and didn't see anyone else I knew or anyone of interest. I felt eyes again, and turned my attention back to the handsome man on the stage. This time, I caught him glancing at me before he turned away. I was actually intrigued by his lack of interaction with anyone around and I wondered if he had been brought to the dance like I had. Maybe he wasn't a Mormon, either! I decided to introduce myself, and so I walked across the gym and sat down next to the stranger on the stage.

He had very broad shoulders and the first thing I noticed when he looked at me were his beautiful blue eyes. As I looked into them, it was as if I saw his soul and a reflection of myself and the universe. For a brief moment, I felt an incredible thrill shoot through my entire body. I *knew* him. I had to look away for a moment, feeling almost shy. With his athletic build, he appeared to be a football player, and his face was even more attractive than I had realized from across the dimly lit room. We introduced ourselves, and he said his name was Sam. He announced outright that he would not be staying long since he had come with a friend.

"What stake are you from?" he asked.

I was confused and told him I didn't belong to this church and that I had come with a friend.

Over the next thirty minutes, I learned several things about Sam, including:

1. He was finishing his last classes at a local university and getting a degree in International Affairs. *Requirement one on my mental checklist: must have a degree from college—check!*

2. He had served a mission for his church in the Azores near Portugal, where he enjoyed teaching and learning about the culture of the people there. *Requirement two: digs international travel—check!*

3. He was a logical person, had lots of common sense, and was an

authentic gentleman—he didn't just act like a gentleman for show. *Require-ment three: trustworthy, gentle, and genuine—check!*

As we talked, a new thought went through my mind, followed by the images I had conjured when I was dreaming about the perfect man for me: Sam was *the one*! I was absolutely surprised at this thought, since at the time I was just over twenty years old.

Soon enough, Sam's friend came, and it was time for him to leave the dance. He seemed to be having some kind of inner battle, and then he rushed out to the car. A minute later, he came back in and asked me for my number. It was a positive sign. Soon after Sam left, Rebecca asked if I was ready to leave. I knew I had met someone special that evening and I shared my experience with Rebecca on the car ride home. Now it was up to Sam to determine if he had met someone special too. I would not seek him out; if it was meant to be, he would find me.

Two weeks passed and I didn't hear from Sam. I wondered if he had lost my phone number, or if perhaps wasn't as interested in me as I had been in him. Two nights previously, I'd had a really intense dream about him, but still no contact. That evening I was working at the cosmetics counter at a store in the mall when Sam stopped in. He attempted to act very casual, but I saw through his ruse right away.

"Hey, Melissa," he said, with a half shy but charming smile that melted my heart. "It's good to see you. I just stopped in to see if you have any sug-gestions on what I could buy as a gift for my mother."

"Sam, this is Victoria's Secret!" I said, giving him a look that said, *I see right through you!* "No guy comes in here looking for a gift for his mom!" He laughed, but undaunted, continued with his plan. Before actually leaving with some perfume for his mother, he asked if I would go on a date with him and arranged a time and place to meet. I did my best to act casual, but I was thrilled.

Our first date was nothing like we planned because I had forgotten that I had agreed to watch my friend's young son for the evening. Instead of choosing to cancel the date, I asked Sam if he wanted to come along with me. Within a short time, we both recognized that there was a powerful connection between us. The evening ended up being absolutely perfect. As Sam and I played together with my friend's son, I had the opportunity to discover the depth of this amazing man—the humor, love, and light that I had never encountered in anyone before.

By the time the evening was over, there was no mistaking the intense attraction between us. However, because of past relationships, we agreed to let our friendship develop slowly. We spent hours and hours in conversation, and I learned so much about him. He outdid any other guy I'd ever known, but I was wary and suspicious. Too many times before I had allowed myself to get hurt emotionally, so during our dates I would investigate Sam, quietly putting him under scrutiny. I'm sure sometimes it had to be uncomfortable for him. Here he was, attempting to get to know me better, and I was checking to see if I had overlooked a critical flaw in him.

I became frustrated when I didn't find something that would startle me and be a deal breaker. I started to wonder if I had lost my talent for finding flaws. The more I learned about Sam, the more I thought he was the perfect match for me.

Because I couldn't find any serious character defects, I had no excuses for keeping things shallow and superficial. In the past, that had been my comfort zone. But with Sam, I felt so deeply for him that I began to expose my most vulnerable self to him. The only person I had really done that with was Tania, but being male, Sam was clearly a much bigger challenge for me. I completely trusted Sam, something I had not done since Sean. When I looked into his eyes, I knew that he would never abuse me, that he would not betray that trust. I lowered my walls of defense for him, and therefore I felt a stronger, deeper, truer emotion of love than I had ever felt before. I shared things with him about my dad, and about many of the things in my past that had wounded or frightened me. I also told him about how my past had made me a much better, stronger, more compassionate woman. It scared the heck out of me, but this relationship with Sam was the closest thing to heaven I had ever experienced with another human being.

I was on a date with Sam when we entered one of my favorite stores: Barnes & Noble. We were headed to pick something specific up when all of a sudden, I froze and began sobbing. I really scared Sam because I was not one to show emotion. He knew me as a very strong girl, not prone to drama. There in front of me, in a huge endcap was the book my father, the serial murderer, had crafted with a famous author. From the rumors I'd heard and what I saw in front of me, this book described in graphic detail the murders he had committed. I couldn't look at it, let alone pick it up. Sam went to grab one to see if my name was printed in it anywhere and I got angry. I demanded that he put it down and I stalked out of the store. I made Sam promise me he would never read it, and he agreed. I didn't talk about the book again. I knew the Jesperson side of the family was in an uproar about it, but I didn't want anything to do with it.

Around this time, Sam and I were spending more and more time together, and we both knew things had begun to shift into something more serious.

After three months of blissful summer dating, the driven man who hadn't planned to marry for several years got down on one knee in front of me before a pond at Manito Park.

"Melissa, I don't want to go another day without knowing we'll be together always. Will you marry me?"

This was a critical choice, for him and for me. I didn't answer right away, and it made him nervous. Sam was asking me if I would trust him enough to plan my whole life with him. He was asking if I would bear his future children and if I would trust him with my well-being and financial care. Sam was so responsible with all of his obligations, and I knew that he would never change his character—it was built into him.

Let go and trust.

I let go and I trusted—deeper, farther, wider than I ever had before.

"Yes, Sam, I would love to marry you!"

That evening we shared the wonderful news with our families and some friends. We would be starting our own life together. There was just one catch: Sam was Mormon. I had been told that they were not Christians. *Was religion that big of a deal in a marriage?* Sam's family wondered the same thing, but from the opposite perspective. I trusted that the issue would work out over time.

We kept our engagement and were married that fall. In a little white wedding chapel with only his sister as the witness, I married my best friend. In March, we had a large ceremony for all of our family and friends at the Bozarth Mansion, and it was beautiful to see my family come from both the Jesperson side and the Zerbos side. Besides all of the joy and celebration there was a lot of healing that took place that day. I got to have my happily ever after, too.

38

❦

the awakening

Our first home together as a newly married couple was a townhouse in the South Hill neighborhood of Spokane. Sam had heard from a friend in his geography class that there was a place for rent. It was only $400 per month, including utilities. We were expecting our first child and needed an affordable place right away. Sam thought this would be the perfect fit for our new little family.

When I first saw the rundown townhouse, I was disappointed in the orange walls and rough wood floors. Underneath the chipped paint and flooring, however, was a charming old world look that could be brought out with some paint and sanding. I asked the landlady for permission to paint the walls and she agreed. Sam and I signed the lease and moved in right away.

The neighborhood was fantastic. We were surrounded by colorful, historic craftsman and Victorian homes. A few blocks away was Manito Park where Sam had proposed to me. The whole feel of the South Hill was casual yet sophisticated. I wanted our home to match the feel of our neighborhood, so we started working on it right away. Sam stained the hardwood floors and transformed the orange walls to a warm and elegant beige.

Our home felt welcoming, even without much furniture. Everything we had was from Sam's bachelor days. This included an old southwestern-style couch and a black leather recliner. Sam's grandmother had given us her old box television, and his mother donated to us her old green craft table for our dining room. There was a small room that fit our new baby's crib perfectly, along with a small dresser. Both were gifts from Linda,

Sam's mother. We were anxious to welcome our new little girl, Aspen, into our lives.

While Sam was finishing his class load for graduation, he worked part time in the evenings unloading trucks for UPS. Every evening he would leave around 10 PM and come home around three thirty in the morning. With Sam gone at night, I felt uneasy and slightly paranoid about my safety. Ever since the night Robert had kicked down our steel front door, I was fearful of an occurrence like that happening again with a stranger. Every sound in the night would wake me up. I didn't realize I had post-traumatic stress disorder.

The months flew by as Sam finished college and graduated with his degree in international affairs. Before long we welcomed little Aspen into our arms. She was beautiful with her tiny fingers and toes. Sam took some time off to be home with me and our new infant. I was able to stay home with Aspen and I loved watching her take her first bath, then later her first steps. Life was changing every day for our little family, and I enjoyed every moment of it.

Several months after the birth of our baby girl, I became increasingly aware of the vast differences in my religion and my husband's. Sam had converted to The Church of Jesus Christ of Latter-day Saints at the age of four when his parents were baptized in 1979. Two missionaries had appeared at their door in Alaska, and his parents had felt prompted to investigate the Church.

My pride was now preventing me from seeing the faith of Sam's family from a new perspective. All I could see was the pain of their disapproval for our new marriage. I had little to no understanding about what my husband's family felt he was risking by marrying me. I had just begun to see what a treasure of a man I had married. Sam was cultured and well-trained from his Portugal Mission. Without any knowledge of the faith of my husband's family, I had taken their disapproval of our marriage quite personally. I had felt rejected for something I could not understand, and the pain of that rejection caused me to put up a defensive wall against his family. All of their requests to help me investigate the Church were ignored due to my frustration and hurt.

My mother-in-law, Linda, had put pressure on us to have our newborn baby blessed in the Mormon faith. I quickly rejected her idea, in fear that it was like the Catholic way of claiming the baby as a member of that faith. This was very hard on Sam's family, and there were a lot of tears and strife. I had been brought up in Catholicism, but as an adult, I felt locked in an epic struggle for truth. My childhood religion had appeared too complex and too formal, and all of the other churches I had attended in later years seemed to preach vastly different beliefs. The more I investigated other churches, the more confused I felt.

When my daughter was almost a year old, we were out for our morning walk to Manito Park. We passed two missionaries who appeared friendly and greeted us cheerfully. It occurred to me that I had been very prideful and had not given the Mormon church a chance. My heart knew that it was only right to at least learn as much about my husband's religion as I had other religions. When Sam got home from work, I told him about my conversation with the missionaries and was surprised to find that he was not as happy as I thought he would be. Sam had always been a strong member of his church until a few years before he met me when he had a disagreement with a local church leader and another member. Sam was actually shocked to learn that I wanted to know more about his church. He let me know that if I was serious, I would have to let go of my occasional Corona and morning cup of java.

He also told me flat-out that he was not ready to go back. He did agree, however, to sit in on what the missionaries called "discussions," or lessons, and he would often join in animatedly. I realized that this wonderful man of mine had a very strong spiritual side. I also realized he had never lost the testimony of his faith.

While admirable, Sam's faith wasn't enough for me to make any major decisions, especially because I was having a hard time with some of the principles. After several lessons, I was about to give up the idea of having any more discussions. The missionaries invited Sam and me to study some scriptures and then to pray. I honestly had not prayed much since I had met Sam. Our life had seemed so stable that I didn't really think I needed to pray.

Now that I had something important to pray about, I was fearful that God would not answer my prayer. There was still a frightened little girl inside of me who was afraid of being abandoned again, afraid of feeling like God didn't know that I existed or that he would judge me as unworthy of His love or His answers.

Humbly, I remembered that little girl who had pleaded with God to be with me when my father was jailed for murder. Looking back, I saw that each of my prayers were answered in some form or another. As an older child, I had pictured God with my own father's characteristics, which obviously led to a twisted spiritual mentality. I was relearning about God, and the peace and unconditional love that I remembered floated through me and caused sweet tears to escape my eyes. Never before in my life had I cried in joy. Those joyful tears spread when I was baptized into the Mormon church. I felt my body being cleansed from all of the horrible situations I had faced at such a young age. I was clean and felt reborn—brand new. My joy was only added to when I found out that my best girlfriend Tania had also been baptized. She had moved out of state with her husband, Mark. Unbeknownst to each other, we had been baptized on the same day. I knew there were no accidents, and I thought how beautiful it was that Tania and I could now share this important part of our lives together too.

At this point, I believed that my transformation was complete. However, the One who had guided me and protected me so often seemed to have additional plans for me.

39

the shattering

There was always a dark and lonely place in my heart from my past traumatic experiences. I had come to terms with the fact that I would always have to carry the heavy burdens of shame, guilt, and insecurity. Even though the people around me were not free from such emotions, somehow I felt inferior because of my great secret—my father's identity. I felt that if the people I associated with really knew my past, they would deny me their support, their care, and their love.

Since joining this new church, it was becoming more difficult to maintain my friendships without giving any detailed information about my parents or childhood. I only let them see me as the good friend, the volunteer who helped with the children's classes at church, and now—with the birth of our son, Jake—the loving mother of two children. No one knew I was the daughter of a serial killer.

In the early spring of 2008, Aspen was in first grade. One day she came bouncing up the driveway from school and gave me a huge hug. Since I was running a day care in my home, I was watching the children play. Aspen chatted about the things they had talked about in school that day. Then she moved to stand directly in front of me so my focus would be on her.

"Mommy, where is your daddy?" my seven-year old daughter asked me, her eyes full of open curiosity. "Everybody has a daddy. You have to have a daddy, too, don't you?"

The question caught me off guard, and I was not prepared to deal with it. I was not expecting my seven-year-old to be curious about extended family members, especially ones she never saw.

"He's in Salem, Oregon," I said quickly. Then I waited to see if she would ask another question or drop the subject. To my relief, she was satisfied with the answer and ran off to play. Her question struck a deep pain inside me, and I realized that one day it would be necessary for my children to know the truth about their grandfather. How would I tell them? I knew that his actions would be a blemish on our family tree forever.

And when it was time for them to ask those questions, what if they wanted to have a relationship with their grandfather? Was it healthy? Should I allow it? Should I oppose it? What if my father pursued it himself? I didn't know the answers. I had never been to therapy for any of the experiences I survived as a child, and I was unsure about my own relationship with my father.

I realized that I was going to need to know sooner rather than later, so I started to do some research, becoming determined to find whatever resources were out there: programs, support groups, self-help books. In the past I had acquired a talent for seeking out materials on subjects that I knew little about. The more I learned, the more empowered I felt.

This time, however, when I searched for materials on this subject, there were none to be found! While there were plenty of resources for victims of crime, there didn't appear to be any kind of resource for those whose loved ones had committed heinous crimes. I would have to figure this one out myself.

There was no way I would allow my lack of knowledge to impact my children. I was afraid that if I did not handle this issue correctly it could actually harm my children in the long run. Based on personal experience, I knew what kind of effects inappropriate information could have on a child. My father consistently talked about subjects that most adults would blush at. In some ways, my innocence was stolen. I did not want to have that happen to my children. I also refused to leave them in the dark. That had been another problem with how I was raised: there were many times when no one spoke at all.

After looking for a week, I decided to write in to the Dr. Phil show. I had come to respect Dr. Phil's opinion, and he seemed to line up with me as far as my beliefs on common sense. We also both had strong opinions on the well-being of children. I realized that if I was way off-base on this one, the man to set me straight would be Dr. Phil.

I organized a query and sent it off, not knowing as I did so that my life was about to change forever.

I received an answer the next day, asking for more information. I wrote about how I was concerned for the mental and emotional health of my children, and how I did not want a relationship with my father, a serial killer, to impact their lives in a negative way.

Over the next few weeks, I was asked specific details of my life, and then came the request to make video dairies of my questions for Dr. Phil. While I was responding to the assignments, I began to be fearful of exposing the truth about my father's identity to the public. Everyone in my surrounding community—schools, church, neighborhood, and so forth —only knew about me: my choices and my faith. They made judgments based on my lifestyle, not knowing about my father. I did not want that to change. It was a huge secret, one that I had told only to my most intimate friends and family. It was hardly spoken of, and I often felt ashamed of my father. Ever since I was a teen, I had worried that people would judge me based on *his* actions, rather than mine, perhaps before they even got to know me. I was ashamed to have anything to do with him.

Before I knew it, the Dr. Phil Show had invited me to come out to film a Get Real Retreat with thirteen other participants from varied walks of life who had their own issues and circumstances to work through. We would enter an intensive retreat environment at the Dr. Phil House to come to grips with our deepest fears and our sickest secrets, and to assist each other in bringing them to light. I was excited because I knew I would also be learning some useful tools for my relationships to take home.

Agreeing to participate in this experience was one of the scariest things I had ever done, and part of my fear was because this would mean revealing family dynamics on public television. For a family that didn't say a word to each other on the day my father was jailed for murder (and who then expected everyone to get up and go to school the next day, like normal), this was a huge risk. I wasn't sure how many of my family and friends would stick by me once this was out in the open. My mother, though she signed the release papers, was petrified. My brother and sister were completely supportive, but wary of the media. They didn't want me to get hurt. My loving husband was prepared to go the distance with me, whatever that took.

As I prepared to catch a flight to the Dr. Phil Studios on Father's Day weekend, 2008, I knew the Get Real Retreat would require intensive homework, taking risks, being conscious, and stepping up for myself and for the other participants. It was fun traveling to LA, but I already felt lonely. I was used to having children with me 24/7 and a husband that liked hanging out with me.

When we met the other participants, it was interesting to see the plethora of backgrounds and issues they had selected to showcase: alcoholism, rape, domestic violence, racism, serial killing, suicide, lack of intimacy, too much intimacy, and so much more.

When Dr. Phil learned about my background, he told me that I got a "shitty deal." He helped me realize that I had been taking on the blame, shame, and guilt that my father should have taken as his own. Dr. Phil told me it was necessary for me to separate my father's crimes from my life, and that there was nothing that I should feel ashamed about. It sounds very simple, but his words went very deep. Fears, remorse, shame, guilt—I had been carrying all of those things around since I was a child and I didn't even know that I had the choice to be rid of it! I came away from the show feeling confident in my own choices and aware of the separation between my father and me. He could not control me any longer. As for my mother, she had made some poor choices that had ended up hurting me and my siblings, but now she and I could work on our relationship. Because of the show, I was also able to see her very loving side. Before I kept silent, never expressing how I felt, for fear she would reject me.

Dr. Phil's Get Real Retreat opened an awareness that allowed me to shatter the silence, break open the secrets, and find sanity.

40

aftermath

For weeks and even months after the Dr. Phil Get Real Retreat, I felt like I was in a time warp. It seemed to me that time had stopped long enough for me to really taste life for the first time, like a veil of fog had been lifted from me. I was centered on the moment and felt very conscious and alive. It felt almost strange that everyone else's lives around me just continued as they had before when there was suddenly so much color, emotion, and vitality all around me. It was as if I had woken from a black and white dream. I wanted others to share it with me, to experience what I had—this reawakening to the richness of life.

There was also the other end of the spectrum—the thoughts, feelings, and emotions I had covered up for years that now made their debut with great force at certain times. Once I allowed myself to venture out from the safety of the emotional numbness I had used for survival, I got to taste both the ups and downs of daily life and memories. There were full days and weeks that I spent immersed in intense joy and gratitude. Then, there were other days that the fixed beliefs I had carried about myself and others for so long stared me right in the face. Sometimes they were so ugly, I didn't want to stare back.

More than ever, though, I began to find the fortitude to work through it. It was like I had emerged from my travels down the rabbit hole and I would never see life the same way again. Hitting some of those highs meant I had to hit some of the lows too and, layer by layer, more and more issues were brought into the light.

In the process of writing this book, my coauthor and I made a trip to the Yakima area, where I had grown up before my parents divorced. While there, I was flooded with childhood thoughts and feelings. When I had experienced them for the first time, they had been so nightmarish that I never thought I would survive to face them again. Letting myself feel them and work through them as an adult in a safe environment allowed me to look at them more objectively and with a higher perspective. I came to see why I had developed certain behaviors and beliefs about myself and the world around me.

A major example of this was a belief that had affected my everyday life since I was a freshman in high school. I had believed that people would always judge me for my father's actions and that they would automatically assume that I was a cruel person just because I was The Happy Face Killer's child. I was terrified of people finding out who my father was, since I believed they would never get to know me for who I really was, inside. I finally came to grips with the fact that people only know what they've been told. We are all a product of our belief systems, our upbringings, and our socialization. Sometimes we are gifted with the absolute miracle of a life- and perception-changing experience. For me, one of these experiences was attending my therapeutic retreat and all that followed, but I believe we are all gifted with those experiences a few times in our lives—if we choose to have them.

I watched my new friends from the Dr. Phil retreat experience the same kind of belief-shattering moments, and I saw what a miracle it could be. Whether they were or not, I believe that neither of my parents felt wrapped in the arms of love. Their childhoods and their choices in adult- hood have shown me that neither of them believed they were worthy of truly loving relationships. I do not believe it was their intention to live a life of love-scarcity, but it was the natural course of things because of the choices they made based on their beliefs. I became aware that my father had a lot of influence in my development and my thought patterns.

Now that I am older and wiser, I have the right—and duty to myself— to question where I get a belief, in case it came from an unreliable source. What a relief to give myself permission to do that. I am learning, little by little, to trust more in that spirit that assisted me in making choices when I was a child, into my teens, and now in adulthood. The more I trust my feelings, intuition, and the promptings that spirit gives me, the better my choices are and the more those choices are founded in beliefs of love.

Because of my father's callous comments, one belief I've worked to shed was my perception of my body as an object. For me, this belief affected the way I treated my body, particularly regarding food. Like many women, I have struggled with body-perception issues. It is so easy to do this in our culture of hype, air-brushed models, and the plethora of diet pills and magazines we see every day on television and in the grocery store checkout lanes. In addition to that, I had learned that I was seeking comfort from food and not people. Where people had turned away from me in times of great stress and trauma, food always provided comfort in stressful moments. However, this created a vicious cycle for me that didn't work. It took me quite a bit of time to see the correlation between stress and my behaviors of survival.

Before, I didn't want to acknowledge that I was binging and I certainly did not know why I binged in stressful moments. I did not see a relationship between how I treated food and my emotions. As I began to face the fears I had lived with for years, I realized I had made a friend and an enemy of food. I had attached energy and emotions to it and had created an unhealthy relationship. Sorting out my past issues, experiences, and behaviors had helped me to overcome this belief and these behaviors. I now find so much more joy in people than I do in food. By being able to relinquish my fear of their love and acceptance—by simply loving them no matter what—I have come to truly cherish and enjoy people. I may not always agree with what they say or do, but I love them for who they are. Family, church, and work get-togethers are filled with people now, and the food is just icing on what the true, delicious cake really is. I never realized how starved I was for one of the most vital parts of life: human connection. Now I feast on it, and the lessons and sharing that come with it. As I do, I become more and more content. What a wonderful way to live!

Perhaps one of the hardest false beliefs I faced was my previous—and erroneous—thought that I had a father who was capable of remorse and who would never harm me. This belief was shattered when my Grandpa Roy confided to me that at one point my dad admitted to seriously considering murdering all of his children and then committing suicide so that we wouldn't have to face the inevitable anger, shame, and humiliation that would come.

This disclosure rocked me to the core, the realization of it affecting me for weeks. When I could begin to get past the shock and fear of it, however, light began to dawn on the many times that I had been protected from my father's psychotic thoughts. I couldn't help but remember the day at breakfast when I now realize he was thinking of telling me everything and would have had to kill me if he had second thoughts about turning himself in. After I read his book, I realized that my father straddled that line for years and that he ended up killing any woman he told about his past.

Sometimes I don't know why I am alive, and that is a thought that used to slowly drive me crazy. My compassion for my father's victims, and also for the families who had lost them, tortured me. I started having more dreams about them and sometimes woke up wishing it was me instead of them. I finally had to realize that I was claiming responsibility for my father's actions *again*. I wanted to live, and so did those women. He spared me my life, perhaps by a hair, and while I am forever grateful, I am forever haunted as well. I don't have to let it get to me, but I do get to make my own contribution to the world. I can never make up for my father's monstrous actions. Ever. And finally, I realize it is not my responsibility to do so. Still I know very clearly that because of what I have been through, it is my passion and my purpose to inspire, motivate, and above all, protect women and children whenever I am able.

I reveled in this new *knowing*. While I had absolutely no control over how my parents treated me and how they felt about me, I suddenly realized that I could control one very important thing—how *I* responded or reacted. I was in charge of how I let them affect me. I could create the love I was seeking for myself, and with God's help, it was all right within me. I felt reborn.

41

❦

enlightenment

Some time later, Sam and I settled in for our talk together at the end of the day. The kids were asleep, and a peaceful air had descended on the house. My husband reminded me that a letter had arrived for me earlier in the day from my father. I had set it aside, as I often did, allowing Sam to read it to me first to see if there was anything of merit or value in it. Sometimes there was; many times there was not, only the angry tantrums of a frustrated man who was no longer in control of his life or that of others.

I sighed, the peaceful feeling already broken.

"Go ahead," I said, not bothering to appear nonchalant. Sam knows me so well I don't try to hide feelings from him any longer. Not that it ever worked, anyway.

He made his way across the room and snatched the letter from the mantel. He opened it, scanning it carefully. I could tell some of the material must have been disturbing. He kept reading further, and turning the pages back and forth, as if searching for something. Then I realized he was searching for a way to tell me what was in the letter without being hurtful. Apparently, there was no way to do that.

"Essentially he's saying that if he gets the death penalty, it will be all your fault," Sam said grimly. I started to laugh. It was ludicrous, and it was liberating to see how absolutely ludicrous it really was!

"He says that because he read your article in the *Seattle Times* and you called him 'sick' and don't want anything more to do with him, then that's that. He won't write you anymore. He said to hell with everything. He's given all the details to his writer on one of the murders, and that particular

217

information may incriminate him so deeply, he'll likely get the chair . . . or whatever it is, wherever that particular state's penalties are."

I thought about my father's words and insinuations, and I got it, I finally got it. I did not invite any street women, transients, girlfriends, or others into my space and strangle them. I did not write letters admitting my guilt and then send them to newspapers to torture victim's families. I did not revel in anyone else's sufferings. *I was NOT my dad.* A part of him was in me, but I had created a different life than his. And while I had certainly made mistakes and had my own regrets, I finally realized some important things.

He showed me one side, but because of who I am, I made another choice. He played in darkness. I chose to surround myself in and grow in love and light. He chose to take away the rights of others, and wanted to use guilt and manipulation to get me and anyone who would listen to him to do what he wanted them to do. I choose to honor myself and honor others. I thought about the word I had learned in yoga class: *Namaste.* It had the most powerful, beautiful meaning I had ever heard: "The divine in me celebrates and honors the divine in you." This includes honoring the things within my father that he himself cannot recognize.

I thought about the 1.5 million people currently in our prisons. Every one of them is a father or a mother, a brother or a sister, a son or a daughter of someone else. I know that what my father did is more heinous than what many have done, but nonetheless, family members can suffer greatly when someone they love goes to prison. How many of them secretly carry the shame and guilt of what their loved one has done? How many of those family members feel helpless and hopeless? How many feel guilty because they truly love that person, but not what that person has done? How many dare not shine because of what their loved one has done?

I tried to get a handle on the sheer number of people that must be affected by this same problem. I knew my father's cruelty had personally affected several people in his family. I could name at least fifty people directly affected by my father's actions, and many more who had been affected indirectly. I began to calculate the number of people nationwide that must be affected by loved ones in prison. It was staggering to me the amount of shame and grief that must be out there. This is why I have chosen not to be silent. I want to bring an awareness of the plight of many people who, like me, do not know what to do when a person they love dearly chooses any hurtful behavior, whether immoral, unethical, or in my case, deadly.

In Dad's last letter, he wrote:

> When asked: Are you the daughter of Keith Jesperson, the killer? Tell them you are Melissa Moore. Not the daughter of a killer. Just a woman that minds her own business. Or simply "NO!" and walk away. My best advice.

(This from the man who said if he was executed it would be my fault.)

What I have learned is that I am not here to please everyone, which is an impossible task anyway. I choose to share my intensely personal experiences to bring a greater understanding that we can overcome abuse and live rich and joyful lives. There was a time when I was convinced that there was no solution for the profound suffering I had gone through. I had the remarkable opportunity to learn otherwise, and now I want to dispel the myth that our past mistreatment, abuse, or trauma has to remain and predetermine our future happiness. I am here to let my light shine for the countless who have not seen a light in the secret, innermost darkness within themselves. There are some lines by Marianne Williamson, often quoted because they ring with such truth.

> Our deepest fear is not that we are inadequate. Our deepest fear is that we are powerful beyond measure. It is our light, not our darkness that most frightens us. We ask ourselves, "Who am I to be brilliant, gorgeous, talented, fabulous?" Actually, who are you not to be? You are a child of God. Your playing small does not serve the world. There is nothing enlightened about shrinking so that others won't feel insecure around you. We are all meant to shine, as children do. We were born to make manifest the glory of God that is within us. It's not just in some of us, it's in everyone. And as we let our own light shine, we unconsciously give other people permission to do the same. As we our liberated from our own fear, our presence automatically liberates others.

History has always been written by the victors. Victors were the ones who destroyed the enemy and had the power and resources to write the history books. That time is changing as humans become more compassionate and refuse to be ignorant. Look at how our society has now recognized the Holocaust, Darfur, Serbia, and so many other horrendous situations. In order to keep atrocities from happening, we *must* learn from them. It begins with someone having enough courage to shatter the silence and provide education into the darkest side of man—the side that we are all capable of. Once we acknowledge it and refuse to sweep it under the carpet again, then we have eyes to see it in the light of day. This is humanity's massive step toward change, and we must all contribute to the forward movement of that journey. That is when humanity will not be able to claim itself as a victor, but as absolutely victorious over its worst enemy—the darkness within itself.

While my father was a conqueror in the old regime of "might makes right," I am rewriting history. It may not be the history of the world, yet I go forth, conquering in a very different realm than "survival of the fittest." That era is ending, and I believe that the more we open to it, the faster a new era will come. Healing, temperance, tolerance, charity, love, and joy: these are the trophies of a new world.

Like many others, I grew up in the belief that we are to be forgiving of other's trespasses. I used to assume that I must accept family members' behaviors, regardless of their violating act. Now I know that forgiving and forgetting are not the same thing. We can forgive by moving forward with our lives, but we don't have to continue to live with abusive actions.

To my father, playing the good little girl means to mind my own business. I have grown up, and I am minding my own business. To do that now means to take care of myself, to take precious care of the loved ones God has given me to watch over and protect. Continuing in shame, secrecy and victim hood would not serve my children, nor be the example I deserve to set. Therefore, I am the mother who has shattered her own silence, and I a victim no longer. I live in the light. I am victorious.

epilogue

❦

blossoming branches

Every story, even a true one, has an ending. Fictional stories have concrete endings, but the funny thing about non-fiction accounts is that life goes on and the journey continues. I have realized that my life is like a living, growing, expanding tree—every leaf and branch has played an integral part in who I have become, even the bare ones. Ever since my awakening, I have healed many old wounds. I have learned that it is not selfish to prune the areas of my life that are unhealthy and not working. When I focus on the abundance of new green growth in my life and the beautiful blossoms of miracles that happen all the time, I find power and tangible joy that I never realized I was worthy of experiencing. I have so much to be grateful for.

My sister, Carrie, finished school and went on to work in a satisfying career. She has a beautiful family of her own, and we have grown closer in the last few years. Our relationship is precious to me. My brother Jason has also become successful and is married to a wonderful woman who supports him in his career. I am so proud of both of them.

My mother is still with Robert. She has recently gone back to school and is getting ready to graduate. I am delighted by the many new decisions she is making in her life.

After reading an early manuscript for this book, my husband wanted to know what had happened to Sean. He wondered if people like that ever really change. A few days later we discovered that just a few months before our inquiry, Sean was arrested and that he has served time in jail for domestic violence. When we learned this, I was so grateful that I learned my lesson young and that I have since chosen to get out of any relationships that were abusive or unhealthy.

The most abundant, flowering growth I have discovered has been in the nurturing of my own sweet family. Despite the emotional turmoil that took place in finding the courage to speak out, my relationship with Sam has only deepened; the love and respect I have for him has grown every day. Enjoying my children and being absolutely present for them at a core level is beautifully satisfying.

Not only is my tree rich, full, and alive, it is laden with delicious fruit. For the first time, I feel equipped to assist others who are struggling with the kinds of issues I faced. Now that I am on the other side of the horror and tragedy, I have sweet fruits of wisdom that I would like to share with anyone who may be struggling, no matter how big or small the problems you face.

1. Listen to your intuition. Some people may call this your inner *knowing*, your spirit. Whatever you call it, begin to trust that still, small voice inside of you.

2. Shatter the silence. Refuse to hold in secrets any longer. You really *are* only as sick as your secrets. I'm not saying that you need to bare your soul on national television. I did, but that was because I couldn't find any other resources that dealt with my specific situation. I felt there was nowhere else to turn.

To begin, I would suggest opening your heart to a close and trusted friend. Go and see a therapist if that suits you or enroll in a core-level accountability training program to rid yourself of past issues and bring in new energy to your life. Join a support group, or, better yet, start one yourself. You will be amazed by what happens when you make a clear decision to heal. Make that choice, and all kinds of resources will suddenly be at your disposal.

3. Be the chain breaker. Refuse to carry on the shame of those close to you. You are not responsible for other people's actions, particularly their hurtful behavior. Teach yourself and your children the healthy habits of physical, emotional, and mental boundaries. Refuse to carry on acts of violence or shame from past generations. It doesn't matter what you've done in the past. Ask for forgiveness and start fresh today.

4. Take accountability. You are not responsible for other people's actions, but you are always, always responsible for your own. Have integrity. Care enough for yourself to surround yourself with good people and to hang out in places where great things are happening. If you choose to put yourself in questionable situations, you can expect questionable—and perhaps even dangerous—outcomes. If you choose to associate with positive people doing positive things, you are more likely to be happier with your relationships and your life overall.

5. Make healthy choices in handling stress. You owe it to yourself to stay away from addictions. Drugs, alcohol, food, sex, gambling, shopping excessively, or any other potentially addictive substance or activity will not make the pain go away, it will eventually only increase it. The longer you seek to escape from your problems, the more deeply they will plague you. Instead resolve to keep your body, mind, and spirit healthy. Exercise often and eat a nutritious diet. Involve yourself in listening to nature or attending church. Living a healthy lifestyle is the perfect way to get grounded and centered, and it increases your ability listen to your own intuition.

6. Keep a journal. I suggest four powerful ways of journaling: to remember what you are grateful for; to release hurt, fear, and painful circumstances; to see your challenges clearly and outline as many solutions as you can think which will help you realize you are not stuck; and finally, to outline specifically what it is you want out of life. Writing has helped me heal immensely, and I believe it is a powerful catalyst for change.

7. Find your passion. I cannot stress this enough! Everyone has unique gifts and talents, even you. No matter what your past life has been, or how poor your circumstances have been to this point, you are have a unique spark of life and there are things that only you can do. What excites you? What makes you happy to jump out of bed in the morning? What makes you want to embrace your day? If you don't know, it's time to find out.

8. Be of service. We are all here on earth with the same mission—to do our best with what we are given. But we cannot succeed in becoming our greatest selves unless we help others to do the same. It is not enough to push through obstacles. We are all here to be teachers as well. Once we master a new challenge, we then have the tools to teach another how to overcome a similar challenge. Service to others dispels sadness, loneliness, pain, and discontentment. From personal experience, I know it is impossible to feel the problems of your own day when you are lifting a burden for someone else.

9. Seek knowledge. I have learned that knowledge gives you the power to make better choices. And better choices ultimately allow you to create your destiny. There is so much information freely available to us that can empower us to create a better world.

10. Begin anew. No matter where you've been, no matter how dark your past, you can step in a new direction the moment that you *choose* to. Healing is a journey, that is for certain, but it starts with a choice. The moment you choose it, your past can be your past—it no longer has to haunt your future. Whoever you are, whatever road you've been down, all you have to do is *decide* to make a change, and you will find it easier to see a new path. Follow up your decision with action and keep moving toward the life of your dreams.

In a way, we are all artists in a sense working on our greatest masterpiece—our own lives. Each choice you make is a brushstroke that paints a grander picture of your legacy. Don't keep waiting for your life to start. It's right here, right now. When you believe in yourself, you can become more than you ever thought you could be.

about the authors

Melissa G. Moore is the daughter of Keith Jesperson, a man infamously known as the Happy Face serial killer. Melissa's intuition and courage forged a drive within her to create a new way of life—one rich with contribution and full of meaning. As an author and international speaker, she shares a dynamic message of the unlimited power of choice. Melissa is a strong advocate for protecting victims of violence and keeping children safe. Her passions involve raising a healthy, beautiful family and developing resources for the emotional, physical, and spiritual needs of other children and families.

Photo: Andrew McAlpin

M. Bridget Cook is an author, speaker, and life coach who has been writing stories of transformation since she was young. Always curious about and awed by the extremes of human behavior, she co-authored *Skinhead Confessions: From Hate to Hope* with former high-ranking gang leader TJ Leyden. She loves to inspire and be inspired by people from all walks of life—from youth to leaders of successful organizations. The delighted mother of three creative children, her other greatest passion lies in discovering and sharing the dynamic possibilities of each human soul.

acknowledgments

There are many individuals that became a living moral compass to me through my journey and to whom I owe many thanks and gratitude. Each one of these people has chiseled into my character a new personal trait and an increased drive toward integrity.

First to my mother, who has shown me to think outside of myself to find happiness and purpose. To my sister Carrie—you taught me to laugh through pain and to look for the comedy in tragedy. And to my brother Jason, who has demonstrated through his actions how to face fear head-on and defend the defenseless.

To Grandpa, and all my aunts and uncles on the Jesperson side, thank you for giving me shelter and a sense of belonging to something bigger than myself—a caring family. While our past has not been ideal, or of our choosing, I take great comfort that we have made it through together. To my aunts especially, you have shown me that I can be a self-reliant and strong person that deserves a better lifestyle—free from abuse. Thank you for your empowering example.

To my new family, the Moores, thank you for accepting me into your hearts and raising a fine and intelligent son whom I get to claim as my husband. Much gratitude to Dan and Linda for being wonderful in-laws and grandparents to our children. To Lori and Dusty for being such a shining example of service.

To my husband, Samuel, and my children, I am so grateful to you for being my inspiration to create a new way of living, one that will transform the future of our family tree. I will strive to be an example in your lives and hopefully show you how to stand up for your beliefs and personal rights.

To M. Bridget Cook whose dedication to learning about my past and helping me to get everything down on paper will never be forgotten. Thank you for being a source of comfort as I explored painful memories. Our friendship has impacted me greatly, and I admire your caring manner and talent. I cannot imagine how many late nights you suffered. Your skill has enhanced and shaped this book in a way I never could have anticipated. I also cannot forget TJ Leyden whose inspiring story, *Skinhead Confessions*, led me to Bridget. Thank you for your courage to change and to show others what light can come from darkness when we choose it. Thank you also to Bridget's family for sacrificing hours, weekends, and family time for this cause.

To Shari, Racheal, and Tania M. you will always be as family to me. Tania, you are such a dear friend and you will always be. I believe that Heavenly Father sent you to be my companion as I trudged through horrific ordeals. Thank you for growing up with me.

To Cedar Fort, Inc.: Lyle Mortimer, Liz Carlston, Heidi Doxey, Heather Holm, and Nicole Williams for believing in my story before it was even fully heard. Your dedication will surely change the hearts of so many young women, children, and families suffering silently from abuse and violence. Thank you for having the courage to voice the unpleasant realities of abuse.

To "Sterling and Amanda," your love for each other mapped out a higher expectation for my own marriage. Thank you "Amanda" for making me feel beautiful. Many thanks to Grandma "Frances" for opening her home to us when we were in need. To my younger brothers, your talents and personalities will help you open up a bright future. I look forward to seeing you create your own destiny.

A special thanks to all of the shelters that housed my family after an attack. Because of your dedication to the well being of my family, we were safe while in your care. Thank you to all the Habitat for Humanity volunteers that continue to help families live in suitable homes. Because of your care and time, I was able to have a clean and safe home. I am also grateful to all the officers and detectives who treat and handle domestic abuse situations. You may never know what an impact for good you have on the families and especially the children you serve. Your tireless drive protects many more women than you know! Thank you for making our nation a little safer.

To "Rebecca" for introducing me to a nice guy to date, one who became my husband. To the missionaries that never gave up on teaching me that I am a child of God. Much appreciation to all the young women I have had the opportunity to serve. You have taught me how to dream again. You give me more than I could ever give back, and I am inspired by your virtue. To Shalise and Craig, thank you for your unconditional friendship.

My gratitude extends to Dr. Phil McGraw for providing me the opportunity to open my eyes to a new perspective. I appreciate and love the thirteen individuals who shared a journey of a lifetime with me.

I believe God allows special people to enter our lives at the right moment in time to help us on our journey. Some of those special people are in our lives just a moment and others remain forever. No matter how long we are together, the timing is always arranged by divine care.

—Melissa

Tender and heartfelt thanks to my precious and loving children: BreeAnna, McKenzie, and Brent for always believing in me and for your patience as this extensive project developed. Doug, your deep love, inspiration and support is a most cherished miracle in my life, for which I am forever grateful. Thank you, thank you, thank you.

Deep gratitude as well to Eric, Matt, Hoss, Dan, Tom, and Stan for believing in me and allowing me to create this alongside our other important endeavors. Much, much gratitude to Bonnie, Michelle, and Emily for your superb assistance in editing this work and for every other service you have provided in support. Your gifts, talents, and your friendship mean the world to me. Special thanks to Sarah, Emily, Linda, Lani, Clarissa, and Steve. Because of your assistance, life has flowed so much more smoothly and sweetly.

Last, but not least, to Melissa and Sam. For the first time, words cannot express what I would like to say. My deepest respect for what you have taken on, and for how you are determined to be a contribution and to serve others.

May all your lives be blessed as richly as you bless mine.

—Bridget

photo history

Me on my first day of kindergarten

Sitting on the couch are my Great-Grandma Bellemy (holding me on her lap), my grandmother Gladys, and my father (holding Jason). I'm about three years old in this picture.

My dad as a young man.

An orchard near our trailer in Yakima. I walked through this orchard every day to reach the school bus stop.

My second elementary school, and the one I was attending when my school bus caught fire.

Our house on Nordin Street, just two doors down from my grandmother's house. When we moved here, I was thrilled that we had a place of our own, and excited to have a real bedroom again.

My dad and Jason during one of Dad's visits.

Our home on Litchfield Street. It was the roomiest home we ever had. Dad bought us a trampoline for the backyard and for the first time, our house was the cool place to play.

Our Habitat for Humanity home.

Here I am in front of Tania's car that she got around her eighteenth birthday. It represented freedom for both of us. Later, when she got another car, Tania gave this one to me.

Tania and me on the suspension bridge at Bowl and Pitcher in Riverside State Park near Spokane, Washington.

Me and Sam on our wedding day at Hobart Mansion in Spokane.

At my wedding, my grandfather walked me down the aisle. He stood in where my father would have been.

Aspen and me.
After my children were born, I began to think about life differently.

In 2005, Sam and I took our children to visit their grandfather in the Salem Penitentiary. This was the last time I saw him.

In this photo I'm standing outside the restaurant where my parents first met. My dad came in to get a burger, but my mom forgot to put a hamburger in his bun. I came to visit it as part of my research for this book.

Me and Sam with our children, Aspen and Jake, in Coeur d'Alene,
Idaho. This is a special place for our family.

A portion of the proceeds from this book will go to the Dr. Phil Foundation. The Dr. Phil Foundation is committed to supporting organizations and programs that build awareness of and offer solutions to address the emotional, physical, mental, and spiritual needs of children and families.

Additional donations may be mailed to:

The Dr. Phil Foundation
137, Larchmont Blvd.,#703
Los, Angeles, CA 90004

To learn more about Melissa's life and current projects you may visit her online at MelissaGraceMoore.com